Why Do They Kill?

Why Do They Kill?

Men Who Murder Their Intimate Partners

David Adams

Vanderbilt University Press | Nashville

11 10 09 08 07   1 2 3 4 5

Printed on acid-free paper.
Manufactured in the United States of America.

Library of Congress Cataloging-in-Publication Data

Adams, David, Ed. D.
Why do they kill? : men who murder their intimate partners /
    David Adams.—1st ed.
        p. cm.
Includes bibliographical references and index.
ISBN 978-0-8265-1568-1 (cloth : alk. paper)
ISBN 978-0-8265-1569-8 (pbk. : alk. paper)
1. Murderers—United States—Psychology. 2. Women—Crimes
against—United States—Case studies. 3. Uxoricide—United
States—Case studies. 4. Murder—United States—Case studies.
I. Title.
HV6529.A33 2007
364.152'3—dc22
        2007007049

Contents

Acknowledgments

Thanks first and foremost to Susan Schechter who started this project with me and, until her untimely death in February 2004, was a valued consultant. Susan was instrumental in both the research design and the early analysis of the data, and even conducted the first victim interview. As the author of *Women and Male Violence* and *When Love Goes Wrong*, and as one of the pioneering advocates for child witnesses to violence, Susan was one of the true originators and leaders of the battered women's movement. Since her work and vision live on, she continues to inspire my work.

Special thanks also go to Michael Ames, the publisher who recognized the significance of the study and encouraged me to write this book. He never gave up on me even during my long periods of attending to other matters. I also appreciate his input on how to structure the book and his advice that I include background information about abusive men.

I'd also like to thank the funders of this project. These were the Gardiner Howland Shaw Foundation, the Boston Foundation, and the Ms. Foundation for Women. Thank you, Tom Coury, for your enduring interest in this project. Thank you, Ed Gondolf, for your encouragement and for advice on the research design.

Several people helped to recruit subjects for the study. These included Donna Kausek, Gale Martin, Michael Coffee, Lucy Murray Brown, and the staff at Womansplace Crisis Center, Transition House, RESPOND, REACH, Help for Abused Women and Children, and DOVE. Of these people, Gale and Donna played additional critical roles as planners and faculty on the national danger assessment and risk management training project. Other important consultants on these trainings and supporters of this book have been Connie Sponsler, Denise Gamache, Edward Gondolf,

Neil Websdale, Susan Cayouette, Rhonda Martinson, Barbara Hart, Jacquelyn Campbell, Catherine Pierce, Diane Coffey, and Lt. Jon Tiplady. I also thank Christopher Hall for his help on the book cover design.

I greatly appreciate the experienced advocates who conducted the interviews of victims. Thank you, Lindsay Baker, Elizabeth Blevins, Lisa Tieszen, Bonnie Gage Anderson, and Maureen Pasik. Thanks also to the staff at the Massachusetts Department of Corrections who helped me to gain access to the prisons and to recruit inmates. These included Janet Knight, Lisa Sampson, Peter Chalapatas, Donna Collins, Joan Milch, Bill Martin, Sherry Bumpus, Scott Anderson, and Jake Gadsden. I'd like to thank my wife, Lisa Tieszen, for being such a great sounding board and source of support.

Finally and foremost, I'd like to commend and thank the victims of attempted homicide for sharing some of their most painful experiences and for speaking for those who can no longer speak. All said they were willing to do so in hopes of helping to prevent more women's deaths. I dedicate this book to you.

1 | **Men Who Kill Their Partners**

Introduction

This book is the culmination of over ten years of work investigating the murders of women by their intimate partners. In 1993, Governor William Weld declared a state of emergency for women in Massachusetts in response to the murders of twenty-eight women and six children at the hands of their husbands or boyfriends. Even *People* magazine took notice, issuing a cover story titled "The Plague Strikes Home" in response to a spate of five wife killings in the town of Barnstable on Cape Cod.[1] Judging by newspaper accounts of these killings, most of the killers had previously battered their victims. Media accounts of the killers pointed to a variety of motives. Some seemed to fit with O. J. Simpson's alleged motive for killing, that of a jealous husband or boyfriend. John Diaz, for example, mistakenly shot and killed Dawn Brown, the look-alike sister of his estranged girlfriend, Kimberly Brown, whom he had intended to kill. Apparently, Mr. Diaz believed Ms. Brown had left him for another man.[2] James St. Cyr was another man who reportedly killed in a jealous rage. Mr. St. Cyr broke into the apartment of his estranged girlfriend, Tara Hartnett, who was a college senior and young mother. After stabbing her to death, Mr. St. Cyr set the apartment ablaze in an attempt to cover up his crime.[3] Other killers appeared to have a clear history of alcohol or drug abuse, and judging from the media accounts, some of these deaths were unplanned and even accidental. There were also those who killed themselves as well as their partners. The portraits that emerged from these killings seemed to fit those of suicidal depression and mental illness. In some cases, though, very little was known about the prior histories of the killers and their victims. For the most part, friends and neighbors said they were shocked and had no clue about what motivated the fatal attack.

As someone who has counseled men who batter for nearly thirty years, I also wondered what, if anything, was unique about these cases. Are abusers who kill more violent, or more jealous, or more suicidal, or just plain crazier than those who don't kill? What could have deterred these men? Despite the sensationalistic headlines and media coverage, very little was really known about wife killings. A few studies had tried to make sense of these situations by interviewing friends and relatives of the murdered women. But even these studies left out the two most important sources of information: the victim and the perpetrator. This is the first study in the United States that sought to gain information directly from men who killed their partners.[4] In seeking to interview killers, I never expected them to provide completely honest accounts, just as I knew from my work with batterers that the picture they paint is often skewed. In fact, I knew much of what the killers would say would be self-serving. They still had much to hide, and even more to justify or excuse. I knew that the best sources of information were dead. While it was impossible to talk to the deceased, we decided to do the next best thing: interview women who came closest to being killed, victims of attempted homicide. This study included in-depth interviews with twenty victims of attempted homicide and nineteen additional women who were victims of potentially life-threatening assaults. These subjects were recruited through district attorney offices in Massachusetts and from battered women's programs. By seeking information from both killers and victims of serious assaults, we sought to increase the understanding about what leads to women's murders by men.

"Is He Going to Kill Me?"

For the first time in a long time, Elizabeth Wilson felt she had something to look forward to as she drove home from her sister's house one late November evening. She was returning from an annual tradition for the Wilson family: dinner following the last hockey game before Christmas. It had felt so good to be where she was so accepted and could just be herself. She had four days off from her job as an office manager. Most of all, she felt relieved not to have encountered her estranged husband, Mark. She realized that Mark was likely aware of her whereabouts that evening because he'd seemed to make it his business to know where she was at all times since she'd filed for divorce in September.

This was their first Christmas apart after four years of marriage and she guessed that he might be ruminating about this, and probably drinking too, this being a Thursday night. It was now nearly midnight and she was almost home free. Maybe he'd been too drunk or high to remember her annual family tradition. It was somewhat a relief to know that he was without a car. Just a month earlier, he'd tried to force her car off the road when she had been on her way home after an evening out with friends. She found out later that Mark had been waiting and watching for her outside her friend's house, though she didn't know how he'd known she was there. It could have been a lucky guess or he might have tailed her after she'd left work. Elizabeth had obtained a restraining order after Mark had repeatedly shown up at her work to try to talk to her, or just to scream at her. He'd told her that he'd ruin everything for her. The last time she'd seen him, she had been frightened to see how his appearance had deteriorated. He'd lost weight and his color was pale. He'd grown a beard and his hair was long and unkempt. She'd heard from a friend that Mark was smoking crack, something he'd never done while they were living together. She'd also heard that he'd stopped showing up for his job as a mechanic and had been fired. She also knew that he had cashed out his retirement account. It frightened her to see him going downhill so fast and she was worried for her safety, especially after he'd started making threats to kill himself.

Elizabeth was less than a mile home when a white car pulled up to hers along a suburban stretch of highway. Almost instantaneously she recognized the other driver to be Mark. Just as she'd imagined in so many bad dreams, he was pointing a gun out his window and motioning for her to pull over. She sped up just as he fired, and two bullets struck the rear driver's side window, just behind her head. Seconds later, he again pulled up to her car and fired two more shots. Both bullets hit her driver's side door this time. In a blind terror, Elizabeth headed toward the police station that was less than a mile away. Tailing her closely, Mark fired three more shots into her car, missing each time. Not deterred when Elizabeth pulled into the police station lot, Mark pulled alongside her car, pointed his gun, and pulled the trigger. The gun jammed and he sped off into the night.

Mark was later arrested at his home and held without bail. He was ultimately convicted of assault with intent to commit homicide, illegal possession of a firearm, and violation of a restraining order, for which he received a prison sentence of eight years.

Elizabeth was lucky on a number of counts, not the least of which was escaping serious injury or death after having seven shots fired at her. Prosecutors say that convictions for assault with intent to commit murder are not always easy to try for, since there must be evidence "beyond a shadow of a doubt" that the assailant intended to kill the victim. Since intent is often unknowable, juries are hesitant to assume the worst about a person's motivations. For this reason, many potential cases of assault with intent to commit homicide, particularly those involving strangulation, stabbing, and bludgeoning, are often pled down to lesser charges such as assault with a dangerous weapon, aggravated assault, or even simple assault and battery. Even cases of shooting must contain irrefutable evidence that the person intended to kill and not merely to maim or to scare the victim. In Mark's case, his heavy use of alcohol on that December evening might have helped convince the jury that he might well have succeeded in killing Elizabeth had he not been so impaired. His past suicide threats, quitting of his job, and cashing out of his retirement plan also helped paint a picture of someone who'd decided he had little to live for. Elizabeth had been right to be fearful about Mark's potential to kill not just himself but her as well. Annually, about 30% of the 1,300 killings of women by their intimate partners in the United States are murder-suicides.[5] A sizable proportion of the other murders are preceded by suicide threats or attempts by the killers.

As will be discussed later, there are different motivations for the perpetrators. In some cases, it appears that their primary aim was to kill their partners and then to choose death over life without their partner and/or life in prison. In contrast, some of the men I interviewed said that they had intended to kill themselves but lacked the courage to do so. At the last minute, they changed targets from themselves to their partners.

Intimate Partner Homicides

Approximately 1,800 adults are killed by their intimate partners annually in the United States. This current rate of killings is a decrease of 40% from 1970-2000, when there had been about 3,000 intimate partner homicides per year. Paradoxically, however, the number of male victims has decreased dramatically during this period, from 1,400 to 500, while killings of women have only moderately decreased, from 1,600 to 1,300.

Over twenty-five years, the proportion of female victims relative to male has actually increased from just over half in 1976 to over 70%.[6] This is surprising given the widespread increases in legal protections and services available for battered women. Some researchers have speculated that men have been the primarily beneficiaries of enhanced protections for abused women since more choices are now available to those who in the past might have killed their abusers. It has long been known that battered women commit a sizable proportion of husband killings. According to a study by Angela Browne of battered women who kill, these women are often subjected to more serious and frequent physical abuse than other battered women.[7] While some of these killings were in self-defense, many others were acts of desperation committed by women who perceived no other means of escape from tortuous and life-threatening relationships.

Research by Brown and others has helped to expand previous notions of self-defense beyond the narrow legal definitions that still exist in many states. These generally require that a person be in imminent danger from his or her attacker and that the actions taken in self-defense use the least force necessary to protect oneself from harm or death. Legal advocates for battered women have argued, sometimes successfully, that these narrow definitions work against women who are usually less able to defend themselves physically than men. They argue that a man who is being beaten by his female partner is usually better able to defend himself physically without using a weapon. Given the disparities in size and strength between men and women, however, the minimal and safest defensive action available to a woman being attacked by her husband may be to shoot him.

Self-defense laws also specify that a person's first duty is to retreat in face of an attack, and that all retreating actions should be exhausted prior to using physical force. Advocates and researchers have pointed out that this action is not always the safest recourse for battered women. In fact, many studies have shown that battered women are most likely to be killed when attempting to flee their abusers or to end their relationships.

Assessing Danger

Even though increased numbers of battered women have left their abusers without being killed or otherwise harmed, leaving is still a major risk for women who are subjected to the most dangerous abusers. Undoubtedly, many of these women do not leave because they know the risk is too great. Often, their abusers have repeatedly told them, "If you leave me, I'll find you and kill you," or "If I can't have you, nobody else can." Investigations of femicides often find a history of threats backed up with prior acts of serious violence or attempts to kill the victim or others to whom she turned for help.

One relatively new tool of law enforcement in helping to prevent killings of battered women has been threat assessments, sometimes known as lethality assessments. These typically consist of checklists of risk factors that have been shown to increase the odds for serious assaults or violence. Such factors include prior threats of homicide or suicide by the abusers, past use of weapons to scare or to injure the victims, past acts of strangulation or other serious violence, drug or alcohol abuse, estrangement, stalking behavior, and extreme jealousy.[8] Ideally, threat assessments that reveal high risk are followed by safety planning with the victims that is conducted by trained victim advocates. In some jurisdictions, findings of high risk also trigger increased monitoring of the perpetrators by members of law enforcement. Such monitoring might take the form of high bail or incarceration, home confinement, a requirement of frequent visits with their probation officers, drug and alcohol screenings, assignment to certified batterer intervention programs, and monthly case reviews before a judge.

Several problems have been identified with the use of threat assessments. One is that these tend to over-predict homicide since there is a high rate of so-called false positives. A false positive occurs when a particular risk factor is present but the predicted outcome does not occur. Relative to the incidence of domestic violence cases—even including those that have elements of high risk—femicide is still a very rare event. According to the FBI's National Crime Victimization Survey, American women experienced 588,000–1,100,000 crimes of domestic violence annually between 1993–2001.[9] Even by these conservative figures, the proportion of women killed relative to those who are battered is one-tenth of one percent.

Given that certain risk factors (such as threats to kill) far exceed the number of killings, it is difficult to know which particular cases most warrant the extra resources. One solution would be to provide enhanced monitoring of all perpetrators who have been found to pose serious risk. This may not be practical for some jurisdictions, however, given the large numbers and the resources involved. This solution also leads to another problem with lethality assessments—that of false negatives. A false negative occurs when the feared outcome (e.g., homicide) was not preceded by any or most of the risk factors. Some men kill their partners without having previously threatened them or themselves, for instance. Many killers lack a criminal record or a history of abusing alcohol or drugs. Threat assessments may lead law enforcement and other agencies to focus solely on those cases where the assessed danger score is high and to ignore those cases where it is low.

A related problem in conducting threat assessments is that relevant information may not be available to those doing the assessment. For example, most perpetrators of domestic violence minimize the seriousness and frequency of their past violence for fear of criminal sanctions. Victims, for a variety of reasons, may also minimize or fail to disclose certain risk factors. They may fear retribution should such information be revealed to their perpetrators. Reinforcing this fear, information obtained from a victim for a dangerousness assessment may be discoverable by the defendant's attorney. Because of this, many jurisdictions advise victims about the limits to their confidentiality prior to interviewing them about the violence. Some jurisdictions provide only summary information in their threat assessment reports, without disclosing the specific sources of that information.

Another problem with threat assessments is that they can lead those conducting them to over-rely on the instruments, at the expense of building a relationship with victims of abuse. Victim advocates point out that victims are most apt to disclose information once a relationship of trust is established. Victims are most likely to trust helpers who are nonjudgmental, validating, and respectful. Information about abusive behavior is revealed over time with the development of a trusting relationship. Sometimes the most useful information provided by the victim is not the presence or absence of particular items on a threat assessment checklist, but a more contextualized history of the perpetrator's abusive behavior. Some victims may be put off by evaluators who want to know "just the facts" and who appear more concerned about filling out a form as opposed to trying to get the whole story. Advocates who take down the histories of victims find that victims are better able to remember and to articulate relevant events when asked open-ended as well as guided questions. The

Danger Assessment tool developed by Jacquelyn Campbell, for instance, includes a step during which the evaluator uses a calendar to prompt the victim's memory of abusive incidents during the past year. The advantage of this approach is not only that the victim may reveal more information that is critical to a threat assessment but also she may be more likely to use the helping system that employs this approach.

Most investigations of dangerousness have been based on either large-scale studies or on examinations of individual cases. These are known as fatality reviews. Fatality reviews provide a helpful postmortem of homicides in which investigative and helping agencies pool their information about the victim and the perpetrator for the purpose of identifying which risk factors were present and what might have helped to avoid the known outcome. Some fatality review teams examine the role of each of the helping systems that the victim and perpetrator might have come in contact with, and whether each system responded in an appropriate manner.[10] Information that has emerged from fatality reviews has provided useful information about serious cases of domestic violence, which in some cases has led to enhanced collaboration among helping systems, along with improvements in institutional responses to domestic violence.

One large study of dangerousness compared known cases of homicide and attempted homicide and compared these to less serious cases of domestic violence. This study confirmed the importance of particular risk factors that had already been identified and suggested some additional factors to be included on threat assessment scales.[11] The known factors included

- Past use of a weapon to scare or harm the victim
- Possession of a weapon
- Past threats of suicide or homicide
- Stalking behavior
- Prior strangulation attempts
- Alcohol and/or drug abuse by the perpetrator
- Sexual abuse of the victim
- Violence while the victim was pregnant
- Estrangement

Applying these factors to Elizabeth Wilson's situation at the beginning of the chapter, we see that most of these were evident prior to Mark's attempt to kill her. The couple was estranged and a divorce was pending. Mark had repeatedly stalked Elizabeth during the four months following their separation. Mark had a history of making threats to kill Elizabeth as well as members of her family. He was a serious abuser of alcohol and drugs. He was extremely jealous. He was depressed and had made several threats to kill himself. He had quit his job and appeared to have no plans for the future. Finally, Mark had previously used a weapon—his car—to scare and intimidate Elizabeth.

Understanding Men Who Kill Their Partners

What is there to learn from men who killed their partners?
Why did they do it?
Did they think they were going to get away with it?
Are they remorseful?
Aren't most of them psychopaths?
What would have prevented them from killing?
Wouldn't they just lie about what they had done?

These are just some of the questions people have asked when told about this study. I wondered myself how honest the men would be about their motives and other details about the killings they committed. Having worked with battering men, I expected high levels of dishonesty and denial. In this regard, I wasn't disappointed. Some of the men continued to deny that they had killed their partners. One man claimed that he had been "framed" by the real killer of his girlfriend. Others claimed to have killed in self-defense, despite their convictions for premeditated murder. Many professed never to have previously abused their partners, despite much evidence to the contrary.

Despite their obvious motives to deny or distort the truth, I knew that these men still had critical information to provide. I knew from my clinical work that abusive men often provide useful information when attempting to explain, defend, or otherwise rationalize their actions. Unwittingly, important attitudes and beliefs are revealed. When telling their side of the stories, batterers give clues to how they see their partners and themselves.

They also reveal information about what they expect from women, how they communicate these expectations, and how they respond when their expectations are not fulfilled. In giving this information, they reveal critical beliefs about how and when they see violence as justified.

Thirty-one wife murderers, all inmates in five different prisons in Massachusetts, were interviewed for this study. Finding these killers was not as easy as one would imagine. The Massachusetts Department of Corrections does not classify killers by their relationship to the victims, so there was no list of those who had killed their intimate partners. At each of the correctional centers, I was given a computer-generated list of all the inmates serving time for homicide. Typically, there were hundreds of names on each list. I then spent days reading through inmate files in order first to identify which inmates had killed women, and then to learn whether the woman killed had been an intimate partner. The next step was to ask qualified inmates for an interview. Those who had been only briefly involved with their victims (three months or less) and never lived with them were screened out of the study. Overall, just over half (52%) of qualified inmates who were asked to participate in the study refused to do so. The vast majority of these inmates (72% of the refusers) cited pending legal appeals as the reason for nonparticipation. Another 18% refused on the grounds that they had not committed the crimes of which they had been convicted, while the remaining 10% gave no reason. Demographically, those who refused to participate were very similar to the study subjects. Among both study participants and nonparticipants, there was an equal spread of convictions for first degree murder, second degree murder, and manslaughter, with approximately a third of each group convicted of each crime. Table 1.1 shows the breakdown of killers at MCI-Norfolk, a medium security prison in Massachusetts, from which over half of the killers in this study were recruited.

Those who qualified for the study were asked to participate in a semi-structured interview that ranged from three to six hours. Besides the information obtained from the interviews, I also had access to their inmate files. These included their complete records of past arrests, prosecutions, and case dispositions, as well as the police reports of the murders they committed. The files also included records of disciplinary problems, classification status, and whether the inmates had participated in any mental health, substance abuse, or educational programs while in prison.

Table 1.1: Breakdown of killers at MCI-Norfolk

Total inmates serving time for murder of any kind	**369**
Inmates who had killed a woman	125
Inmates who had killed a female intimate partner	49*
Wife killers asked to participate in study	35
Wife killers who agreed to participate	17

* Fourteen of these did not qualify for the study since they had been involved with their murder victims for less than three months and never lived with them.

Due to prison regulations related to inmate schedules, my interviews with the inmates usually had to be conducted in two or three sittings that sometimes extended over two or more days. Often, merely gaining entry into the particular prison for an inmate interview would exceed an hour due to security precautions and "lock-downs" during which inmates could not leave their cells. As an incentive to participate in the study, each inmate was offered a stipend of thirty dollars. This is a considerable amount for inmates, whose primary expenses are phone calls, cigarettes, candy bars, and recreation room fees.

Each interview included a wide variety of questions about the murder committed and the murderer's background. The background questions were extensive and included queries about the killer's upbringing, school and work history, criminal behavior, physical and mental health, and use of alcohol and drugs. Each killer was asked how each relationship began and ended, how long it had lasted, and whether it had included any physical or psychological abuse on his part. I asked each killer to help me construct a timeline of his relationship with the murder victim, beginning with how they met and when they began living together. The timeline included significant events such as if and when they married, when their children were born, when and why separations occurred, and when and why they changed residences. The men were also asked when and in what ways they and their partners experienced significant changes in their lives such as job losses, new jobs or promotions, arrests, sicknesses, emotional problems, and the deaths of close friends or relatives. I also asked the men to indicate when major conflicts and/or acts of abuse had occurred in order to learn how these acts related to the other events in their lives together. I asked the men to give more detailed accounts of their lives and relationships with their partners and children during the months, weeks, and days that immediately preceded the murders. I hoped that the resulting timeline of significant events would reveal both long-term and short-term factors that might have triggered the murder. Murderers were also directly asked why they had killed their partners and what might have prevented them from doing so. I further asked why they had chosen the particular murder weapon they used, and whether they would have used an alternate weapon. Besides the semi-structured interview, I administered a number of other tools designed to measure psychological abuse, jealousy, child abuse, substance use, and beliefs about wife beating.[12]

How Did They Kill?

I wondered if learning about the killer's method of killing might add to our understanding of when and why he killed. This is the first study of wife killers to ask men directly about their choice of murder weapon. The methods of murder used by the thirty-one killers are listed in Table 1.2. Does the chosen weapon reflect the killer's motives for killing the victim? Was the chosen weapon previously used to terrorize and control the victim? Was the weapon readily available or did he take pains to obtain it? If the weapon was a gun, did its availability make him more likely to murder?

Every scale used to assess danger in domestic violence cases asks whether the perpetrator has access to a gun. Judging from national statis-

Table 1.2: Murder methods of the thirty-one killers

Method used	Number	Percentage of killers
Shooting with gun	14	45
Stabbing	5	16
Strangling with hands	5	16
Bludgeoning/Beating	3	10
Asphyxiating/Smothering	2	6
Stabbing and bludgeonin	1	3
Strangling and running over with car	1	3

N=31

tics of intimate partner homicides, there is good reason for this. Almost two-thirds of men who kill their intimate partners do so with a gun, according to the FBI.[13] Three quarters of the guns used are handguns. This compares to about one-sixth of killers who use a knife and one-twelfth who use their bare hands. Crime statistics concerning murder-suicides involving intimate partners and familicide reveal a still greater proportion of gun use, one approaching 95 percent.[14]

Considering the prevalence of guns as murder weapons, does their mere presence in the home increase the risk of wife killing? Several studies suggest this to be the case. One investigation of 220 intimate partner homicides of women in eleven American cities found that in just over half the cases, a gun was present in the house during the twelve months leading up to the murder.[15] In contrast, guns were present in the homes of just 16% of the control group of abused women. These investigators conclude that when a gun is present in the house, an abused woman is between five and eight times more likely to be killed. As widespread as gun ownership is among men in general, it appears that serious wife abusers are more likely to have guns and certainly to use them to threaten and to kill their partners.

Why Guns?

Could some women's murders be averted if not for the killers' easy access to guns? I asked the men who had shot their victims whether they would have still killed if a gun had not been available. Fourteen of the thirty-one killers (45%) used guns to kill their partners or ex-partners. Eleven of these men (78% of the shooters) said that they would not have killed if a gun had not been available, while the other three said they would have merely used another weapon. For those who said they would not have used an alternate weapon, their reasons varied, as can be seen in Figure 1.1.

For the most part, these men said that the ready availability of a gun "made it easier" to kill, as one of them put it. There is an obvious self-serving aspect to this claim, particularly when the person making it asserts to have killed with little or no premeditation. For many people, particularly friends and family of the victim, the distinction between a planned murder and an unplanned but still voluntary one may seem arbitrary. The end result is the same. But for the killers and those who prosecute and

Figure 1.1: Shooters' reasons for not using another weapon to kill their partner

"I was intoxicated . . . and didn't have the strength to stab or choke her."

"It happened too fast. . . . I would have come to my senses in the time it took to take out a knife."

"A gun depersonalizes. . . . I wouldn't have gone through with it if I had time to think about it."

"I hate knives. I've been stabbed."

"I had no intention of killing her. . . . I was just fiddling with the gun."

"She was waving the gun around, threatening to kill herself. . . . I grabbed for it and it went off."

"A gun is the easier way. . . . I don't have the guts to use a knife; that's butchering."

"Probably wouldn't have killed her mother, and definitely not her sister. . . . I would have just gotten out of there."

"I didn't want her to suffer; that's why I killed her in her sleep."

---

sentence them, the difference is substantial. In most states, first degree murder carries a mandatory sentence of life without parole, while sentences for second degree murder generally range from twenty years to life. By contrast, the sentence for voluntary manslaughter can range from as little as five years to as many as twenty. Even with the longer sentence, there is the possibility of parole in as few as five years.

Most of the eleven men who claimed that they would not have killed without a gun appeared to be saying that it was the *guns* and not *them* that killed. In describing the minutes and hours before the killing, many of these men claimed to have been "in a fog" during which they were not aware of their actions. Several asserted that they did not specifically recall picking up the gun or firing it.

One such man, Edward, said that he would not have used any other weapon because "a gun depersonalizes," adding that killing with a knife or with his hands might have made it seem "more real." Elaborating on this theme of "unrealness," Edward said that immediately after killing his wife, Sylvia, he went to a local amusement park where he played video games for several hours. On his way back home, Edward said that he picked up a half dozen donuts, including "three of Sylvia's favorites."

Once home, Edward made coffee, put the donuts on a plate, and "went into the bedroom to awaken Sylvia. When I saw that she was dead, I sat on the bed crying." Edward then called the halfway house for retarded women where he worked as an assistant director to say that he would not be in. He then called his mother to tell her that he'd killed Sylvia.

Four men claimed to have brandished the gun with the intention of killing themselves and not their partners, and to be perplexed about how the gun went off. It bears noting, however, that none of these men subsequently killed themselves and that each eluded arrest for periods ranging from several hours to three weeks. One man, Gerald, shot his partner in the face at close range with a sawed-off shotgun and stated that the weapon went off "by accident." Gerald said that, just prior to shooting Pamela, he had shot at a trashcan in the back yard during an argument with her, "just to show her how frustrated I was."

In some of the cases where the killer claimed he would not have killed without a gun, I did not believe him, given the facts. Judging from the killers' court records, neither did their juries, who found them guilty of murder in the first or second degree. These were cases in which the killers appeared intent to kill, regardless of how convenient the weapon. In most of the cases, the gun had been convenient because the killer brought it with him to the murder scene. In the cases of two of the killers, however, there is strong reason to believe that the murders might have been averted if not for the ready availability of a gun. In both cases, the perpetrator had been significantly impaired by heavy use of alcohol and drugs just prior to the killing. Neither killer appeared to have had any longstanding motive for killing his partner, such as to prevent her from ending the relationship. Neither had taken pains to secure a gun just prior to the killing.

At age twenty-one, Kevin was the youngest of the killers we studied. Kevin and Rebecca's relationship had apparently revolved around alcohol and drug use with their mutual friends. There is no evidence that Rebecca had planned to end their relationship in the months leading up to her murder. On the night Kevin killed Rebecca, they had been out "drinking and drugging" for several hours with four friends. Back at his apartment, Kevin slapped Rebecca several times after she complained that he'd "stranded her" at the house of an earlier party. Kevin's roommate, Rob, intervened and he and Kevin began to "throw punches at each other." After being bloodied by the much bigger Rob, Kevin retreated to his room to get his semi-automatic assault rifle. While Rebecca was on the phone calling for a friend to pick her up, Kevin shouted, "Be a tough guy now!" to Rob before "spraying" him with bullets. According to Kevin, Rebecca was hit in the elbow and stomach because she was standing behind Rob, and that he had had no intention of shooting her as well. At Kevin's trial for double homicide, one witness essentially supported Kevin's version of events. He was found guilty of second degree murder on two counts. Explaining his actions of that evening, Kevin said, "I felt humiliated due to Rob getting the better of me. . . . without the gun I would have just screwed [left]." Kevin had legally purchased his rifle six months prior to the murder.

In contrast to many of the shooters who had showed obvious premeditation and perseverance of effort, Kevin's actions seem to have been at least partially determined by the easy availability of a gun. One can imagine that neither victim might have been killed if the same scenario had unfolded on the street or in someone else's apartment where there had been no gun, though Kevin might have subsequently sought revenge in some other way.

It bears repeating that guns are disproportionably involved in killings where there is more than one victim. For a killer intent on killing more than one person, a gun is the practical choice. Killing with a knife or one's hands takes far more time, giving the additional intended victims more opportunity to escape. If the killer's second intended victim is himself, as in the case of a murder-suicide, killing with a gun offers the additional benefit of ending life with less suffering.

Killing additional people reflects different motivations on the part of abusers who commit murder. For some, like Kevin, killing the additional people may reflect the happenstance of the moment, such as who intervenes or is merely present. For others, killing additional people such as the victim's relatives, friends, or other lover is an essential part of their retribution program. In these cases, the killer's motivation is sometimes revealed by the order of killing. For instance, a sadistic killer may spare his partner until she has first witnessed the killing of those who are dear to her such as her children or parents.

One of the killers in our study, Henry, first murdered his wife's mother and shot her sister before killing his wife. This reflected Henry's desire to inflict one last measure of revenge against his wife for having left him and "taken my children away." At the same time, Henry settled scores against his mother-in-law and wife's sister, whom he blamed for turning his wife against him. Before shooting his mother-in-law, Henry yelled at her, "Die, bitch!"

Several victims of attempted homicide that we interviewed echoed this theme of sadistic vengeance on the part of their abusers. One woman said that her abuser had repeatedly threatened to kill their daughter in front of her. Another victim, Lynette, reported that her boyfriend, William, had continually threatened to kill her mother and brother in her presence. During one evening of heavy drinking, William made Lynette play Russian roulette with him. He first pointed a gun to his head and pulled the trigger before handing it to her and demanding that she do the same. Lynette said that she had been so terrorized and "resigned to dying" by that point that it would have been a relief to "get it over with." She also felt that her death might prevent William's killing of her mother and brother. Three times following William's "turns" with the gun, she pointed it at herself and pulled the trigger. During her last turn, Lynette pulled the trigger, only to hear William's cackling laughter and taunting that he'd "forgotten" to put in the bullet. A year following this incident, William broke into Lynette's apartment shortly after she had ended the relationship and bludgeoned her with a baseball bat until she lost consciousness. William then held Lynette's two young children hostage for several hours before being apprehended by a police SWAT team.

Where Do the Guns Come From?

No large-scale studies have investigated how men who shoot their partner get their guns. In our study, I asked the fourteen killers who had used guns how they had obtained their guns and whether they had had legal access to them at the time of the murder. Nine of the fourteen men admitted that the guns they had used were illegal. Owning a weapon was illegal for four of these men due to their criminal records.

Gerald, the man who had shot a trash can before "accidentally" shooting Pamela in the face, was one of these men. Gerald admits that he had been on the lam for fourteen months prior to the murder. Gerald had previously served six different jail terms for armed robbery. He had violated the terms of his most recent parole by siphoning gas from someone's car and by failing to appear for his court arraignment. Despite the open warrant for his arrest, Gerald had continued to support himself by stealing from homes. One of the tools of his trade had been the sawed-off shotgun that he used to kill Pamela. Gerald had purchased this gun from a partner in crime shortly after his release from jail.

Five of the men who had shot their partners did not have legal access to guns due to active protective orders against them. Enacted in 1994, a federal law bans those under a protective order from owning a weapon. Two men with active protective orders had failed to surrender their firearms to legal authorities. Three others had no guns to begin with but simply obtained theirs illegally without applying for a license to own a firearm. The first killer had purchased a handgun "from someone on the street" the night before he shot and killed his estranged girlfriend. The second borrowed a gun from a relative about a month before coming into his wife's restaurant and shooting her. A week prior to killing his wife, the third man drove to Maine to purchase a Civil War-era sidearm and black powder in an antique shop. Since sidearms or rifles that use black powder are not defined as guns in Maine, buyers of these weapons are not subjected to the same restrictions as buyers of modern guns. For instance, they are not subjected to the three-day waiting period before they can purchase the weapon, during which the local police department checks for past felonies or other grounds for prohibiting the pending purchase. Indeed, buyers of these vintage weapons are not required to have a firearms license at all, leaving them as free to buy a gun as they are to purchase any other "collectible."

Other Weapons

What about the men who had stabbed, strangled, or bludgeoned their victims to death? Had they considered using guns instead? Six of the killers had stabbed their victims to death. Four of these men said they would have used a gun if one had been available. None of these four men said that he had owned a gun or had taken any steps to gain access to one in the days or weeks leading up to the murder. At first glance, one might be tempted to view knife killings as more spontaneous and less premeditated. Judging from the court findings for these stabbers, however, this did not seem to have been the case. All six of these men were convicted of murder in the first or the second degree, meaning that there was strong evidence of premeditation. In all these cases, there was evidence that the killer had used forethought. Several of these men had brought the knife to their estranged partner's residence shortly before killing her. According to trial testimony, two of these men had previously told friends of their plans to kill their partners.

Two of the stabbers admitted that they had considered using guns instead. Each man said that he had had access to a gun and could easily have used it as the murder weapon, but each also said that he'd decided not to use a gun because it would have made too much noise. They had had different reasons for wanting to avoid noise, however. One man who had stormed into his estranged wife's house and stabbed her said that a gunshot would have aroused the neighbors and therefore lessened his chances of being able to flee the police. The other man said that he did not use a gun because he had not wanted to awaken his children. (This man, John, is profiled in the later section about possessive beliefs.)

I also asked the men who had strangled, bludgeoned, or used some other weapon to kill their partners whether they had considered other weapons, such as a gun or a knife. Five men had strangled their victims, one had asphyxiated his partner by forcing his hands down her throat, one had smothered his wife with a pillow, one had bludgeoned his wife to death with a hammer, and one had beaten his partner to death with his bare hands. One additional man had strangled his estranged girlfriend and then finished her off by running over her repeatedly with his car.

Four of these ten men said that they would have used a gun if one had been available. One man, Louis, who is profiled in chapter 5 (on short courtships), said, "If I had a gun I probably would have killed her earlier. That's why I didn't keep one around." The remaining six men said they would not have used a gun or a knife to kill their partner. All claimed to have had no intent to kill their partner on the day of the murder, and therefore lacked the forethought to have used a gun or a knife unless it had been immediately available. One of these men explained, "I would have come to my senses in the time it took to take out a gun or a knife." All six of these men claimed to have killed "in the heat of the moment" with no prior planning. In four of these cases, there was some evidence to support their claims. All four had been convicted of voluntary manslaughter, meaning there were no strong indications of premeditation. One man, Vincent, had killed his girlfriend with a single punch to her head.

She had died ten days later of a brain aneurism. Another killer, Lee, had strangled his partner after she threw a cup of hot tea on him. At his trial, Lee had mounted a defense of "temporary insanity" by claiming that the hot tea had triggered a flashback to his experience in the Vietnam War. To bolster this claim, Lee had produced evidence of a prior diagnosis of post-traumatic stress disorder.

It is important to note that a manslaughter conviction is not proof that a killer acted without forethought or malice—only that there was insufficient evidence to establish the presence of these conditions in court. Prosecutors say that it is often more difficult to establish premeditation on a killer's part when the murder weapon was his bare hands. Such cases can also result in plea bargains in which the defendant agrees to plead guilty to manslaughter in exchange for a shorter sentence.

Where Do They Kill?

I also asked the killers to tell me where the murders had occurred. The location of a murder often provides clues about the killer's motivation and degree of premeditation. For instance, a murder committed in an estranged victim's home points to motives of revenge or jealousy and also suggests some degree of premeditation. Murders committed in a bedroom sometimes suggest a sexual component. The most common site of death for the thirty-one victims of homicide was in their bedrooms. Ten victims were in their bedroom when killed. Seven of these women were lying in bed when attacked, and three were asleep. Eight victims were attacked when they were undressed or partially undressed. One of these women was killed while in the bathroom.

This indicates that many women are killed in very vulnerable positions, when their ability to fight back does not exist or is greatly compromised. In nearly half the cases, the killer broke into or came uninvited to the victim's house to kill her. One broke into his estranged wife's house in the late evening when she was out at a party. He waited for her to come home and remained hidden while she put the children to bed and went to bed herself before attacking her with a knife. Three of the killers waited for their partners to fall asleep before killing them. One of these men had plied his wife with alcohol so that she would fall asleep before he stabbed her and bludgeoned her over the head with a bat. Another man cajoled his estranged girlfriend to stay with him "for one last night" at a hotel with the promise that he would leave her alone after that. He then shot her in the head while she was lying in bed shortly after having sex with her. Four of the killers said that they had had sex with their estranged partners, or had been attempting to do so, shortly before killing them. I will say more about this in the section about sexual violence.

Next to the victims' homes, the next most common murder sites for estranged men were outdoors or in cars. Shortly after his girlfriend broke off relations with him, one killer lured her into his car, where he shot her. Another convinced his girlfriend to go for a ride with him before strangling her. He then pushed her out of the car and ran over her several times. A third man asked his girlfriend to go for a walk before strangling her and throwing her body in a canal. Two women were fatally attacked while leaving a friend's house where they had been staying. Both killers admitted that they had stalked their victims. Table 1.3 provides a summary of the murder sites.

For couples still living together, the most common location for murder

Table 1.3: Murder sites

Location of murder	Number in this location
Victim's home or premises	11
Couple's home	10
Perpetrator's home	3
Outdoors	6
Hotel	1
Victim's workplace	1
	N=32*
Room where killing occurred	**Number in this location**
Bedroom	10
Living room	6
Kitchen	5
Bathroom	1
Hotel room	1
	N=23

* One murder is counted twice because it occurred outside but on the victim's premises.

was the living room or the kitchen. In these cases, there was no apparent connection between the room and the weapon used. Only one of the men who killed his partner in the kitchen used a kitchen knife, for example. All five other men who killed in the kitchen used a gun that they had carried in from another room or from outside the house. One of these men had recently bought the rifle he used and hidden it in an outside shed. One man who stabbed his wife in the living room used a screwdriver that he had taken from the basement. Among the intact couples, only one killing occurred outside of a home. This murder occurred in a cemetery where the killer bludgeoned his girlfriend to death with a large rock. The couple was homeless at the time.

2 | **Recognizing Abusive Men**

Before proceeding with the analysis of killers, it is necessary to step back to review what is known about abusive men in general. In giving this overview, I draw upon my twenty-nine years of experience working with men who batter as well as the growing body of research findings about men who are violent to their intimate partners. One hypothesis about abusive men who kill is that they share many of the same characteristics as abusers who don't kill. Some victim advocates have argued that serious and less serious abusers exist on the same continuum and that their primary differences are matters of degree more than of substance. Men who batter cover a wide spectrum in terms of the severity of their violence. Many have committed very little or no physical violence but have been primarily verbally and psychologically abusive. Other batterers exhibit similar levels of violence, and even more, to those who kill their partners. Judging from our interviews with victims of attempted homicide and serious abuse, it is clear that some abusive men have not killed solely due to poor planning, poor execution, or rapid medical responses to the victims they have attempted to kill.

Myths About Men Who Batter

Despite increased public attention to domestic violence, much continues to be misunderstood about perpetrators of abuse, and popular stereotypes about them persist. Perhaps one of the most enduring myths about men who batter is that they are easily identifiable. Related to this myth are the common stereotypes of batterers as alcoholics or as mentally ill. Other common myths about batterers are that they are predominantly uneducated or unemployed, or that they are criminals or "tough guys." Clearly, some batterers do fit these stereotypes, and perhaps in substantial enough numbers that these myths are reinforced. For instance, most research has indicated that batterers are more likely than nonbatterers to be substance abusers. Further, there is some evidence that substance abuse is most likely to be found among men who batter at the most severe levels. Even among this group of abusers, however, there are many batterers who do not abuse substances. Most studies have found rates of alcoholism among batterers that fall in the 40%–60% range.[1] The intake data of over 1,600 abusive men attending batterer intervention programs in Massachusetts during 2005–2006 showed that two-fifths had a history of substance abuse.[2] Edward Gondolf's study of 840 men undergoing batterer treatment in Pennsylvania, Texas, and Colorado found that just over half could be characterized as problem drinkers. Thirty-one percent of the men had severe problems connected with drinking such as drunk driving, fighting and arrests.[3]

Are men who batter psychologically ill? Similar to alcoholism, the proportion of batterers with a diagnosable mental illness is less than what is popularly believed. The previously cited study by Gondolf found that batterers have less severe psychological problems than most other clinical populations that have been studied.[4] Based on their test scores on a common measure of psychological disorders, less than half showed evidence of a personality disorder. However, about 40% of the men exhibited characteristics common to narcissistic or anti-social personality disorders. Despite this, less than a fifth of the abusive men were deemed to have severe personality dysfunctions and one-quarter were classified as moderate cases. Personality disorders did not even appear to be more common among the recidivist batterers in this study. Only 11% of the men who committed more than one re-assault during the fifteen-month follow-up period were deemed to have psychopathic disorders.[5] Alcoholism was found to be a far better predictor of multiple re-assaults. Independently of this, about half of the men also showed signs of depression. It was unclear, however, to what extent their depression was a stable feature or situationally related to their arrests, marital separations, and other consequences of their violence.[6]

Another stereotype of men who batter is that most are criminals. In reality, the vast majority of abusive men do not have criminal records other than their arrests for domestic violence. Even the majority of killers in our study had had no prior convictions. Twenty of the thirty-one killers had not previously been convicted of a crime of any kind. Again, there is a substantial minority that fits the criminally involved stereotype. In our study, 26% of the men had been previously incarcerated and 16% could be characterized as career criminals.

A third myth about abusive men is that they are mostly uneducated or unemployed. Again, the overwhelming evidence points otherwise, though there is a substantial subgroup of abusers who fit the stereotype. Most studies have found battering to occur across all educational and income levels, though abusive men from lower economic levels are more likely to be arrested and prosecuted for domestic violence.[7] Gondolf found that 37% of the 840 men attending batterer intervention programs in three different states held white-collar jobs, while 64% had blue-collar ones. Sixteen percent of the men were unemployed while an additional 12% worked part-time. Three-quarters of the men were high school graduates and 36% had attended some college or more.[8]

Perhaps most difficult to dispel is the myth of the abusive man as a "tough guy" or someone with stereotypically "macho" characteristics. Since these are traits that are hard to define operationally, there is no research that compares abusive men to nonabusive men on these characteristics. However, there is considerable empirical evidence from treatment programs for batterers about abusive men's public personas. For the most part, abusive men do not come across as violent or abusive to their friends, neighbors, or co-workers. Anecdotally, most abusive men in my practice say that their peers do not view them as violent. There are two reasons for this. First, for the most part, they have not exhibited any aggressive or violent behavior toward people other than their intimate partners. Second, they usually have not disclosed their domestic violence to their friends or co-workers. Unless they are arrested, their domestic violence remains hidden from others. One study of twenty-nine abusive men attending batterer intervention programs in Massachusetts found that only a small minority said that their employer knew about their domestic violence. Most also said that their domestic violence had not impacted their work in any obvious way so as to invite attention to their home life.[9]

Also adding to abusive men's ability to avoid detection is that many are well liked and respected by their peers. We have not only abusive men's claims about this to go by but also the testimony of victims. Very often, victims report that their abusive partners are well liked by others. Quite often, in fact, abusive men enjoy better reputations among their peers than do their victims. One reason for this is that domestic violence affects victims more than it does perpetrators. Domestic violence affects victims in a variety of ways, including depression, anxiety, social withdrawal, guilt or shame, distrust toward others, and protectiveness toward their children. Domestic violence often adversely affects victims' work performance more than it does for perpetrators.

Another reason that abusive men are so well liked is that they often put considerable energy into maintaining a positive image among their friends and peers. Many victims of abuse complain their abusive partners are overly ingratiating to others, at the expense of how they themselves are treated. Even victims of severe violence often say that their abusive partners come across as "charming" to people outside the family. Eighteen of the twenty victims of attempted homicide in our study rated their abusers as "charming to others."

Many batterers avoid detection by their friends, neighbors, and co-workers precisely because they do not fit the stereotypes that persist of them. I have written elsewhere that these same myths about batterers lead medical and mental health professionals to under-identify batterers. One additional reason for this is that batterers rarely self-identify as abusers even when they are seeking help for medical or psychological problems.[10]

Regardless of the severity of their violence, I've found that virtually all abusive men show features of jealousy and possessiveness. Similarly, many batterers are rigid in their attitudes and beliefs. Most often, the worldview that batterers reveal is a highly self-centered one. While they often come across to others as likeable and sociable, their public personas are belied by abusive and selfish behavior that is usually reserved for their partners and children. At their cores, most battering men display a lack of empathy for their partners. In batterer intervention programs, this lack of empathy is often manifested as insensitivity to their partners' feelings and concerns.

Group leader: Can you describe your most recent act of abuse?

Mark: I came home and Barbara was all over me about something, bitching about this and that.

Group leader: What did you do?

Mark: I told her to stop bitching and to shut up. I was tired and just wanted to go to bed.

Group leader: What time was it?

Mark: Nine o'clock, something like that.

Group leader: What happened next?

Mark: She kept on bitching, and I slapped her.

Group leader: In the face?

Mark: Yeah.

Group leader: Anything else?

Mark: I don't know, I think I grabbed her and threw her down to the floor.

Group leader: Then what?

Mark: I just went to bed.

Group leader: What was Barbara upset about?

Mark: I have no idea. She's always complaining about something.[11]

Like Mark, many abusers cannot articulate their partner's perspective when asked to do so because they do not know it. Most can remember and relate their own concerns in great detail, however. One key trait of self-centeredness is a lack of empathy for the feelings and concerns of others. This can exist at several different levels. Mark demonstrates the deepest level in his inability even to identify Barbara's feelings or concerns, much less identify with them. Somewhat more commonly, the abuser is able to identify his partner's feelings or concerns but is indifferent or hostile to them.

In a previous study that compared abusive husbands to nonabusive ones, I found that abusers were significantly less able to empathize with their partners and showed far less positive regard for them, and while abusive men did not score any differently than nonabusive men on tests that assess attitudes toward women in general, they consistently communicated more negative beliefs about their partners. The predominant attitude of the abusive husbands seemed to be, "I like women in general but the one I have is defective." This reflects, I think, a rather compartmentalized way of thinking about women. By upholding idealized notions of "good women," abusive men appear to set themselves up to find fault with real women.[12]

Denigrating Their Partners

For abusive men, denigration of their partners appears to serve several important functions. First, by devaluing their partners' worth, abusers appear to be elevating their own virtues and worth. For example, one man attending a batterer intervention program complained frequently about his wife's "stupid mistakes." "For all her education, she's dumb," he said, adding, "She doesn't have an ounce of common sense." This man's group leader pointed out that many of the mistakes about which he was complaining about, such as leaving the lights on when she left the house, were neither stupid nor mistakes but rather reflected her different concerns and values. By labeling his wife "dumb," the man seemed to be warding off his insecurities about his own lack of education. Later on in the program, he admitted that he envied his wife's education.

A second major function of partner denigration for abusive men is that it helps them avoid or alleviate any feelings of remorse for their abusive actions. As one batterer once told me,

> It sounds strange but I really didn't feel bad about my violence or how I treated Lindsay because I really didn't take her seriously as a person. I mean, I had more respect for my car and my things. She always used to complain about that, and she was right. I did take better care of my *stuff*. I just didn't respect her. I figured anything I did was okay and if she didn't like it my attitude was "where to hell are you going to go?" I thought she was lucky to have me. I don't now, but I did then.[13]

This level of insight is rare among abusive men, even those in recovery. For those abusive men who do make changes, the development of remorse and empathy appear to be key to their progress. With empathy comes the man's ability to see his abusive actions from his partner's perspective and to recognize its damaging effects on her.

Blaming the Victim

Beyond bolstering feelings of superiority and avoiding feelings of remorse, partner denigration serves a third important purpose for abusers: it provides them with grounds for avoiding responsibility for violence by shifting blame unto the victim. For most batterers, their denigration of their partners is fueled by their numerous complaints and grievances about their partners. When asked to describe their violent actions, most batterers begin describing how they were incited or provoked by something their partner did or did not do. Figure 2.1 shows intake data provided by abusive men upon their enrollment in batterer intervention programs. After giving a written or oral account of his most recent act of violence, each man is asked to give a reason for acting in this manner.

As can be seen from the above, literally any action or inaction by a woman can be cited by an abuser as provocation for his violence. As one victim noted, "what seemed to provoke him was so contradictory. Some-

Figure 2.1: Examples of how batterers blame their partners for their violence

What was your reason for committing your most recent act of violence?

"She wouldn't keep her mouth shut."
"She has a big mouth."
"She's always got something to say."
"She didn't talk to me respectfully."
"She's got a big mouth."
"She's not sexual enough."
"She's not good enough in bed."
"She makes me jealous."
"She was being a slut."
"She didn't respond quickly enough."
"She's too stubborn."
"She's not as nice as she used to be."
"She jokes around too much."
"She was battered in her first marriage."

Source: Adams 2004.

times he would get mad if I didn't get dressed up but if I did get dressed up he'd accuse me of looking too sexy. Sometimes he'd be upset if I asked him what was bothering him and at other times he'd be mad if I didn't ask him."[14]

Our research suggests that killers denigrate and blame their partners even more than abusers who don't kill. Perhaps the most surprising single finding about these men was how much rage they still held toward the women they had killed. I had expected, perhaps naively, more of the men to express remorse about their actions or sadness about their deceased partners, but remarkably few of them did. For the few who did express remorse, it appeared to revolve around their loss of freedom rather than their partners' loss of life. Interestingly, the only killer who expressed remorse for his victim was one of the two who had attempted to kill himself following his partner's murder. Immediately after strangling and stabbing his wife, this man had turned the knife on himself, surviving only due to the rapid response of the emergency medical team that had been summoned by a neighbor. This man had later pled guilty to murder in the second degree, refusing an offer by the prosecutor to reduce charges to manslaughter.

Minimizing Violence

The vast majority of men who batter do not voluntarily seek help for their violence. Overwhelmingly, men who attend batterer intervention programs are mandated into treatment by the courts that have convicted them of domestic battery or violation of a protective order. In Massachusetts, for example, 84% of the men attending a certified batterer intervention program in 2003 were mandated by a court to do so, while an additional 9% were referred by the child welfare system as a condition of their "service plan."[15]

Are those men who seek help voluntarily more committed to change? Not necessarily. Many of the "self-referred" men are not seeking services to change their behavior so much as to save their relationships. For the most part, these are men whose partners have left them or threatened to do so. Many of these men are seeking help in order to stave off criminal charges or protective orders that would require them to vacate their homes. Some are attending only because their partners have demanded that they do so. For this reason, some practitioners refer to these men as "partner-mandated."

Most batterers do not seek to change their behavior because they deny or minimize their problems. As already discussed, they also blame their partners. Two major goals of batterer intervention programs are to help men recognize their abusive behavior, and beyond this, to accept responsibility for ending it. One obvious motive for the abuser to minimize his violence is to avoid legal sanctions. However, some minimize also because they do not characterize much of their intimidating behaviors as violent. The following are examples of this by two men engaged in a batterer intervention program.

Counselor: Have you been violent to your wife?
Client: No.
Counselor: Have you ever hit her?
Client: A couple of times maybe.
Counselor: You don't consider that to be violence?
Client: I thought you meant when you get someone down on the ground, you know, beat someone up. I've never done that.[16]

Counselor: Can you tell me about the last time you were violent toward your wife?
Client: We were arguing about something and one thing led to another and then I just lost control.
Counselor: Did you hit her?
Client: I would never hit her like a man!
[*This client went on to explain that he had slapped his wife in the face with an open hand, leaving her with two black eyes.*][17]

One aspect of helping abusers to overcome their denial is to provide information that broadens their understanding of what constitutes violence. One batterer intervention program provides the following definitions of violence:

1) Any behavior that is intimidating or frightening to your partner
2) Anything that forces your partner to do something she does not want to do
3) Anything that prevents her from doing something she wants to do[18]

Within these frameworks, such acts as yelling at one's partner while standing over her, disabling her car or telephone, or locking her in or out of a room would qualify as violent. While yelling at one's partner is not inherently intimidating, it is all the more so when it has been preceded by physical violence or threats of violence. By yelling or even by raising his voice toward his partner, the abuser is reminding her, wittingly or unwittingly, of his past violence and his potential to repeat it.

Batterers not only resist change by minimizing their actions but also by mimicking change in ways that are designed to avoid legal and other consequences. Some experts have referred to this as the "quick fix strategies" of abusers.[19] Examples of "quick fixes" include apologizing for one's violence or promising that it will never occur again. Rather than reflecting the abuser's real commitment to change, however, these actions are often an attempt to manipulate his partner to remain in the relationship, or if she has already left, to reunite with him. Revealingly, some voluntary clients in batterer intervention programs drop out of treatment once their partners have reconciled with them or dropped legal charges. Others drop out when their partners file for divorce. As one such client explained, "I came here to save my marriage. This has been a waste of my money."[20]

Capable of Change

A major challenge of batterer intervention programs is to help abusers recognize the need for genuine and lasting change. Over time, many abusers do come to recognize that becoming nonviolent is not just something that they must do to placate their partners but rather a necessary first step toward building better relationships with their partners and children. While abusers rarely seek help on a voluntary basis, there is some evidence that many benefit from such help once it is mandated. Most outcome studies of batterer intervention programs have found a positive effect. One overview of twenty-two batterer intervention program outcome studies found offender recidivism rates that ranged from 7% to 47%, with an average rate of 26%.[21] The wide variation in outcome was attributed to a variety of factors, such as quality and duration of the program, length of the follow-up period during which new acts of violence were recorded, and strength of court monitoring of the offenders. The studies also varied according to the sources of data they relied upon to determine recidivism. While most relied upon police reports of new arrests, others additionally sought input from the men's partners about new acts of violence. One outcome study in Seattle that relied solely on police reports found that offenders engaged in a batterer intervention program had a recidivism rate of 23%, compared to a rate of 62% in a control group of offenders who did not receive treatment.[22] By comparison, the studies that included partner reports of new acts of violence found an average recidivism rate of 32%.[23]

Nearly all the studies have found that offenders who complete their batterer intervention programs do better than those who do not. Aggregately, these studies have found that program dropouts are one-and-a-half to three times more likely than program completers to re-offend.[24]Program dropouts have also been found to re-offend more frequently and more severely.[25] Given this, several researchers have noted that program noncompletion is a significant predictor of an offender's likelihood of committing new and escalating levels of violence. One factor that appears to influence program completion rates significantly is the strength and consistency of court monitoring of the program participants. In some jurisdictions, more consistent court monitoring of offenders has been achieved as a result of creating specialized domestic violence dockets or courts. In such courts, judges, prosecutors, and probation officers receive specialized training in the handling of domestic violence cases, and sometimes handle these cases exclusively. This creates more consistency and collaboration in creating safeguards for victims, and also in the sentencing and monitoring of offenders. Studies have increasingly pointed to the improved outcomes of these systems with specialized domestic violence protocols. One researcher evaluated the impact of mandatory court reviews of all batterers sentenced to attend a batterer intervention program in Pittsburgh. Program participants were required to go before a magistrate after thirty days, and again after sixty days to review their cooperation and progress. As a result, the rate of program "no shows" (men who failed to enroll in the assigned program) had dropped from 36% to 6%. It was also found that the rate of program drop-out had been reduced from 65% to 48%.[26]

These findings suggest that courts can play a key role in getting offenders to the right programs and in keeping them in these programs long enough for them to move beyond quick fixes. But, as one team of researchers noted, "Not all mandating systems are alike in their effectiveness to compel wife assaulters to seek treatment. They also differ in the consistency with which no-shows are actively penalized for failing to comply with court orders to attend treatment."[27] For example, program evaluators of court sentencing of offenders in Seattle found that 58% of the program noncompleters attended no sessions at all. Despite this, only 37% of these men had their probation revoked.[28]

3 | Killer Profiles

The murderers we interviewed were not representative of men who kill their partners in one important respect: none of them had also killed themselves. For two of the men, this had not been for lack of trying. Immediately after strangling and stabbing his partner, one man had plunged the same knife into his neck and slashed both wrists. In an attempt to finish himself off, he had then attempted to stab himself in the chest. By that point, however, he had been too weak from loss of blood to penetrate his rib cage and passed out. This man had survived only due to the rapid response of the EMTs. I will describe this man, Allen, in more detail in the later section about the suicidal type of killer. The other killer who had attempted suicide had shot himself in the chest immediately after shooting his partner in the neck and head. He was hospitalized for two months in recovery. In profiling the suicidal type of killer, I will draw from other research findings.

Including the men who we characterized as suicidal, I found all thirty-one killers could be classified under at least one of five broad types. These types were *jealous, substance abusing, materially motivated, suicidal,* and *career criminal.* I also found that there was considerable overlap among these types. We classified more than half of the men as belonging to more than one of these types. The largest overlaps were between the jealous and the substance abusing types. There was also a considerable overlap between the career criminal and the materially motivated types. I will say more about these overlaps in the section about men who pose multiple threats.

There are any number of alternative ways that killers, like any other individuals, could be classified. One possible classification scheme would be according to personality type. I did not undertake to classify the killers in this manner because it is already known that murderers have many personality types. I wished instead to focus on assessments of behavior and attitude. Though there might be some value to assessing which personality types are most common, the added time it would have taken to administer personality assessment tools would have been at the expense of the structured interviews and the attitude and behavior measures.

Similarly, I did not attempt to categorize the killers formally according to mental health diagnoses. One reason was that this also would have been time consuming and at the expense of other information. Secondly, classifications based on psychopathology are notoriously hard to understand and impractical for those who intervene in domestic violence cases, and even more so for the general public. For instance, to say that some killers have narcissistic personalities or even anti-social ones is useless as a guide for assessing dangerousness since most people charged with assessing danger do not use, and are not qualified or trained to use, psychodiagnostic measures. One such measure, for instance, is the psychopathic checklist.[1] This is used by forensic psychologists and other trained criminal justice workers to assess for psychopathy, one major aspect of anti-social personality disorder. It is known that high proportions of violent offenders, particularly killers, have such traits.[2] While some of these are behavior traits, such as chronic lying and exploitative behavior, others are more subjective, such as the lack of remorse or guilt for one's actions, glibness or superficial charm, having a grandiose sense of self-worth, being irresponsible, and having shallow affect. Discerning these traits is not only difficult for the lay public but also among law enforcement professionals, and among trained therapists as well. Even the shortened version of the psychopathy checklist takes at least one hour to complete by a trained professional. Usually those judged to be high in psychopathic traits have already amply demonstrated their high potential for violence and for other crimes against people. Perhaps the most useful aspect of such diagnostics is to match the individual with the form of treatment that might be most effective. It is commonly advised that individuals who are assessed to be high in psychopathy will not benefit from outpatient therapy and should only receive treatment in a highly structured environment. Further discussion of psychopathy will be provided in the sections about materially motivated and career criminal types of killers.

I sought to categorize killers according to their behavior patterns and relationship histories more than on their psychological characteristics. These behaviors are easily discernable for victims of abuse as well as those who work with them. In classifying each killer, I relied upon his own testimony as well as police reports and newspaper accounts of the murders. Such accounts often provided background information, such as quotes from witnesses and friends and relatives of the victims. These witnesses often had information about the perpetrator's prior abuse of the deceased. I also had access to each killer's criminal record, as well as trial transcripts in some cases. To confirm the validity of each of the categories of killer, I relied upon information from the victims of attempted homicide that we interviewed. From these interviews, a more detailed picture of perpetrators of near-fatal abuse emerged. Demographically, the perpetrators of attempted homicide were very similar to the killers. Judging from their victims' accounts, they also exhibited similar attitudes, expectations, and patterns of abuse. The killers and near-killers were also similar in their rates of substance abuse and mental health problems, as well as their exposure to violence in their upbringings. The more detailed information provided by victims of attempted homicide, particularly about perpetrators' abusive behavior, was indispensable in completing the picture of men who kill. In this way, the victims of attempted homicide served as "stand-ins" for those women who could no longer speak.

Each of the five types of killers profiled had somewhat distinctive ways of meeting women and of forming intimate relationships. I found that each type also had unique patterns of behavior within those relationships, as well as unique complaints and grievances toward their partners. Though all five types of perpetrators exhibited abusive or coercive behavior toward their partners, it seemed to be motivated by factors that were unique to that particular style. Moreover, the fatal and near-fatal assaults appeared to be triggered by these same factors. For each type of killer, I found that the man's short-term triggers were not new but were consistent with his longtime grievances toward the woman he killed.

Jealous Type

Most of the killers came across as extremely jealous. This was the largest category of killers, with seventy-one percent fitting the criteria for membership. It is probable that the actual percentage is higher, but we did not have sufficient information about some of the killers to screen them in as jealous types. According to information from the victims of attempted homicide that we interviewed, eighteen of the twenty perpetrators (or 90%) were extremely jealous. The criteria I used for categorizing a killer as a jealous type included the following four characteristics and behaviors:

1) The perpetrator frequently had jealous suspicions that his partner was sexually involved or interested in others. He was preoccupied with these jealous thoughts.
2) He frequently made jealous accusations to his partner, and frequently asked jealous questions.
3) He often made attempts to confirm his suspicions by monitoring the victim's whereabouts and activities.
4) He'd committed at least one act of abuse or violence toward the victim or toward her alleged romantic partner in response to his jealous suspicions or beliefs.

All twenty-two of the killers whom we characterized as extremely jealous exhibited at least three of the above characteristics. It is important to note that criteria number three by itself did not qualify a killer as being jealous since his monitoring may have had another motive besides jealousy. Some of the killers, especially the materially motivated ones, monitored their victims' activities not with any jealous notions but with intent to oversee their activities. The purpose was not to confirm or disconfirm a jealous suspicion but to determine whether the victim was following through on things that he expected of her. For example, several killers admitted that they often monitored their partners' spending. Other killers said that they often monitored their partners' social activities to ensure that they were not associating with people the men considered to be "a bad influence." Often these "bad influences" meant people who might seek to take steps to end the relationships. One killer admitted that he forbade his partner from seeing certain relatives whom he said had "put ideas in her head about being a battered woman." Several of the other killers said that they had often listened in on their partners' telephone conversations with friends and relatives to monitor what might be disclosed about the women's activities and plans. Some killers seemed not to worry about the existence of another man as much as the possibility that the victim would end the relationship. These men could be said to be possessive more than jealous. I will say more about possessive control and stalking in later chapters.

In many cases, the killer's monitoring of the victim appeared to have a dual purpose: to confirm a jealous suspicion and also to look for signs of compliance or noncompliance on her part. In determining whether certain killers fit the jealous profile, it was necessary to go beyond their self-assessments about jealousy since many downplayed any jealous tendencies. Even some of the men who claimed to have killed their partners in a "jealous rage" avowed not to be abnormally jealous individuals. As one killer put it, "I'm a reasonable man but she drove me to be jealous with what she was doing." This man cited no solid evidence that his partner was being unfaithful, though he had continuously spied upon her and sought to verify her accounts of her activities. During this man's murder trial, the victim's family and friends strongly refuted his claims that she had been having an affair and said that the victim had often complained to them about his jealousy.

Killing from Jealous Rage?

One of the most popular and persistent ways that the media portray domestic homicides is as "crimes of passion" in which a jealous husband kills an unfaithful wife and sometimes her lover as well. Unfortunately, both investigators and reporters sometimes glibly offer this phrase as an explanation, as if to distinguish these killings from others that are portrayed as more "heinous" and "cold blooded." But is that ever the whole story? When a murderer claims to have killed out of jealous rage, this should never be accepted at face value. When domestic violence has been part of the equation, the man's accusation of the woman's infidelity must be examined within the context of an abusive relationship. Was the killing a moment of "temporary insanity" prompted by the killer's discovery of an affair? Or was it the final culmination of possessive control and escalating violence within the relationship?

To answer this question, I examined each case in which the killer claimed that the murder had been primarily prompted by his partner's involvement with another person. Thirteen of the thirty-one killers (65% of the jealous type of killers and 41% of the total) made such claims. It should be noted, however, that twelve of these men said that the murder also had been prompted by the victim's decision to end the relationship. Seven of these victims had already separated from their future killers and an eighth, who had never lived with him, had broken off any contact with him. Interestingly, only one of the thirteen men who claimed to have killed out of a jealous rage had been convicted of manslaughter. Seven were convicted of first degree murder while the remaining five were convicted of second degree murder. This means there was overwhelming evidence that these men, claiming to have killed in a jealous rage, had in fact acted with considerable premeditation.

One killer, Dennis, claimed to have found an unused condom on his estranged wife's night table, prompting him to stab her in the chest. Strong evidence of premeditation, however, was presented at Dennis's murder trial. The couple had separated a year earlier when his wife, Susan, took out a restraining order and filed for divorce. Over the year before her death, Susan had accused Dennis of violating her restraining order by entering her house on three different occasions when she wasn't there and by making threatening phone calls on two other occasions. Susan had begun dating another man shortly before her divorce from Dennis was finalized. Meanwhile, Dennis's gambling problem had escalated to the point where he was tens of thousands of dollars in debt. According to the police investigation of Susan's homicide, Dennis carried a hunting knife with him when he broke into her house on the evening he killed her. There was also evidence that Dennis had made several phone calls to track Susan's whereabouts that day. The medical examiner reported that Susan had been stabbed at least nine times.

In eight of the cases where the killers claimed to have killed out of a jealous rage, there is no independent evidence that their partner had been involved with someone else. In four of these cases, friends and/or relatives of the deceased provided strong testimony to the contrary, saying that any infidelities on the victim's part had been solely in the imagination of the jealously possessive perpetrator. Table 3.1 summarizes our findings about this.

In some cases, it was hard to discern whether the killer sincerely believed that his partner had been involved with someone else or whether his allegations were fabricated in order to win sympathy from others, including court juries. For some of the killers, their continual allegations of infidelity appeared to have been a major part of their attempts to control

Table 3.1: Findings relevant to the killers' claims of killing out of a jealous rage

Total number of men claiming to have killed out of a jealous rage	13 (42%)
	N=31
Of these thirteen men:	
Number convicted of first degree murder	7
Number convicted of second degree murder	5
Number convicted of manslaughter	1
There is evidence the victim was involved with someone else	5 (38%)
There is no evidence the victim was involved with someone else	8 (62%)

and to isolate their partners socially. Many victims of severe abuse said that their abusers' frequent allegations had caused them to curtail or cease contact with friends and relatives. One victim said, "I just gave up with my friends anyway because if I did make an effort to see them, he would always badger me with questions and make my life miserable."

For battering men, their jealousy provides a nearly perfect excuse for their abusive behavior, making it appear "crazy" or irrational rather than deliberate or calculating. Some batterers go so far as to proclaim that their extreme jealousy is evidence of their deep devotion and passion for their partners. In explaining his jealous rages, one young man told his girlfriend, "I wouldn't do these things if I didn't love you so much."

Jealous Thoughts and Behaviors

According to the victims of severe abuse that we interviewed, the vast majority of their abusers displayed extremely jealous behavior. Nearly 90% of the women said that they were subjected to frequent jealous questions and accusations, often accompanied by abusive behavior such as monitoring, stalking, and threatening or committing violence. At least half of the women said that their partners checked their clothing for signs of sexual activity. Table 3.2 presents findings about how victims rated the jealous feelings of their abusive partners.

In some instances, the abusive men's lists of imagined romantic rivals

Table 3.2: Seriously battered women's ratings of their partners' jealousy

		Percentage of victims who said "yes"
How jealous did your partner get of your relationships with members of the opposite sex?	He was very jealous or extremely jealous	89
In general, how jealous of a person do you think your partner was?	He was very jealous or extremely jealous	7
In response to the following scenarios, how jealous do you think your partner would be		
— We were at a bar together and another man invited me to dance but I politely said no.	He would be moderately to extremely jealous	83
— When buying something at a convenience store, I laughed at something the store clerk said.	He would be moderately to extremely jealous	69

N=35

are very long, extending even to members of the victims' families. Nearly one-quarter of the victims we interviewed said that their abusers had accused them of sexual interest in their own relatives. The women said they found this particularly distressing since these accusations were sometimes accompanied by demands that they stop having contact with the relative. Three women said that they regretted telling their abusers about their past traumatic experiences with incest since it subsequently led to allegations that they had been complicit with the sexual acts or that they continued to have interest in the relative who abused them. In one case, the batterer beat up the victim's father who had sexually abused her as a child. This led to the victim becoming further alienated from her mother and siblings.

Case Example 1

"I knew that I couldn't trust her.
It was the same way with my second wife."

Emmit was thirty-nine and Louise twenty-nine when they first met at the nursing home where they were both working. Emmit had been married twice previously and Louise once. Emmit had two children by his first wife and one by his second. Emmit said that both of these prior marriages ended badly due to infidelity on each ex-partner's part. Conceding that he had threatened violence and sometimes hit or pushed each ex-partner, Emmit insisted that these were "natural reactions to their cheating and lying about it." Emmit's first jealousy toward Louise appeared after their first date, when Louise admitted that she was still living with her estranged husband with whom she had a two-year old son, Brian. At Emmit's insistence, Louise filed for divorce two months later and moved in with her parents. Louise's parents were negative toward Emmit because of his two failed marriages and urged Louise to stop seeing him. In response to this, Emmit confronted Louise's father, having a "fist fight" with him in the driveway. After Louise's father filed a charge of assault and battery against Emmit, Louise decided to find an apartment in which to live with her son. After one month in the new place, Emmit convinced Louise to live with him and the new couple found a larger apartment several towns away. By now, Emmit had taken a new job at a car rental agency and Louise was working in another nursing home in the same town. Within one year, the couple bought their first home and their son Benjamin was born.

Suspicious of Louise's relationships with co-workers, he continuously urged her to quit her job so that she could be a full-time mother. After about five years of this, Louise reluctantly quit her job to work at the seasonal seafood restaurant that Emmit had purchased. Though Emmit worked odd jobs during the winter months, the family had difficulty paying all their bills and fell into debt. Louise convinced Emmit to let her go back to school so she could pursue her nursing license. At the same time, she resumed work as a nurse's aide at a nursing home.

By mid-1994, Emmit began to suspect that Louise was having an affair because she was coming home late on some evenings. After one such incident in early September, he demanded to know where she had been and she insisted that she had been shopping. He rifled her purse looking for a store receipt, and finding none, grabbed Louise by the shirt while calling her a liar. He demanded that she leave, and in response, Louise took the two children to stay with her parents. The following day, Louise returned with the police to get some of her belongings. Meanwhile, Emmit has spoken with several neighbors who all sought to assure him that Louise had been faithful to him. Full of remorse, Emmit drove to Louise's work the next day to leave flowers and a note of apology on the windshield of her car. Louise called him that evening and Emmit begged her to return. Louise agreed to do so on the condition that Emmit stop making jealous accusations. Two days later, however, Emmit's suspicions returned when Louise was one hour late coming home from work. They had a loud argument in which Emmit accused Louise of neglecting the house and she accused him of being short with the children. During this conflict, Emmit knocked over several pieces of furniture and pushed Louise into a wall.

On September 22, Emmit drove by Louise's workplace late in the day to verify whether she was working late as she had told him over the phone. When he arrived at the nursing home, he noticed Louise getting into a car with a man. He followed the other car from a distance until they pulled into a Dunkin Donuts. In a jealous rage, Emmit approached the pair in the parking lot, yelling and threatening to kill both of them. Louise insisted that the other man was just a co-worker and they had just been picking up donuts for a meeting at work. Emmit called her a liar, telling her, "If you want to destroy our marriage, then goodbye." He then drove to Louise's parents house and told her father that Louise was having an affair. Returning home, he told the same thing to twelve-year-old Brian, who quickly left to visit a friend. Emmit then loaded his shotgun with the intention of shooting himself but stopped when Brian returned home with his friend. After putting the shotgun away, Emmit gathered up nearly everything that Louise owned, making numerous trips out to the back yard, where he placed her clothing, shoes, jewelry, pictures, and other keepsakes into a pile. With Brian questioning what he was doing, Emmit poured gasoline on the pile, setting it ablaze. Fearing what would come next, Brian fled to a neighbor's house. Meanwhile, Emmit called his brother, Ronald, to tell him what had happened. Ronald came over to see the still-burning pile and convinced Emmit to come over to his house in order "to calm down." Ronald told Emmit, "If you don't trust Louise, you should just divorce her." He took Emmit out to dinner, but Emmit was continuously sobbing and could not eat. Emmit returned home to find the police. The police told him that Louise had taken out a protective order that barred him from being in the house and from having any contact with Louise. The police also informed Emmit that there would be a court date at 9:00 the next morning for a hearing to determine whether the restraining and vacate order should be continued. They transported Emmit back to Ronald's house. That evening, Ronald and his wife continuously sought to assure Emmit that Louise had not cheated on him.

On his way to court the following day, Emmit stopped at the bank where he cleaned out the joint checking account. At the court hearing, Louise told the judge that she feared Emmit due to his violent jealousy. The judge continued the restraining order, warning Emmit that he was not allowed to have any contact with Louise, Brian, or Benjamin. A hearing was set for ten days later to determine whether the restraining order would be extended for a year and to determine whether Emmit would be allowed to have child visitations. After the court hearing, Emmit stopped back at the bank to tell them he would stop making mortgage payments on the house as well as loan payments on Louise's car. Emmit spent the rest of the day at his restaurant.

That evening, Emmit and Ronald planned to attend a party to be held at a Chinese restaurant by a friend of the family. Knowing that Louise had also been invited, Emmit went out to purchase a new suit in hopes of impressing her at the party. Arriving early at the party, Emmit was anxious to see Louise despite her restraining order against him. He arrived at 5:45, and not seeing Louise, went to the bar where he had four rum and Cokes over the next two hours. During this time, Emmit talked with many friends as they arrived for the party, telling all of them that Louise had cheated on him and kicked him out of the house. Most of the friends had already heard about the situation and tried to tell Emmit that Louise was a good wife who would never cheat on him. At 7:45, Louise arrived with Benjamin, now age eight, and several cousins. Benjamin ran over to sit in his father's lap as Louise and her cousins took a booth in another section of the restaurant. A bit later, when Louise came in to summon Benjamin, Emmit tried to speak with her. In response, Louise told him, "Don't make a scene," and returned with Benjamin to the other room.

Over the next two hours, Emmit had two more drinks while continuing to talk with friends and relatives about the situation. He became increasingly furious that others did not believe his accusations of Louise. Emmit left the restaurant at 10:00 and decided to drive to Louise's house. He parked his car several streets away and walked to her house, trying to avoid being seen by any neighbors. He let himself in via some sliding doors in the back and looked around the house to see if anyone was home. He then sat in a chair and awaited Louise's arrival.

Hearing Louise and the children arrive home at 10:30, Emmit hid behind a chair in the living room. He waited there in the dark while Louise made the boys take their showers and gave them a snack in the dining room before putting them to bed at 11:00. Emmit waited another fifteen minutes before making his move. He first looked into both boys' bedrooms, looking for Louise. He saw that Benjamin was already asleep while Brian was watching television. He then went into Louise's bedroom where he found her lying on her bed with her television on. He walked closer to see if she was asleep, and noticed that her eyes were closed. He touched Louise's arm and called her name. Louise awoke with a start, saying, "What are you doing here?" Emmit told her, "Louise, I love you. Please don't leave me. I don't care what you did. Think of the kids. All I want is for you to see a doctor." As he was saying this, he put his hand on her chest. When she pushed to get up, Emmit pulled a knife from her dresser drawer and jumped on her. He stabbed her several times in the chest, stopping only when Benjamin walked in saying, "Daddy, what's going on here?" The knife was still sticking in Louise's chest with its handle broken off. Emmit told Benjamin to go back into his room and then called his brother, Ronald. Ronald's wife answered and Emmit told her that he had just stabbed Louise. Meanwhile, the next-door neighbor arrived, after having been summoned by Brian. Emmit yelled at the neighbor, who then fled the house with the two boys. Before the police arrived, Emmit stabbed himself once in the stomach. The wound was not considered life-threatening. The police testified at Emmit's trial that Louise had been stabbed seventeen times. One witness who had attended the party on the night of the murder testified that Emmit had kept saying, "I'll kill Louise and put her in her grave." Contrary to Emmit's claim that he'd had seven mixed drinks that evening, no alcohol had been found in his system when his blood alcohol level was tested two hours after the murder. Emmit was convicted of murder in the first degree and is currently serving a life sentence.

Emotional Dependence and Instability

The sheer prevalence of extreme jealousy among killers makes it difficult to determine how they are unique, other than from their jealous behavior. Many of their characteristics are similar to those found among the substance abusers who will be profiled in the next section. This is not surprising given the large overlap between these two groups. Both kinds of killers are emotionally volatile, moody, and self-centered. If we separate out the substance abusers from the other jealous men, the remaining men are more stable in terms of their work records and relationship histories. They are more likely to be employed, to be married, and to have children. They are similar to the substance abusers, however, in the frequency and explosiveness of their violence. Their violence may be somewhat more predictable in that it is often prompted by jealous suspicions and not subject to the aggravating effects of alcohol or drugs.

In some ways, it is easier to identify unique features of the jealous types by examining the men who don't fit the profile. This was approximately one-third of the killers. The most obvious difference of these nine men was that they did not display jealous behaviors, though nearly all of them could be said to be possessively controlling. These men did not appear to have worried about the possibility that their partners would become involved with other men. Was it because their partners gave them no reason for concern? Three of these men said that their partners had been involved with other men. In all three cases, the killer said he had not cared about this other relationship since he did not love his partner. Two of these men said that they had left their partners shortly before killing them and three others were estranged from their partners. None said that he wished to reunite with his partner.

Compared to these men, the jealous men appeared much more invested in maintaining their relationships with the women they killed. None who were estranged from their partners said that they had initiated the break-up. All of these men said that they had wanted to reunite with their partners. Jealous men were significantly more likely than their nonjealous counterparts to say that they felt "highly dependent" upon their partners. They were more than five times more likely to characterize themselves as "needy or clingy." Nearly one-third of these men characterized themselves as "helpless much of the time." By contrast, none of the nonjealous men viewed themselves this way. There were no differences between these groups of men in the proportion who characterized themselves as "impulsive" or as "explosive." However, the jealous men were four times more likely to say that they were "set off by little things." They were also more than twice as likely to say that they were "sensitive to insult" and to characterize themselves as "moody." A summary of these self-perceptions is provided in Table 3.3.

The jealous killers came across as more emotionally volatile and moody than the other killers, though they were no more likely to abuse alcohol or drugs. The jealous killers also distinguished themselves in how much they were influenced by their relationships. They rated themselves as being much more emotionally dependent on their partners, as well as more emotionally needy or clingy. This suggests a much bigger investment in their partners' loyalty and emotional availability. One killer said, "I didn't realize how bad off I was emotionally. I thought in my heart I could get her back." When asked if there was anything his estranged partner could have said to have avoided being killed, another man said, "If she told me she wouldn't leave me. I was so vulnerable, I would have believed her."

The jealous men were more likely to say that they had wanted frequent sex with their partners. Given their jealous thoughts, frequent sex may have been a way for these men of continually confirming their primary status with their partners. The jealous men were also more likely to

Table 3.3: Comparison of jealous and not-jealous killers on how they see themselves (by percentage)

Jealous trait	Jealous men	Not-jealous men
Moody	70	30
Sensitive to insult	68	30
Feeling needy or clingy	57	10
Impulsive	52	50
Feeling highly dependent on my partner	52	30
Set off by little things	42	10
Explosive	36	30
Feeling helpless much of the time	31	0
	N=22	N=9

say that they had wanted sex immediately following an act of violence toward the victim. The perpetrators' expectations of sex after violence are discussed in more detail in the section on sexual violence.

A higher proportion of the jealous types of killers reported that they had no friends, and on average, they had fewer friends than the other killers. This was especially true when we separate out the jealous men who did not have substance abuse problems. Seven out of the eight non-substance-abusing jealous men said that they had no friends. These seven men also had been far less likely to want to engage in social activities with their partners. None said that he and his partner had spent any significant time with mutual friends. When asked why, one of these men said, "I didn't trust her friends." He went on to explain that several of his wife's friends had encouraged her to leave him due to his violence. Two other men said their jealousy had been the reason for not socializing with other couples. Both had strongly suspected their wives of having affairs with other women's husbands. These men had not only refused to accompany their wives on evenings out with other couples but had also attempted to dissuade their wives from doing so. One man, Gregory, had been so suspicious that his wife was having an affair with the husband of her best friend that he had followed her on several occasions when she said she was having dinner at a restaurant with her friends. Gregory admitted that he had peered through the windows of the restaurant to make sure that his wife was "with who she said she was with."

Triggers for Homicide

I found that each type of killer had somewhat distinctive triggering factors that led him to murder. In examining each homicide, I looked at two kinds of triggers: longstanding ones, such as grievances against the victim, as well as recent events, such as estrangement or a suspected affair. Often, the immediate triggers were simply continuations of longstanding ones. For example, the jealous killer's "jealous rage" leading to homicide often seemed but a culmination of his longstanding jealousy. As previously mentioned, over half of the jealous men said that the murders they committed had been primarily triggered by jealous rage about their partners' alleged involvement with other men. About half of these men named a person whom they had believed to be sexually involved with their partner.

Two men said that the immediate trigger had been their partner not admitting to an affair they had assumed she was having. One of these men said, "If she had said 'I'm sorry,' or 'I don't want to be with you,' I would have killed myself instead." The other man said, "If she had just admitted it, I would have just left." This man had lured his estranged partner to a hotel for one last night with her and then demanded that she admit an affair.

Four men said that their murderous rage had been motivated not by suspicions about a specific rival but by the idea that their partners would end the relationships and eventually replace them with someone else. One man said he had been infuriated by the idea that "someone else would have her." Beyond their jealous vengeance, the vast majority of the jealous men said that the murders also had been triggered by anger at their partners for ending or attempting to end the relationships. The two most commonly stated motives for killing were to punish the partner for ending the relationship and to prevent her from leaving. Asked his motive in killing his recently estranged partner, one killer said, "To stop her from hurting me, and to keep our family together." This man went on to explain that his having sex with her one last time before killing her had been "a way of preserving us as a couple forever."

Most of the men said that their suspicions about their partners ending the relationships became more frequent over time. Three-quarters of the jealous men said that they became "obsessive" about their partners in the hours and days leading up to the murder. Three-quarters said that they also had become increasingly "desperate." By contrast, only 10% of the other killers said that they had felt desperate or obsessive just prior to killing their partners. Several men said that they had not slept for days before the murder. One killer said, "I was obsessed, every waking moment." This obsession had been accompanied by increased monitoring, and in many cases, stalking of their partners.

One killer, Harold, said, "I suspected Jenaya was making plans [to end the relationship] but I didn't know for sure. The more distant she became . . . it got worse. And it got to the point where I was obsessed with knowing . . . what she was thinking." In the weeks before he shot Jenaya to death in a hotel room, Harold had begun to take more and more time off from work to monitor her activities. From observing her interactions with a fellow tenant, Harold had become convinced that Jenaya was planning to leave him for the other man. Unbeknownst to Jenaya, Harold had quit his job two weeks before the murder in order to devote himself full time to observing her. He would leave the house in the morning at the usual time, as if he were going to work, and then park his truck down the street from where he would spy on Jenaya.

Another killer, Anthony, had also quit his job in order to spy on his wife, Robin. Two days before the murder, Anthony had bound Robin's feet and wrists with duct tape and held her hostage all night while threatening to kill both of them. The next day, Robin had obtained a protective order, requiring Anthony to leave their house. Desperate to enlist their support, Robin had visited Anthony's parents to tell them of her decision to file for divorce. She did not know that Anthony was sitting in the stairwell, listening to their conversation via a baby monitor. He had overheard Robin telling his parents that she would take the children to Cape Cod the following morning. Anthony's parents had been so fearful that he might kill Robin before she fled that they had insisted he make an emergency appointment with his psychiatrist for the following morning. Throughout that night, they had taken turns standing watch outside his bedroom to make sure that he didn't leave.

Early the following morning, Anthony had called a cab from his room and then told his parents he needed to go outside for a smoke. He had then fled in the cab to Robin's house. When he arrived, Robin had just put the two boys in the car and had gone back inside to get some bags. Anthony told the two boys to stay quiet before going into the house to find Robin. Trapping her in the bathroom, Anthony stabbed Robin in the chest and lower back with a fishing knife.

While Anthony had monitored Robin's behavior throughout their eleven-year marriage, he reported that this behavior became more frequent during periods of separation or pending separation. During one prior separation six years earlier, Anthony had hired a private investigator to conduct surveillance of Robin. Reflecting back on the intense energy he had devoted to "worrying" about Robin's plans, Anthony said that he felt a great relief after killing her. "It was almost like having an orgasm," he added.

Potential Deterrents

I asked each man a variety of questions to identify what might have prevented from killing his partner. Some questions related to potential immediate deterrents while others concerned long-term measures such as counseling, criminal sanctions, and other kinds of interventions. I found that each of the killer types was somewhat distinct in the kinds of potential deterrents that they identified. I asked each man to look over a list of potential deterrents, and to indicate which "would have" and "would not have" prevented him from killing. This list included

a) a judge putting me in jail with a warning that any further violence would result in more jail time
b) attending a batterer intervention program
c) a clergy person talking to me about my violence
d) a police officer threatening to arrest me for any further violence toward my partner
e) a family member urging me to stop my violence toward my partner
f) a friend or relative of my partner threatening to beat me up or kill me
g) being on probation
h) being on probation and having to wear an ankle bracelet that notified police whenever I came close to my partner
i) my partner wearing a beeper that notified the police whenever I came close to her
j) my partner having a restraining order against me
k) having my violence toward my partner publicized in the local newspaper
l) realizing I would spend the rest of my life in prison

Nearly all of these men said that a batterer intervention program might have helped them to stop their violence at an earlier stage. Despite this, none of these men had attended such a program, either voluntarily or as ordered by a court. Such programs were not as available during the early to mid-nineties when many of these murders occurred. Those who counsel batterers say that the biggest barrier for these men to seek help is their denial of abusive behavior. The jealous killers I interviewed were no different in this regard, other than perhaps having an even higher level of denial. Most denied having been abusive to their partners, and therefore would not have seen the need for treatment that focuses on domestic violence. The jealous men who were also substance abusers were more apt to admit a problem with alcohol or drugs than with domestic violence, though (as we will see in the next section), neither did they seek treatment for this.

Those without a substance abuse problem tended to view their partners, and not themselves, as the ones with the problems. As one man put it, "She couldn't keep her pants on, that was the main problem in our relationship." Other jealous killers were more specific about their partners' involvement with particular men. When asked to identify the biggest problems in his relationship with his partner, Harold said, "That man upstairs," meaning another resident with whom he suspected Jenaya was romantically involved. In response to this same question, James, who had smothered his partner, Corinne, with a pillow, said, "her uncle," citing her alleged past sexual involvement with her uncle.

James was the only killer I interviewed who had previously attended a batterer intervention program. One year prior to killing Corinne, James had agreed to attend such a program during his incarceration for a past assault of Corinne. Unfortunately, James had stopped attending this program after twelve sessions when he was released from prison, and did not heed the program's recommendation that he continue treatment in a community-based program. Interestingly, James credited the batterer intervention program with helping him to recognize, at least temporarily, that his jealous feelings concerning Corinne and her uncle were unwarranted and had been destructive to their relationship. As James put it, the program had motivated him to "stop throwing her uncle in her face." Asked whether he had continued to do so following his release from prison, James said, "No, but I ruminated about it when we was separated, I guess out of insecurity." James added that if he had continued his treatment, he "probably" would have been better able to handle his jealous and insecure feelings. While there is certainly no guarantee of this, had James continued his batterer intervention and substance abuse programs, he might not have violated Corinne's restraining order on the night he killed her. James admitted that these feelings "flared up" when he was drinking. James is profiled as a jealous substance abuser in the later section about men who pose multiple threats.

Outcome studies of batterer intervention programs have consistently shown that program completers are significantly less likely to commit new acts of violence, particularly serious ones, than noncompleters. One goal of such programs is that abusers strictly obey the conditions of protective orders. Programs also commonly require participants to commit to sobriety, sometimes with the additional requirement of submitting to random drug screens that are conducted by court personnel. Batterer intervention programs also provide participants a weekly opportunity to discuss any ruminations, obsessive thoughts, or forms of "negative self-talk" such as jealousy or anger toward their partners. One common intervention is to help abusive men identify such negative thoughts in their earliest stages, before they escalate, and to replace them with more constructive ways of thinking, which in turn will help them to make better choices. The need to choose an alternative course of action was best articulated by one of my former clients, Kendrick, who had a history making jealous accusations to his partner.

"Yeah, I'd just run with those feelings [his anger and jealousy] and then I'd do something stupid like going . . . to the bar and showing up at her house and talking shit. . . . Now, I go to a meeting [Alcohol Anonymous] or call my sponsor."[3]

Though Kendrick's words suggest someone with self-motivation, he is like many abusive men who do not voluntarily choose to attend a batterer intervention or a substance abuse program, and only do so because of a court order. Without court monitoring, many abusive men do not remain in such programs long enough to make lasting changes. Outcome studies of abusive men in batterer intervention programs have shown that program completion, as well as desistence from violence, are most likely when program participation is accompanied by consistent monitoring by the courts.[4]

Substance Abusing Type

Next to the jealous type, the largest category of killers was those who abused alcohol or drugs. Nineteen of the killers, or 61%, fit this category. In comparison, 75% of the perpetrators of attempted homicide were classified as substance abusers based on the victim's reports of their alcohol and drug use. Classification for the killers was based on their self reported use of alcohol and drugs as well as their responses to the Addiction Severity Index (ASI).[5] Questions on the ASI require respondents to indicate both lifetime use of alcohol and drugs, as well as their use during the past thirty days. I also asked the men to rate the frequency and amount of substance use during the thirty days immediately preceding the murder. Each man was asked to estimate the number of days he used alcohol and particular drugs during this thirty-day period. To put this in context, I also asked each man to talk about any increases, decreases, or other changes in his substance use during the complete duration of his relationship with the woman he murdered. Each man was additionally asked to describe any consequences of his use, such as arrests for drunk driving or drug possession, or problems in the relationship related to his own or his partner's use of alcohol or drugs. Table 3.4 provides a summary of alcohol and drug abuse by the killers.

Based on their patterns of use, all the men in this group fit the profile of an alcoholic or a drug addict. Just over half of the substance abusers could be classified as polydrug abusers since they abused more than one substance. Aside from alcohol, the most commonly abused drug was marijuana, reported by eight of the men. Eight of the men also reported overusing one or more medications that had been prescribed to them or that they had illegally obtained. These medications included Valium, Elavil, Xanix, Codeine, Percocet, Demerol, or Darvon. Four of the killers reported heavy use of cocaine or crack, while two said they were addicted to heroin.

When assessing an abusive man's potential for homicide, there is some evidence that substance abuse by itself is a significant risk marker. There is more evidence, however, that *frequency* of abuse is especially significant and that the risk of homicide increases dramatically when the abusive man is abusing alcohol or drugs on a daily basis. The incidence of daily use of alcohol and drugs among the substance abusers is shown in Table 3.5.

Table 3.4: Patterns of substance use among killers (by percentage)

Substance abuse profile	Substance abusers	All killers
Abused alcohol only	26	16
Abused drugs only	21	12
Abused alcohol and drugs	52	32
	N=19	N=31

Table 3.5: Daily abuse of substances among killers (by percentage)

Substance abuse profile	Substance abusers	All killers
Daily abuse of alcohol only	57	35
Daily abuse of drugs only	52	32
Daily abuse of alcohol and drugs	31	19
	N=19	N=31

Does Substance Use Contribute to Murder?

Our findings about alcohol and drug use by the killers are consistent with those of Jacquelyn Campbell and her colleagues based on their investigation of 445 intimate partner homicides and attempted homicides of women.[6] This study found that half the perpetrators were problem drinkers and that half used illegal drugs of some kind. There was a substantial amount of overlap between the alcohol and drug abusers. This same study found that one-third of the perpetrators had used alcohol at the time of the homicide or attempted homicide while 12% had used drugs. In about one-quarter of the cases, the perpetrator had used both alcohol and drugs on the day of the homicide or homicide attempt.[7] Pooling the data from the thirty-one killers and the twenty victims of attempted homicide in our study, we found somewhat higher proportions. Half of our killers said that they had been drunk or high or both on the day that they killed their partner or ex-partner. Meanwhile, half of the victims of attempted homicide also reported that their perpetrator had appeared to be drunk or high on the day of the near-fatal assault. For most of the perpetrators who used alcohol or drugs on the day of the murder or attempted murder, alcohol or drug use was not a departure from their usual pattern. Nearly all, from the killers' and victims' accounts, had habitually abused alcohol or drugs on a daily basis. However, this does not mean that alcohol or drug use was not a factor in the fatal and near-fatal assaults. When asked if they thought alcohol or drugs had been a strong factor in their partner's near-fatal assault, half of the victims of attempted homicide said yes. Generally, victims gave two rationales for their answers. A few said that their partner's violence had always been more severe when he had been drinking or using drugs. One woman said that her boyfriend had physically abused her *only* when he was drunk. As one woman put it, "He didn't hold back as much when he was drinking." Another said, "He was more honest about what he really thought when he had alcohol in him," citing his jealous accusations and threats. These women were essentially saying that alcohol or drugs seemed to trigger their partners' violence, including the men's attempts to kill them. Most of the women, however, gave a different reason for thinking alcohol or drugs had played a strong role in their abusers' near-fatal assaults. These women said that their partners' alcohol or drug use had escalated and seemed a part of an overall deterioration that they had noticed in the days or months leading up to the assaults. In most cases, the victim traced her abuser's deterioration to when she had separated from him or otherwise taken steps to end the relationship. Besides increased alcohol or drug use, some victims said they'd also noticed other signs of deterioration such as neglect of hygiene, depression, lack of sleep, or loss of a job. Here is one victim's account of this.

> Interviewer: Were there any other changes you noticed in the three months prior to the homicide attempt?
> Vickie: He seemed to be coming apart. . . . I could tell he wasn't bathing and he'd lost a lot of weight. . . . And his sister told me that he'd been fired from his job.
> Interviewer: Do you know the reason?
> Vickie: She told me it was from his going to work drunk.

Several other victims said that their partner's deterioration was accompanied by increasing levels of violence and "paranoid" behavior in the three months leading up to the near-fatal assault.

> Interviewer: Did you notice anything else?
> Kelly: Well, he was always watching me.
> Interviewer: How do you mean?
> Kelly: Even when I was sleeping, he would be awake and looking at me.
> Interviewer: Why do you think he was doing that?
> Kelly: I think it was because he was suspicious of what I was up to.
> Interviewer: You mean jealous?

Kelly:	Not just that. Paranoid. He was always paranoid but he became even more so. He thought everyone was against him, not just me.
Interviewer:	Do you know why?
Kelly:	The only thing I can think of was the cocaine just because that was never a big thing for him before.

Despite this testimony to the effects of alcohol and drugs, half of the victims of substance-abusing perpetrators said that they did not think alcohol or drugs had been significant factors in the near-fatal assaults. Most of these women thought that their partners would have done the same thing anyway, and several women said they thought alcohol use was merely incidental to the attacks. Further evidence of this is provided by the court findings concerning the killers. Compared to the other killers, those who abused substances were more likely to have been convicted of murder in the first degree (42% compared to 25% of the nonsubstance abusers). A conviction of murder in the first degree indicates "irrefutable" evidence of premeditation on the killer's part. Despite this, over one-third of the substance-abusing killers did not show strong premeditation, according to the court, and were found guilty only of manslaughter. Judging from the court findings and sentences, the substance-abusing killers were mostly on opposite ends of the premeditation scale, suggesting that they had either carefully planned the killing or hardly at all.

How do substance-abusing killers differ from those who do not abuse alcohol or drugs? I found that they are more severely and frequently violent. They are also younger, less likely to be married or to have children, and more likely to be unemployed. In many ways, the substance abusers appeared less stable and more volatile than their nonsubstance-abusing counterparts. Many of the substance abusers talked of a progression of abuse that had corresponded with their increased consumption of alcohol or drugs. More often, their relationships had been short-lived, including their relationships with the deceased. On average, these relationships had lasted two years prior to the murders. This compares to five and a half years for the nonsubstance abusers. Their relationships with the deceased had not only ended faster but also started faster as well. I found that the substance abusers had significantly shorter courtships with the women they killed; two and a half months on average compared to five and a half months for the other killers. Short courtships will be discussed in more detail in a later chapter, since we found this to be a separate risk factor that was not confined just to substance abusers.

Severe Violence

Some researchers and service providers have reported that substance-abusing batterers exhibit more severe levels of violence than do other batterers.[8] There are two primary theories about this. According to proponents of the "disinhibition theory," alcohol and some drugs directly contribute to violence in a variety of ways. These include physiological effects such as loss of motor control and ability to control one's impulses.[9] Personality effects include a lowered ability to tolerate frustration, self-centeredness, avoidance of problems, black-and-white thinking, and being more sensitive to insult. There are also lifestyle consequences that can include financial losses, unemployment, and social alienation. All of these factors can greatly contribute to a person's likelihood of using violence in an intimate relationship.

Proponents of the "deviance disavowal" theory argue that people react very differently to alcohol, and whether a person resorts to violence is determined by one's *beliefs* about drinking.[10] They point to famous lab experiments in which subjects who are led to believe they are drinking alcohol-laced punch at a party, when in fact there is no alcohol in the punch, become more aggressive than those subjects who had actually imbibed alcohol. Other experimental studies have shown that subjects who falsely believe they have imbibed alcohol administer higher levels of electric shock to individuals who give wrong answers to tests they are asked to give.[11] These experimental results suggest that individuals use alcohol as an *excuse* to act out or become violent. By saying "alcohol made me do it," such individuals seek to avoid responsibility for actions that otherwise might get them in trouble.[12]

At least two of the men I interviewed appeared to be using the alcohol or drugs to downplay responsibility for murder. These men claimed that they had consumed large quantities of alcohol or drugs just prior to killing their partners. Drug tests administered to them immediately after their arrest, however, showed that there had been no alcohol or drugs in their systems. This does not mean that alcohol or drugs did not contribute to these killings in other ways, however. Both men did in fact have long histories of alcohol and drug use that may well have contributed to their decisions to kill their partners. Each fit the profile of an advanced-stage alcoholic who had experienced multiple negative effects as the result of alcohol use. One was homeless and had not held a job of over two months for the previous ten years. The other had committed multiple robberies and other crimes to support his drug habit. Though neither was in fact drunk or high on the day of the murders, alcohol and drugs appeared to have greatly influenced their lifestyles and narrowed their choices.

Regardless of whether alcohol or drugs cause these men to be violent, the substance-abusing killers appeared to have committed more frequent and more severe prior acts of violence toward the women they killed. They were almost twice as likely as the other killers to admit past violence that had occurred on at least a monthly level. They were approximately twice as likely to have previously injured their partner. Several of the men had committed past acts of severe violence that could have easily resulted in the deaths of the victims. These include the following incidents by five different men:

1) Bludgeoned the victim repeatedly over the head with a pipe until she lost consciousness and required hospitalization for over one week
2) Threw the victim over a stone wall onto a busy highway
3) Strangled the victim into unconsciousness
4) Punched and kicked the victim repeatedly while throwing her around a room (for about twenty minutes), resulting in many severe lacerations to her head and body
5) Repeatedly drove drunkenly and recklessly with the victim in the car, once crashing into a set of gas pumps and setting them ablaze

For about one-third of the substance-abusing killers, the homicide appeared almost as an inevitable culmination of their highly violent and reckless behavior toward the victim. For two of the men, their fatal assaults were arguably not the most severe acts of violence they had committed toward the victims.

Case Example 2

"She'd always do the opposite of what I'd tell her."

One year prior to killing Carol, Vincent had assaulted her while they were out "drinking and partying" with mutual friends. Enraged that she was "being too friendly" with a mutual friend, Vincent had hit her in the face with a beer bottle. Carol had sustained a deep laceration over her eye for which she'd required at least twenty sutures. Approximately six months later, Vincent had again assaulted Carol while they were out drinking with some friends. This time he'd punched her in the face, breaking her jaw. Vincent had been arrested and served three months in jail.

One night shortly after his release, Vincent and Carol went out partying with mutual friends. Both of them consumed a great deal of alcohol, according to Vincent. Vincent went to the liquor store six times during the course of the evening, buying and helping to consume six pints of peppermint schnapps, four quarter-pints of hot (cinnamon) schnapps, a half gallon of vodka, and about sixty dollars' worth of whiskey. They arrived home at 9:30 p.m. and began to argue. Carol complained that Vincent had stopped up the toilet by throwing some macaroni in it. Vincent tried to unstop it with a broom handle, and then broke it over his knee in frustration. After Carol yelled at him, Vincent punched her in the leg and arm several times and then backhanded her in the face, giving her a bloody nose. He then gave Carol a towel to wipe her face and sat down to watch TV while she went to bed. That evening Vincent slept on the couch.

When he awoke, Carol's face was swollen and he offered to take her to the hospital. She refused his help and instead called the police while he was taking a shower. Vincent was arrested. Ten days later, while Vincent was still in jail awaiting trial, Carol died of a blood clot to her brain. Vincent was convicted of manslaughter and received a ten-year prison sentence.

Asked if a jail sentence for his serious assault of Carol a year prior to her death would have made a difference, Vincent said, "Not really, I would have gone back to her. She'd always do the opposite of what I'd tell her but I was infatuated with her. I'd do anything for her. I'd take her out for Chinese four times a week, buy her flowers. Twice I bought her kittens."

Economic and Emotional Instability

The substance-abusing killers were most distinct from the other killers in their lack of stability. I have already mentioned that their relationships with the deceased had faster beginnings and endings. They also appeared to be less stable in a multitude of other ways. They were twice as likely as the other men to be unemployed at the time of the killings. Overall, their work histories were more sporadic. On average, they changed jobs much more often and held jobs for shorter periods. They were almost three times as likely to have been fired from a job. Their annual incomes were considerably less than those of the other killers. They were three times less likely to own a home. However, their level of education was similar to that of the other killers. Just over half had completed high school and one-quarter had attended at least one year of college.

A pattern of instability was also reflected in the substance abuser's relationships. Despite the fact that they were an average of six years younger than the other killers, the substance abusers had more relationships that preceded their involvement with the women they killed. These relationships were more short-lived and more likely to have ended due to abusive behavior. The substance abusers were half as likely to be married to the murder victim, and three times less likely to have ever married. They were also half as likely to have had children. Those who did primarily appeared to have been abusive parents. More than half admitted to assaulting their children verbally or physically on a regular basis. Compared to the other killers, substance abusers also appeared to have been less involved with their children. Half admitted to having no contact with their biological children following the dissolution of their relationships with the mothers. Some admitted to being unable or unwilling to tolerate children's emotional needs.

Compared to the other killers, except for those we deemed financially exploitative, the substance abusers were most likely to have depended financially upon the murder victims. Given their long periods of unemployment and underemployment, this often extended through most of the relationships and often had been a point of contention with their partners. One man, who had been on extended disability, said that his wife had repeatedly questioned his inability to work. Several of the men said that they had resented their financial dependency on their partners and believed that it had given their partners too much power over them. One man added that "she lorded it over me every chance she got." Two men said that they were more suspicious and jealous toward their partners when they were unemployed.

Compared to the other killers, substance abusers seemed more emotionally volatile. They rated themselves as quick to anger but also said they were often depressed. Two-thirds of the substance abusers rated themselves as being moody. This is over three times the proportion of other killers who perceived themselves this way. Despite this, they were no more likely to rate themselves as being depressed. Half of all killers said that they had been depressed for significant periods of time.

Another distinguishing feature of the substance abusers was that they were much more likely to report that they had had many friends and an active social life. The median number of friends claimed by the substance abusers was five, compared to one for the other killers. Substance abusers were also more than twice as likely to say that they had spent at least one day or evening per week with a friend or friends independently of their partners. Overwhelmingly, these friends were fellow substance abusers and their times together had revolved around alcohol or drugs or both. Four of the substance abusers said that they had spent more evenings with their friends than with their partners. As well as their solo activities with friends, most of the substance abusers reported that they frequently had seen friends with their partners. About two-thirds of the substance abusers said that, together with their partners, they had spent at least one evening per week with mutual friends. This compares to just one-quarter of the other killers. One-third of the substance abusers said that they and their partners had spent *most* of their evenings out with friends, while none of the other killers reported this. As with their solo friends, the killers reported that most of these mutual friends were also heavy users of alcohol or drugs. This choice of friends may explain why so few of the substance abusers had voluntarily sought help for their drinking or drug use. As one killer put it, "They wasn't [sic] going to tell me to stop [drinking] 'cause they was all doing the same thing." This man went on to say that he had retained the same group of "drinking buddies" since childhood and that most had been arrested for alcohol-related crimes such as disturbing the peace, drunk driving, and assaults.

Blaming Alcohol and Drugs

The substance abusers were least likely to express self-regrets, next to the materially motivated killers. When asked to check off whether they "sometimes felt like a failure," only 17% of the substance abusers gave an affirmative response. By contrast, 40% of the other killers checked "yes" to this. Given their poor economic and employment status relative to the other killers, one would expect substance abusers to feel more like failures. However, many substance abusers are known to maintain grandiose self-images. Substance abusers often use alcohol and drugs to avoid self-doubts and to bolster their self-regard. This can become a vicious circle. The more negative consequences the substance abuser incurs due to drinking and drug use, the more he may want to further imbibe in order to forget the past. Drinking also becomes a way of excusing or rationalizing failures. When discussing their failure to advance their careers, a number of the substance abusers I interviewed expressed "I could have been a contender" sentiments. As one man put it, "Alcohol messed me up" in reference to his long periods of unemployment. Not surprisingly, the substance abusers were far more likely to blame their violence on alcohol or drugs. More than half of the substance abusers said that they would not have killed their partner had they not been drunk or high on the day of the murder. Only one of the nonsubstance abusers made this claim.

Triggers for Homicide

Many of the substance abusers revealed longstanding grievances against their partners, but part of the long-term picture for these men was also that their partners had had longstanding grievances against them. Quite often, these grievances had revolved about the man's substance use, lack of financial stability, and general lack of responsibility. Victims had also complained about the men's abusive behavior. As mentioned earlier, these men's violence was often more frequent and more severe than that the other types of killers. Without exception, their physical violence was accompanied by economic abuse. Compared to the other killers, substance abusers were more likely to be unemployed or underemployed and to drain finances on alcohol and drugs. Alcohol and drug use also commonly resulted in additional costs such as drunk driving injuries and fines, damage to one's car as well as other property, and medical costs associated with poor health. Substance abusers often engaged in a wide variety of psychological abuse that typically included name-calling, lying about their whereabouts, having affairs, and not following through on promises.

Despite this, substance abusers were half as likely, compared to the other killers, to be estranged from their partners at the time of the homicide. For those who were no longer living with their partners, estrangement appeared to be a prominent triggering factor for the murders they committed. Nearly all of these men also qualified as jealous types of killers. For the substance abusers who were still living with their partners, the immediate triggers to the murders appeared to have revolved around more mundane grievances. Nine of these men said that the immediate trigger had been that the victim was complaining about something. According to the killers, these nine victims had complained about the following:

1) His drinking and wanting her to go into a particular bar
2) His staying home from work. Killer said he had been upset that neighbors would hear her yelling and they would be kicked out of their apartment
3) Him having stopped up the toilet by throwing macaroni in it
4) Him having left her at a party to go out with his friends
5) He had stolen her heroin
6) He had taken some of her money
7) He had broken a flowerpot
8) His not getting help for his depression
9) Something that the killer cannot recall

There is no way of knowing how accurately the killer is reporting these triggering events. However, the victims of attempted homicide whose partners had been substance abusers cited similar triggering events, even though these victims often said that the near-fatal attacks had come not in response to their complaints about their partners' behavior. In some cases, there had been major complaints about the men's drinking, violence, or controlling behavior. Just as often, victims said the complaints triggering the murder attempts had been minor ones. Some women said they had made no complaints at all, and their partners appeared to be reacting to some imagined slight.

Potential Deterrents

The majority of substance abusers identified alcohol or drug treatment as the biggest potential deterrent for them. Despite this, only 36% had received any kind of treatment for their alcohol or drug abuse prior to the murders. Moreover, more than half the men who had sought treatment only stayed in treatment for short periods that ranged from a single meeting at Alcoholics Anonymous to three to four sessions with a substance abuse counselor. All of the four men who had received longer treatment did so as a prisoner or as a condition of probation. This usually consisted of attending a residential detox program of ten to thirty days followed by a period of group education. Two of the men who had attended detox said that this had been their only period of sobriety during their entire adult lives. Most of the substance abusers admitted that their abuse of alcohol or drugs had begun in their teen years, some starting as early as age eleven.

I also asked each man whether he had experienced any mental health problems as a child or as an adult. Just over half of the substance abusers said that they had suffered from depression or bipolar disorder at least once, though some had never received a formal diagnosis for these. Interestingly, these men were more likely to have sought treatment for depression than for their substance abuse. All eleven men who had depression said that they'd sought some form of treatment for it. For two of these men, this treatment came only when they were children and had been triggered because of conduct problems at school. For two others, the treatment they received had been in prison or as a condition of probation. One of these men, John, had been ordered to attend treatment following his conviction for animal abuse. One year prior to killing his estranged wife, John had poisoned over 10,000 migratory birds in his Cape Cod neighborhood. According to John, neighbors had complained about seagulls, and working as an exterminator, he had volunteered to take care of the problem.

Of the entire list of potential deterrents listed in the previous section about jealous killers, none were selected by more than half of the substance abusers. By contrast, a majority of the other killers (ranging from 62%–75%) checked off six of the ten items. Half the substance abusers believed that being jailed by a judge and having to wear an ankle bracelet would have "very likely" prevented the murders. The least likely potential deterrent selected by the substance abusers was "a clergy person talking to me about my violence." The other killers were three times more likely to say that this would likely have prevented them from committing murder. The substance abusers' low endorsement of this item reflects their general lack of participation in formal religious activities. Less than one-third of these men said that they attended religious services on a regular or occasional basis. The proportion of church-going among the other killers was somewhat higher at forty percent. Only two of the substance-abusing killers said they had ever discussed marital problems with their clergyperson. Neither, however, had disclosed his domestic violence to the pastor.

Most substance abusers rejected all other potential deterrents in favor of measures that would have prevented them from drinking or using drugs on the day of the murder. Short of being in jail or some other controlled environment, few of the men had any ideas of how this might have been achieved. Only one of the substance abusers had been on probation. One of the conditions of this man's probation had been that he submit to random tests to detect whether he had used alcohol or drugs. The last screening he had undergone had been three months prior to the murder, and the results had been negative for alcohol or drug use.

Compared to the other killers, substance abusers were least likely to have sought informal help or advice from other people. This may be because many of their friends were fellow substance abusers. When asked if friends who had witnessed his domestic violence had ever intervened, one killer said, "Nah, they was all doing the same thing." Only one of these men said that a friend had ever intervened. This was Kevin, the young man who shot and killed his friend, Rob, when Rob was trying to stop Kevin from hitting his girlfriend, Rebecca. After killing Rob, Kevin fired his assault rifle at Rebecca, killing her too.

A few of the murder victims, including Rebecca, appeared to be substance abusers. Several of the victims of attempted homicide said that their abusers had often pressured them to drink or to use drugs along with them. In two cases, victims said that the perpetrators had been their prime suppliers of drugs. If a victim is abusing substances, she may not have as much credibility to courts, police, child welfare workers, and other helpers as other victims of abuse. Many battered women's programs do not accept victims who are actively drinking or drugging. This creates a considerable gap in services. Our helping systems need to be better trained and equipped to deal with the special needs and challenges of substance-abusing battered women. Safety planning with these victims is essential as they may be less aware of the danger they face or less able to take steps to protect themselves and their children.

Even victims who do not abuse substances often need help to recognize that substance abuse does not cause their partner to batter, though it may well make the abuse worse. When the batterer abuses alcohol or drugs on a daily or near-daily basis, the level of danger grows exponentially worse. Those who assess danger with victims should therefore always ask detailed questions about the perpetrator's pattern of alcohol and drug use. Sometimes, batterers can be prosecuted for their drug crimes more easily than for domestic violence since such prosecutions for drug crimes don't require the battered partner's testimony. Two victims of attempted homicide said that their perpetrators were never prosecuted for domestic violence since the women had been too fearful to call the police or to file criminal complaints. In both cases, however, the perpetrators ultimately received substantial jail sentences for drug trafficking.

Materially Motivated Type

The term "materially motivated" conjures someone who commits murder for profit. Though it is known that some men murder their wives purely for monetary gain, this was not the case for any of the killers I interviewed, including those I have characterized here as materially motivated. In this context, materially motivated killers are those whose primary interests in their relationships with women related to money and other material assets. Following from this, the murders they committed appear to have been primarily motivated by grievances concerning money, possessions, and other material benefits. These murders were not committed for profit but rather to avoid material loss. The term "material" is important here since it encompasses more than money. It includes possessions, such as a house and a car, but also the benefits that such possessions confer. In the case of a house, the material benefits include not just having equity as well as status within the community, but also having a place to call home, with all of the attendant privileges. In the context of an intimate relationship, the material benefits of home also include the comforts one receives from a committed partner, such as sexual intimacy, emotional support, and companionship, as well as housework and childcare. What stood out among the materially motivated men was their unilateral expectation of such services without assuming any reciprocal responsibilities. Perhaps more to the point, they seemed to expect such services while having no emotional attachment or loyalty to their partners. Many of the other killers, such as the jealous men, similarly expected services from their partners. However, they also displayed some degree of emotional attachment to their partners, even if it had been often communicated in an abusive manner. All of the jealous killers said they had loved their partners either throughout or for some period in their relationship with the women they killed. None of the materially motivated men said this.

The criteria for membership in the materially motivated group of killers includes the following features:

1) He exhibited very few jealous feelings and little jealous behavior.
2) He was materially exploitative and/or possessive. His grievances primarily revolved around money and other material benefits.
3) He had an overwhelmingly negative view of women.

Lack of Jealousy

Materially motivated killers were unique among partner killers in their relative lack of jealous thoughts and feelings concerning their partners. This is because jealousy, whether within the normal or extreme range, requires an emotional investment in one's partner. The materially motivated killers showed no signs of having made such investments. None of these seven killers revealed a history of having been emotionally attached to the deceased or to any previous partners. While all of the other killers admitted some degree of jealousy, ranging from normal to extreme on the two jealousy scales that we used, none of the materially motivated men reported having even normal degrees of jealous thoughts or feelings. Initially, I was highly skeptical about these claims, all the more so since some of the men admitted that they had monitored their partners' activities. When asked about this apparent discrepancy, the men said that their monitoring had been motivated not by jealous suspicions but by their wish to know their partners' plans, and in particular whether the women had been planning to file charges for domestic violence, obtain protective orders, or seek to end the relationships. Our interviews with the victims of attempted homicide also provided some evidence about the lack of jealousy among this subgroup of perpetrators. Four of the twenty victims of attempted homicide that we interviewed rated their partners as being "not jealous at all" or only "mildly jealous." As one woman said, "He didn't care about me or worry about me being with someone else; he just cared about the house and all the things in it."

Violence, for the materially motivated perpetrators, was not triggered by their own jealousy but more often by that of their partners. All four of the victims who said that their partners had not been jealous also reported that their partners had been continually involved with other women, and that their complaints about this had triggered violent responses from the men. Most of the materially motivated killers also complained about their partner's jealous complaints. For some, these jealous complaints represented an attempt to "own me," as one man put it.

These men did not appear to have worried about losing their partners so much as the money and other material benefits connected to the relationship. For some men, this would have meant loss of a home. For those who were unemployed, it meant loss of their primary source of "income." Ideally for some, the relationship would have ended without the loss of such financial support. In fact, two of the men admitted that they had continued to receive money or gifts from ex-partners with whom they had continued to have sexual relations during their relationships with the women they killed.

Contempt for Women

All seven of the materially motivated killers painted an overwhelmingly negative picture of their partners. Not once during the four-hour interviews did any of these men communicate a positive sentiment about the women they had murdered. When asked directly, none could think of a positive attribute of his partner. Each man went to great lengths to demonize the deceased, as if perhaps to rationalize the murders they had committed. While this may be true, it was also clear that this hostility had been a longstanding feature in their relationships with their partners.

Abusive men in general tend to have highly critical opinions of their partners. In my previous study that compared abusive to nonabusive husbands, I found that abusive husbands had significantly less positive regard and empathy for their wives, and much more antipathy towards them.[13] Despite this, the vast majority communicated *some* positive regards toward their partners, and most professed to love them. This was even true for the majority of killers I interviewed, though as a whole, their negative feelings and attitudes toward their partners appeared to outweigh their positive ones. Their overall attitude seemed to be, "I couldn't live with her and I couldn't live without her," revealing a sometimes begrudging acknowledgment of affection or perhaps dependency. The materially motivated killers were the only type of perpetrator who appeared to have had *no* positive regards or sentiments toward their partners. Their overall attitude seemed to be something akin to "good riddance for someone I never liked to begin with." Their contempt for their partners appeared to be an extension of their contempt for women in general. These were the only men I interviewed who revealed an *overt* distain for women. The other killers appeared to like women, at least in theory. In practice, however, they could never seem to tolerate the one they were with. By contrast, the materially motivated killers were more consistent; they held all women in contempt, including those with whom they had been partnered. These men tend to view women primarily as objects of complaint, and perhaps more to the point, as restrictors of their liberties. Referring to his many arrests for domestic violence, Everett said, "Women have always gotten me in trouble." For Everett, "trouble" came not from his violence toward women but from women's complaints about it. Several of the materially motivated men did express regrets for having killed, but their regrets seemed to revolve around their loss of freedom rather than their partners' loss of life. For some, their incarceration appeared to be their final grievance against the deceased, as if to say, "Look at the problems she's caused for me now."

The open contempt that materially possessive men held toward their partners was accompanied and fueled by many longstanding grievances and grudges. It should be noted that all of the killers had held grudges against their victims or felt aggrieved in some way. For most, however, these grudges appeared to have been short-lived and episodic, as in the case of jealous rages or alcoholic binges. These periods of anger had often been followed by apologies, retractions, and periods of conciliation. There appeared to have been many highs and lows in their relationships, and considerable emotional flux on their parts. The materially motivated killers, however, did not report this same pattern of highs and lows, or of emotional storms with their partners. Instead, these men appeared to have exhibited more of a pattern of contemptuous detachment toward their partners. Their animosity toward their partners had resembled a "slow burn" rather than a "quick fuse." While 62% of the other killers characterized themselves as being "moody," none of the materially motivated men thought of themselves in this way. Compared to the other killers, these men were the most guarded and evasive about discussing the events that had led up to them murdering their partners or ex-partners. Only one of the seven men acknowledged any intent to kill his partner. In fact, two denied committing the murders altogether. Three others claimed that shooting their partner had been "an accident," while another claimed it to have been in self-defense. Despite this, five of the seven men had been convicted of first or second degree murder. This suggests that, on average, these men were more calculating killers than the others, and ones who were also more likely to attempt to cover their tracks.

Judging from their relationship histories, the materially motivated killers did not look to women for love but primarily for sex and material benefits, such as money, place of residence, housekeeping, and some cases, childcare. Despite this overall commonality, I found that there were two distinct types of men in this category: those who were *financially exploitive* of women and those who were *financially possessive* in their relationships.

Financially Exploitative

The three men who fit this profile appeared to view women as interchangeable, and disposable, objects of exploitation. These men had had twice as many prior relationships, relative to their ages, as the jealous killers. Their past relationships had also been more short-lived and overlapping and they often had been involved with several women at one time. Consistently, these men had sought to appropriate the financial resources of each woman with whom he had been involved. All three of these men acknowledged that they had also stolen money or possessions from past partners. None of these men had married the murder victim or had children with her. Each had lived in her house or apartment and had contributed little or no money to the rent or mortgage. Each said that he had lived primarily off of his deceased partner's income.

All three of these men said that he had been sexually involved with other women during his relationship with the woman he killed. Only one-third of the other killers made such claims. Perhaps directly related to this, the materially exploitative killers were most likely to complain about jealousy by the women they killed. For these men, their biggest grievances seemed to be when their partners had complained about their violence, infidelity, or substance use. One man said the biggest problem in his relationship with the deceased had been her complaints about his involvement with a motorcycle club. Most of these men appeared to have longstanding perceptions of their partners as "too bossy," "too jealous," or overly critical. Asked their biggest complaints about their deceased partners, two of the men simply said, "She bothered me." Pressed to clarify what he meant by being bothered, one of these men, Sidney, said, "She'd do nothing but complain." This man went on to describe how his girlfriend would complain about his staying out all night, his not telling her his plans, and his yelling at her. Adding that he had often encountered this problem with women, Sidney said, "They are nice at first but when I move in they get to think they own you." The other man who said that his partner "bothered" him explained that "she was always getting into my business." Five of the materially motivated men killed their partners after the relationships had ended, essentially claiming that the victims had provoked their own murders by continuing to make claims on them.

When asked what he thought had been the biggest problems in his relationship, Everett said, "Her jealousy, without a doubt. Plus her always wanting to fight with me." Everett went on to complain about Monique's frequent accusations of his interest in other women. Despite this, Everett freely admitted that he had had numerous affairs, but justified this by saying she had been free to do the same. Everett also complained that after he had broken off the relationship with her, Monique had demanded payment of money and gifts she had given him, and also accused him of having stolen some jewelry that he had given her. This culminated in Monique showing up at his house to demand he return the jewelry. Though he admitted beating her up, Everett continues to deny shooting her to death as she stood in his parking lot that evening. Despite overwhelming evidence of his guilt, Everett insists that he was "framed" by another man who happened to be visiting with friends that day.

Another killer, Kyle, had left his girlfriend, Hadley, to move across the country eight months before killing her. He said he had returned only because Hadley had told him that she was pregnant with his baby, and that he had wished to convince her to have an abortion. On the day of the murder, he had found out Hadley had lied about being pregnant in order to lure him back to Massachusetts with her. He asked her to go for a walk along the railroad tracks, where he then strangled her and buried her body in the woods. Kyle fled back to Oregon. Though he had been questioned about Hadley's disappearance, he was not arrested until her body was found over a year later.

Financially Possessive

Two of the materially motivated killers, Ambrose and Lester, had been married to their victims and had more stable relationship histories with women than the five men previously described. While the financially exploitative men had relationships with the deceased that had averaged one year, Ambrose and Lester had each been married more than ten years to the woman they killed. Further, each had far fewer prior relationships relative to his age. Both men had had children with his wife. By every measure, Ambrose and Lester had been more economically stable than the other five men. Each had held the same job for more than fifteen years, owned a home, and had longtime stakes in his community. In this regard, they deviated from the pattern of the other five men who collectively owned no homes, had held no jobs longer than two years, and as adults had not lived in any communities for more than a few years. What these two men had in common with the other five was their lack of jealous feelings, contempt for their partners, and their longstanding grievances concerning money and material things. These two men were not financially exploitative of women but rather had been equal wage earners with their partners. But while neither looked to women for financial support, both had been financially possessive in their respective relationships. Each man had frequently accused his wife of being "a financial drain." Each man admitted that he had frequently become verbally or physically violent to his wife in response to her spending or her complaints about his spending or money management. Both men complained that their partners were "never satisfied." In both cases, their relationships had ended prior to the murders, and neither man had seemed interested in reconciling with his partner. However, both were embittered about the division of property arrangements of their divorces. Critical to this was that both men had co-owned a business with their partners. Each had stood to lose half of his share of the business as part of the divorce settlement. One man, Lester, had owned a butchery and deli counter with his wife. The other man, Ambrose, is profiled as follows.

Case Example 3

"You're old and fat and I hate you."

Ambrose and Luisa were both thirty-one when they were married following a two-month courtship. Luisa had an eleven-year-old son, Samuel, from a prior marriage. Stanley, their first and only child together, was born a year later. Luisa had grown up working in her family's sandwich shop, and she continued to work at her brother's shop. Ambrose worked as a cook at another restaurant. Ambrose was restless to own their own restaurant and continually accused Luisa of being too content working for her family. He also complained that Luisa was "selfish" and overly critical of him.

After four years of pressure from Ambrose, Luisa agreed to ask her brother to sell his restaurant to them, and Ambrose quit his other job so they could manage the new restaurant together. Shortly after this, Ambrose was arrested for soliciting a police officer posing as a prostitute, and received a fine of $200. He never admitted to Luisa that this was a regular activity of his. Luisa did find out, however, about his relationship with a younger woman and his visits to strip clubs. When she confronted Ambrose about this, he told her, "You are old and fat and I hate you. I'm only staying with you because of Stanley." Perhaps to sidetrack attention from his own infidelity, Ambrose began to accuse Luisa of having affairs with particular men. Later that year, Luisa obtained a restraining and vacate order after claiming that Ambrose had beat her up. Though he denied even being in the house that day, the order was granted and Ambrose was ordered to vacate their house as well as their business. He moved in with some friends and took a job at another restaurant. Luisa filed for divorce. As part of the divorce settlement, Ambrose agreed to sell his share of the restaurant, receiving a substantial profit from his initial investment.

Ambrose looked into buying a new restaurant. According to Luisa's family, Ambrose continually violated Luisa's restraining order by entering her home and threatening her and Samuel and by making threatening phone calls. Ambrose denies this.

According to the police report, Ambrose walked into Luisa's restaurant on June 6, displayed a .38 caliber handgun, and yelled, "Freeze, motherfuckers!" He then went to the counter to where Luisa was washing pans and shot her in the side. His second shot struck her wrist and arm. Luisa's sister, Mary, then pushed his arm, causing the third shot to miss Luisa. Ambrose then straddled Luisa, who was lying on the floor, and fired two shots into her head and neck at point-blank range. According to several eyewitnesses, he then turned to Mary, smiled, put the gun to her chest, and pulled the trigger but was out of bullets. He fled the restaurant and later called to turn himself in to the police.

Ambrose gives a very different version of these events. He says that Luisa called him the previous day to ask him to come to the restaurant so they could discuss something. When he arrived at the restaurant, Luisa pulled a gun from her purse and pointed it at him. He kicked the gun out of her hand, knocking it into the sink. Luisa tried to grab the gun but he got to it first. They struggled with the gun and it went off, striking Luisa in the head. Despite the police report that he fired five shots, Ambrose says he remembers only one shot. After firing this shot, he grabbed the bag of bullets and ran out of the store.

According to testimony at Ambrose's trial, Stanley, aged six, said that his father had frequently hit his mother. Mary said that Luisa had gotten some kind of venereal disease due to Ambrose's frequent visits to prostitutes. Once, when Luisa complained, he told her, "I will cut you up and fry you." One day when Mary called the house, Stanley answered and told her that his father had broken in and had gone upstairs looking for his mother with a big knife. He had grabbed his father by the leg to stop him but Ambrose had told him he would kill him and his brother. Mary had gone over to the house and Ambrose had answered the door, telling her that Luisa wasn't home. When she persisted, he had let Luisa come downstairs to make coffee. Luisa had denied that there had been any problems but later confided to her sister that what Stanley had told her was true. Shortly after this incident, Luisa had told Ambrose that she wanted a divorce. He told her, "I'm not giving you a divorce; I'll give you bullets in the head instead." He also had written a letter to her saying that he would kill her and Samuel. Two weeks prior to the murder, Ambrose had brought a friend over to Luisa's house to try to convince Luisa to take Ambrose back. When Luisa refused, Ambrose had told her he would kill her. The friend had told Ambrose that he should be nice to Luisa if he wanted her back. Luisa's murder occurred on the anniversary of her wedding. Following the murder, Mary found that Luisa's apartment above the restaurant had been ransacked.

Ambrose was convicted of murder in the first degree. Two subsequent appeals filed by Ambrose have been denied.

Projection

Ambrose's depiction of Luisa as selfish, overly critical, and untrustworthy would seem to be a more accurate depiction of himself rather than of her. This is not coincidental. Ambrose appears to be using a psychological defense mechanism known as projection. Projection is the tendency to see one's own (usually negative) characteristics in other people. By ascribing unflattering attributes onto others, the individual either avoids seeing these same traits in himself or rationalizes that he is merely being like others. Greedy individuals, for example, often justify their venality by saying that they are just doing what everyone else does or wants to do. In a similar vein, many battering men see their partners as selfish and unappreciative because they themselves are selfish and unappreciative. They see their partners as being controlling and vindictive because they themselves are controlling and vindictive. They see their partners as jealous because they themselves are jealous. Many of the killers appeared to use projective thinking as a way of seeing their partners as persecutors rather than as victims. These men frequently complained that they had felt mocked, humiliated, or otherwise "disrespected" by the women they killed. For example, Ambrose said that he had felt "humiliated" having to sell his share of the restaurant. Another man said that he had felt that his wife was "mocking" him by becoming involved with another man following their separation.

This man had in fact flaunted his relationships with other women through-out their marriage by continually bringing other women over to the house for sex when his wife was there and by openly comparing these women to her in highly unflattering and graphic terms.

Similarity to Murderers for Profit

Though there is no evidence that any of these men killed their partners purely for profit, they appear to have much in common with those men who do. The materially motivated men seemed the most calculating and remorseless of all the killers that I interviewed. These appear to be common traits among men who killed their partners for monetary gain. I know of no systematic study of these kinds of killings. Therefore, what we know about them is based primarily on court testimony and media reports.

One potential difference in these media-reported cases is the apparent absence of histories of domestic violence. However, we must remember that domestic violence is often hidden from public view so it may well have existed in many or most of these cases. As mentioned previously, there was strong evidence of prior violence on the part of all thirty-one of the men that I interviewed. Other research studies of killings of women by their intimate partners have found histories of domestic violence in the vast majority of these cases.[14] For instance, one researcher found evidence of prior domestic violence in 85% of the eighty-seven women's homicides that she examined.[15] No research has specifically analyzed rates of prior domestic violence in cases when husbands kill for profit.

However, there have been some high-profile cases in which there was no known history of domestic violence. One such case was Charles (Chuck) Stuart, a furrier store manager, who murdered his pregnant wife, Carol, in Boston in 1989. Mr. Stuart tried to cover up his crime by claiming that a man had robbed and shot him and his wife in their car shortly after they had attended a childbirthing class at Brigham and Women's Hospital in the Roxbury section of Boston.[16] Boston police subsequently arrested and charged an African American man who matched the description that Chuck Stuart had given of their assailant. Subsequently, evidence emerged that Mr. Stuart had enlisted his brother, Matthew, to help him kill his wife so that he could benefit from her life insurance policy. On the evening of the crime, Matthew delivered the .38-caliber handgun that

Chuck used first to shoot Carol. Chuck then shot himself in the stomach in order to bolster his claim of being robbed. Evidence emerged that Chuck Stuart had been involved with another woman with whom he'd been making secret plans to buy and manage a restaurant. Mr. Stuart subsequently killed himself by jumping off the Tobin Bridge once it became clear that he was about to be charged with the murder. According to the extensive media reports, as well as the police interviews with Carol Stuart's friends and relatives, no one had known of any instances of domestic abuse by Chuck. While evidence of prior domestic violence has been uncovered in other such cases, it appears that a significant number of these for-profit killers do not previously batter their wives.

Despite this potential difference, men who kill for profit appear to have many of the same preoccupation with money and material benefits as the materially motivated killers that I've profiled. They appear to fit more closely the profile of the financially possessive men than the financially exploitative ones. This is because they are more often married to their murder victims. This makes sense since the financial gain is greater when the killer is married to his victim and therefore stands to inherit her assets as well as to be the beneficiary of her life insurance policy. Another potential similarity between the profit killers and the financially possessive ones that I interviewed is their ambitions for wealth and social status. Chuck Stuart, for instance, had apparently cultivated an image of someone with high ambitions. He had lavished his mistress with fur coats, a diamond ring, and other expensive gifts. Similarly, both Ambrose and Lester had been business owners with dreams of wealth and of enhanced social status. Each man, like Chuck Stuart, had seen his wife as a hindrance to these dreams.

One perpetrator of attempted homicide, Richard, had already achieved high social status as a physician. Just prior to his attempt to kill his wife, Louise, by poisoning her, he was under investigation for illegal prescribing practices. As his one-time office manager, Louise knew that Richard had been overprescribing to his patients and also fraudulently billing insurance providers. She also suspected that Richard had attempted to financially exploit disoriented elderly patients by "plying them with gifts" and inducing them to become dependent upon drugs that he prescribed. Prior to her filing for divorce, Richard had increased the amount of Louise's life insurance policy and was openly spending time with another woman.

Louise was one of the three victims of attempted homicide who felt that her perpetrator had had a financial motive to kill her. "I was in the way of the life he wanted to have," Louise said, adding, "and he figured my death was cheaper than divorce."

Another potential similarity between for-profit killers and the materially motivated type of killer is that both kinds of men appear to have features associated with anti-social personality. These include lacking empathy and remorse, being manipulative and exploitative of others, and having shallow emotions. Louise spoke of Richard's "complete lack of a conscience," for instance. Three of the materially motivated killers had been formally evaluated as having anti-social personality. All three also qualified as career criminals, based on their lengthy criminal records. The other four men might also have scored high on the psychopathy scale, a test used to identify features of anti-social personality. None had ever received a mental health evaluation or been in a setting that required psychological testing. None had an extensive criminal history. In fact, Ambrose and Lester had no prior arrests at all. Having a criminal record is not a prerequisite for a diagnosis of anti-social personality, however. Many people with this personality exploit others without breaking laws, and even when they do, manage to avoid arrest. Further discussion about the characteristics of individuals with anti-social personality will be provided in the section about the career criminal type of killer.

Potential Deterrents

Compared to the other types of killers, the materially motivated ones were the least likely to have participated in a therapeutic program prior to committing murder. Only three of the seven men had attended any kind of counseling during his lifetime, and for one man, it had been involuntary. This man, Kyle, had been required to see a therapist while in high school because of missing classes and acting out in class. Diagnosed with conduct disorder, Kyle had also been arrested numerous times for stealing cars. Kyle reported that he had dropped out of school after seeing his psychologist approximately ten times.

Two of the materially motivated killers had voluntarily sought treatment, but neither had stayed in treatment for more than ten weeks. In both cases, this therapy had been received more than five weeks prior to the murders these men committed. One of these men, Lee, had attended several group sessions at a Veteran's Administration Hospital for victims of post-traumatic stress disorder. More than ten years later, Lee killed his partner by strangling her and breaking her neck. Lee claimed that this was an "involuntary instinctive response" after his partner had thrown some hot tea in his face. Lee reported that he had been trained to kill people in this manner while serving in the army during the Vietnam War era. The other killer who had previously sought counseling was Gerald, the man who said that he "accidentally" shot his girlfriend, Pamela, at close range in the face with his sawed-off shotgun. Gerald had briefly received treatment for depression during one of his prior incarcerations for armed robbery.

Not only were the materially motivated men least likely to have sought therapy but they also identified the fewest potential deterrents for the murders they committed. Their reluctance to cite factors might well be influenced by the fact that most of these men denied committing murder altogether or avowed that the killing had been in self-defense or otherwise provoked by the victim. As Gerald said, "Nothing would have prevented it because it was an accident." Despite this, six of the men identified some potential factors that might have prevented their victims' deaths. Unlike the jealous killers, few selected participation in a batterer intervention program as a potential deterrent. Only two of the men said that this "might have" helped prevent the deaths of their partners. Interestingly, three men identified two particular technological devices as potential deterrents. They selected "knowing my partner had a beeper that notified the police whenever I came near her" as a factor that "very likely would have" deterred them from killing their partners. They also selected "being on probation and having to wear an ankle bracelet that notified police whenever I came near my partner" as a "very likely" deterrent. When they committed the murders, both of these men had active restraining orders that required them to stay away from their partners. Each man accurately reported that "my partner having a restraining order" had not been a sufficient deterrent.

Everett explained, "If someone does something to me and gets away with it, the only thing that will work is them being away where I can't find them."

These men's endorsement of beepers for victims and ankle bracelets for perpetrators lends support to the arguments of many threat assessment specialists that strict monitoring or confinement are the only effective deterrents for some types of dangerous offenders. The "ankle bracelet" is one form of monitoring that has increasingly been used with sex offenders, particularly those with a history of assaulting children. This system is more aptly known as Global Position System (GPS) monitoring since the ankle bracelet worn by the offender is programmed to send a continuous signal that is tracked by satellites, which then bounce the signal back to the monitoring device. The monitoring device is programmed to keep a real-time record, as well as a map, of the offender's whereabouts in relation to places that are frequented by potential victims, such as schools or playgrounds. Some jurisdictions have recently used GPS to monitor domestic violence offenders. In these cases, the system is programmed to show when the offender comes within a certain distance, say one mile, of certain buildings used by the victim. These typically include her home, workplace, house of worship, and businesses that she frequents. In some cases, the offender's probation officer is automatically beeped whenever the offender comes within the specified distance of any of the selected buildings. One of the biggest drawbacks of GPS monitoring is that it can only detect the offender's proximity to selected buildings, rather than that of the victim herself. Knowing the victim's usual travel route from home to work, a perpetrator could accost her somewhere along this route without alerting the GPS monitor. Another drawback is that the system is only as effective as the response time of the monitoring authorities. Even if a perpetrator accosts his victim in one of the selected buildings, he could easily kill her before the monitoring authorities arrive.

Suicidal Type

Though I did not know it at the time, Jerold was my first encounter with a suicidal abuser. I didn't know Jerold was suicidal since he'd revealed no history of suicidal threats or attempts on the intake form when he enrolled in the batterer intervention program where I worked. During the first three group sessions he attended, Jerold often cracked jokes and appeared to be optimistic about his future. Only after he had missed the next two sessions did I learn from his probation officer that Jerold had killed himself. Despite his denials on the intake form, Jerold's wife, Anita, knew him to be suicidal because he had frequently threatened to kill her, their two children, and himself. Jerold would often repeat this threat when Anita talked about ending the relationship. Fearing that he would make good on these threats, Anita took steps to protect the children and herself by obtaining a protective order that required Jerold to move out the house and to avoid any contact with her or the children. Anita asked some of her neighbors to alert her should they see Jerold in the neighborhood. She coached the children to go to a neighbor's house should their father show up, telling them, "Don't try to talk to daddy, just run to Shirley's house." Despite these plans, Jerold showed up unannounced on early morning with a loaded shotgun. Brandishing the gun, he threatened to "take out the whole family." Anita begged and eventually convinced Jerold to let the children go. After the children fled, Anita said silent prayers in anticipation of being killed. Instead, Jerold walked up to her, saying, "You ruined my life" just before shooting himself in the head.

Jerold's case helped me to recognize that suicidal men are not always easy to spot. I also came to see that for some perpetrators, their suicidality (and overall threat potential) rises and falls according to the status of their relationships with their partners and children. Given the ever-changing situational factors, threat assessments should not be one-time events but need to be repeated when the circumstances change. Factors such as estrangement, as well as changes in a perpetrator's employment, health, mood, and level of drinking, are all extremely relevant to assessing his threat potential. As the situation changes, the level of danger may increase or decrease. Therapists who work with suicidal individuals similarly report that the likelihood of suicide varies according to the situation. When a suicidal individual has been abusive to his partner as Jerold had been, the threat of homicide always looms as a potential outcome. Based on research findings, there is good reason for this. As mentioned earlier, about 30% of intimate partner killings of American women are followed by suicide. The proportion of murder-suicides relative to murder-only cases appears to vary a great deal from region to region in the United States, with western and southern states having higher rates than in the central, eastern, and northern states. Campbell's study of femicides in eleven American cities found the rate of murder-suicides to be 51% in Houston and 38% in Los Angeles, compared to 8% in Baltimore and 13% in Kansas City.[17] During the ten-year period from 1995–2004 in Massachusetts, the murder-suicide rate was 29%.[18] By comparison, the murder-suicide rate in Arizona was 55% during the two-year period from 2000–2001.[19] During the three-year period from 2002–2004, the rate in Florida was 40%.[20] Overwhelmingly, murder-suicides involving intimate partners are perpetrated by men. Various studies have found the proportion of male perpetrators in these kinds of cases to be in the 85%–95% range.[21]

More Stability

Aside from the fact that the killers are mostly male, surprisingly little has been written about murder-suicides involving intimate partners. There is some evidence that these perpetrators tend to be significantly older than their victims. One analysis of data of such cases in six American states found that perpetrators were, on average, over six years older than their victims.[22] Studies of homicide-only cases have not found such a significant age difference between the killers and the killed. In our study, only 17% of the killers were six or more years older than their victims. However, neither of the two men who attempted suicide was six years older. In fact, one was twelve years *younger* his victim. Regardless of whether they are older than their victims, there is stronger evidence that perpetrators of murder-suicide are older than those who kill their partners only. The previously cited national study by Campbell and colleagues found that 11% of the perpetrators in murder-suicide cases were fifty years of age or older, compared to 7% of the perpetrators in murder-only cases.[23]

Compared to men who kill only their partners, another distinguishing feature of men who also kill themselves is that they are more likely to be married to their victims. In Campbell's study, 51% of the murder-suicide perpetrators were married to their victims, compared to 33% of the murder-only perpetrators.[24] Though these killers were no more likely to have biological children of their own, they were more likely to be living with the biological children of the victims. How do we interpret these findings? It is possible that the existence of stepchildren poses additional grounds for jealousy and resentment for these men. Some battered women have reported that their abusers are jealous of their relationships with their own children. Many of the abusive men I have counseled have expressed particular resentments toward their stepchildren. Some have attempted to portray stepchildren as undermining influences on their relationships with the mothers. One man continually claimed that his stepdaughter was attempting to orchestrate a reconciliation between her mother and her biological father. Much of his time during group sessions was spent attempting to portray this eleven-year-old girl as an "evil influence" on her mother. One of the killers, Harold, who had tried to commit suicide after killing his estranged partner, said that he deeply resented Jenaya's adult children because he knew that they were "against" him.

Gun Use

The reader might recall that guns are overwhelmingly the weapon of choice for men who kill their partners. This is even more so for men who kill themselves after slaying their partners. Campbell found that 61% of the women in the murder-suicide cases were killed with a gun, compared to 28% of the women in the murder-only cases.[25] A second study of twenty murder-suicides in Arizona found that nineteen of the twenty perpetrators used a gun.[26] These studies also found that the suicidal killers were more likely than the not-suicidal ones to have had easy access to a gun. The Campbell study found that 81% of those who perpetrated murder-suicide had easy access to a gun over the one-year period leading up to the fatal assaults.[27] This same study found that just over half of these perpetrators had previously threatened their victims with a weapon.

One interpretation of this finding is that easy access to a gun presents the depressed and angry perpetrator with more of a "quick fix" to his problems. Simply having a gun may make it more likely for him to follow through on any impulses to kill his partner and/or himself. This explanation fits research that shows that gun access is one of the leading risk factors to femicide in general, and may be even more so for cases of femicide-suicide. Contrary to this interpretation, substantial premeditation is evident in cases of murder-suicide. For some of the killers in our study, their easy access to guns was not coincidental to their crimes. Many had taken pains to obtain guns with the apparent intention to kill their partners.

Substance Abuse

Suicidal killers may be more likely than nonsuicidal ones to abuse alcohol. In their study, Campbell and colleagues found that 52% of the murder-suicide group of killers had been abusers of alcohol.[28] In their closer examination of forty-two cases, these researchers found that 63% of these perpetrators had used alcohol on the day of the fatal assaults. This same study found no significant differences between the murder-suicide killers and the murder-only ones in their use of illicit drugs. About half of each group had used one or more drugs of some kind. It seems likely that a higher proportion of the murder-suicide group of killers had used prescription drugs since they were more likely to have sought treatment and medication for their depression.

Depression

Most studies of murder-suicide cases have found depression and other forms of mental illness to be prominent factors in the lives of the perpetrators. One of the first studies of such cases in Great Britain, conducted in 1967, found that forty-five of the seventy-eight killers had exhibited some form of "mental abnormality" and that twenty-eight had suffered from depression.[29] A later study that directly compared murder-suicide cases to murder-only ones found that three-quarters of the first group of perpetrators had suffered from depression while none of the twenty-four killers in the latter category had been depressed.[30] The Campbell study judged that 38% of the murder-suicide killers had had "poor mental health" compared to 28% of the other killers.[31] A fourth study accessed coroner files of 121 homicide cases. This investigator found that the men who killed themselves were more likely to have suffered from depression.[32] Not surprisingly, most studies have found these men were more likely to have threatened or attempted suicide.

But how do we account for the surprisingly large proportion of these men with no apparent histories of suicide attempts or depression? It seems likely that, for some of these men, killing their partner had been the primary aim and killing themselves merely an afterthought. Rather than reflecting any longstanding wish to commit suicide, these men's decision to do so may have been a rational choice made after killing their partner: choosing death over the prospect of lifetime incarceration. Others might have arrived at this choice in a less rational manner. Those who killed their partners in blind rage or while intoxicated might have killed themselves in a panic before having the opportunity to think about it.

Much like the other types of killers, the suicidal types appear to fall along both ends of the emotional control continuum. Some exhibit more of an impulsive style while others fit more of an over-controlled personality profile. The impulsive style of abusive man is much more emotionally volatile and prone to frequent rages. In contrast, the over-controlled style of abuser is much more deliberate, calculating and operates more at a "slow burn." This type of abuser tends to accumulate grievances against his partner between his periodic explosions of rages. One team of researchers compared the more impulsive style of abuser to pit bulls and the more calculating ones to cobras.[33] Jealous feelings are common features for both styles of abusers, but as with anger, tend to be communicated very differently. The impulsive type tends to make more frequent and dramatic jealous accusations. He may also be more prone to so-called morbid or delusional jealousy. The more compulsive style of abuser is more likely to keep his suspicions to himself for long periods, while conducting continued surveillance on his partner. Depression can be a feature of both styles. James, described earlier in this chapter as a jealous type of killer, is a good example of how depression looks for someone with an impulsive style. This type of man often uses alcohol and drugs as forms of self-medication. Allen, profiled here, provides an example of how depression is handled by someone with the opposite style.

Case Example 4

"I took the life of a beautiful human being . . .
my wife of 32 years. . . ."

Allen was cited in Chapter 1 as one of the two perpetrators I interviewed who made bona fide attempts to kill themselves after murdering their partners. Due to the serious injuries he had sustained by stabbing himself in the throat, Allen spoke in a voice that seemed halfway between a growl and a whisper. Ten years after the murder, his eerie voice along with his disfiguring scars remained as daily reminders.

Allen was twenty-two and Andrea sixteen when they became involved as a couple, and they married two years later. The couple seemed a mismatch right from the beginning. Andrea was strikingly beautiful, with the petite figure of a model. She was elegant in her style of dress, her way of communicating, and in her overall manner. In contrast, Allen was rather coarse of features, stocky, and usually clad in overalls and flannel work shirts. A Portuguese immigrant, he could barely speak and write in English.

From the beginning of their marriage, the couple fought frequently. Many of these conflicts centered on Andrea's dislike of Allen's uncouth manner and his desire to have sex three to four times a day. During some of these arguments, Allen would grab and shake Andrea. His violence gradually escalated to slapping her in the face and throwing her to the floor.

Their first child was born in 1964. Until 1970, when their daughter, Lori, was born, Andrea worked as a computer software programmer. Allen worked two jobs (one full-time and one part-time) as a machinist. In 1972, Allen started his own construction company, against the advice of Andrea as well as his brother and sister. When the company foundered, Allen became severely depressed and spent much of 1974 in bed. He began to see a psychiatrist but was not prescribed any medications.

By 1976, Allen took a job at an auto plant and his depression lifted. Meanwhile, Andrea had received a promotion at her software company and was now heading her division. Still attempting to salvage his construction company, Allen convinced Andrea to quit this job. When the construction company folded three months later, Andrea felt "too proud," according to Allen, to ask for her job back. Instead, she took a job as a buyer for a clothing store, a job that she continued until her death nearly fifteen years later.

By the time the couple bought a house lot in 1977, they were arguing every day and no longer sleeping together. Allen was rehired at the auto plant and spent nearly all of his off time helping to build their fourteen-room house. During this period, Allen began to suspect that Andrea was having an affair, though he did not confront her about this until years later. A few times, he stopped at Andrea's store and sensed that she was embarrassed by his unsophisticated appearance and manner. Allen complained that Andrea was spending nearly all of her paycheck on clothing for the children and herself. He felt a growing gulf between the rest of his family and himself. At this point, he began to frequent strip clubs once or twice a month.

Allen's depression worsened during the 1980s, yet he refused to seek help at the urging of his family and siblings. Finally in 1990, Allen started seeing a psychiatrist on a weekly basis. He was eventually diagnosed with bipolar disorder with "obsessive-compulsive features," for which he was prescribed Prozac. Allen frequently checked the appliances to see that they were turned off and compulsively tended the yard, mowing it every day. Between 1990 and 1993, Allen's depression continued to deepen to the point where he started neglecting his hygiene and stopped attending to the house and yard altogether.

In August 1993, Allen stopped seeing his psychiatrist. During this period, according to Allen, Andrea would frequently berate him to "snap out of it" and return to therapy. On October 3, Allen's suspicions that Andrea had been having an affair were confirmed. He learned that she been romantically involved with her store manager for several years. When he confronted her, she admitted the affair and told him she planned to move out and find a place of her own later that month. Over the next week, Allen avoided Andrea but became increasingly depressed and agitated.

Allen awoke at 8:30 on October 12 to find Andrea preparing for work. According to Allen, she "blew up at me" for pacing. She also complained that he had become a bad example for their daughter, Lori, who was now twenty-three and still living at home. When she continued to yell and to wave a kitchen knife at him, Allen said he "snapped" and began to strangle her until she passed out. To ensure that she was dead, he took the knife and stabbed her in the neck. Allen then slashed his wrists and stabbed himself in the neck. He tried to stab himself in the heart but by then was too weak to penetrate his ribs due to the loss of blood. When the police arrived, they found Allen lying unconscious next to Andrea's body. He was revived by EMTs and rushed to the hospital. where he underwent surgery to save his life.

During their investigation, police interviewed Charles, the man with whom Andrea had been involved, who confirmed she had made plans to leave Allen later that month and that they had made plans "to make a life together." At his court hearing, Allen rejected an offer by the district attorney for him to plead guilty for manslaughter. Instead, he pled guilty to second degree murder, saying that he deserved to spend the rest of his life in prison. During his sentencing in court, Allen read the following statement in halting English:

I took the life of a beautiful human being . . . my wife of 32 years and the mother of our two beautiful children. My wife was very pleasant, very intelligent. She always worked very hard. Some members of my family and my attorney thought that I should be charged with a lesser crime. I understand and appreciate their feelings and concerns for me but I am the one who has to live with myself and my conscience. When I came to Bridgewater [the psychiatric hospital where he had awaited trial] I was in bad shape emotionally and physically. The help and care that I received is truly overwhelming to me. Before coming to Bridgewater, I could only spell very little; after spending 14 months of school at the institution I now write to my children, to my nieces and even legal material to my attorney. I realize these words and these sentences are not well-written but they are from my mind and heart.

Since there was no trial, it remains unclear how premeditated Allen's murder of Andrea had been. Allen said that he had had frequent, though unexpressed, thoughts of killing himself but denied any forethoughts of killing Andrea.

Judging from his history, Allen is clearly not an impulsive person, but neither does he come across as a calculating and remorseless one. Allen does, however, fit the profile of someone who is emotionally over-controlled. He did not have frequent outbursts of anger but admitted that he had frequently ruminated about Andrea's apparent lack of affection and loyalty to him. His rumination appeared to be a combination of anger toward her and self-loathing. He said that he had frequently felt inferior to Andrea. Allen also said that he had felt "ashamed" about his long bouts of depression during which he had been unable to work and to maintain his house and yard. As Andrea grew more and more distant, Allen had sunk deeper into his depression. The final straw, evidently, had been Andrea's decision to leave him for another man.

Allen was not blameless in the breakdown of his relationship with Andrea. He admitted to frequent sexual coercion and violence, primarily during their first ten years together. Over the last ten years, he had retreated into self-isolation and depression. Andrea's decision to become involved with another man is understandable and even reasonable, given this context.

Triggers for Homicide

Estrangement and jealousy appear to be the immediate triggers in the majority of cases of murder-suicide. In terms of motivation and style, the suicidal type of killer appears most similar to the jealous type that was profiled earlier in this chapter. Suicidal killers are more apt to be married to their victims, and to have had longer relationships with them, and to be older. For some of these men, like Allen, these factors may contribute to the perception that there is no life beyond their relationships with their partners. This sense of no viable future may be greatly exacerbated by these men's suicidal depressions. The existence of depression may also contribute to an abnormal degree of emotional dependence upon their partners. I have known many battered women with depressed partners who have said that they feel overly responsible for meeting their partner's emotional needs. As one woman said, "He was depressed all the time, but he wouldn't get help. Instead he'd blame me and I was supposed to pick him up and make him feel better. It got to be too much." This woman went on to explain that throughout their relationship, she'd felt responsible for preventing her husband from killing himself.

For other suicidal types of killers, the primary triggering factor may not be emotional dependency on their partners so much as their sense of ownership of them, something that Websdale has labeled "obsessive possessiveness." Being left by a longtime partner may signify the ultimate betrayal or defeat for this kind of man. So attached is he to the notion that his partner "belongs" to him, her decision to end the relationship is experienced as an unforgivable insult of him, and a larger injustice than his killing her. This represents a valuing system in which the loyalty and obedience of his partner supercede any beliefs in love or affection.

Daly and Wilson have argued that femicide and familicide are natural extensions of some men's proprietary beliefs concerning their partners and families. They state, "The prospect of losing his family through death apparently strikes the desperate familicidal father as no more disastrous than the prospect of losing them through desertion! Better, perhaps, since at least he has called the shots and exerted his authority."[34]

Potential Deterrents

Two problems are present for the suicidal abusive man: depression and domestic violence. However, treatment for one is not likely to alleviate the other. In fact, there is evidence that each form of treatment may be less effective if not accompanied by the other. Allen said that his treatment for depression, along with his medication, had helped somewhat to alleviate his depression and to ward off thoughts of suicide. He added that he had not been motivated to continue this treatment because of the continued decline of his relationship and because of his growing suspicions about his wife's involvement with another man.

Allen said that he never discussed these suspicions with his psychiatrists, nor did he ever tell the psychiatrist about his domestic violence. It is not unusual for abusive men to not disclose their domestic violence to mental health therapists. Unfortunately, surveys have also shown that therapists rarely ask about domestic violence unless the client broaches the subject. This has been an important matter for therapeutic training, given the high incidence of domestic violence among those in mental health counseling, substance abuse treatment, or family therapy.

Had Allen attended a batterer intervention program (BIP), it is much more likely that his violence would have been discussed, since such programs proactively require their clients to describe their violence as well as the issues, such as jealousy, that trigger their abusive behavior. Such programs also assess for indicators of dangerousness. For some programs, this assessment sometimes includes confidential telephone interviews with the victim, as well as accessing the perpetrator's police reports and criminal history. When strong indicators of dangerousness are identified, these programs alert the victim as well as the criminal justice system. Beyond this, BIPs work to manage the risk by continuously monitoring dangerous perpetrators for signs of escalation, growing desperation or depression, alcohol or drug use, and their overall reactions to changes in the status of their relationships with their partners and children. The following case example illustrates how long-term risk management and treatment were provided by one such program.

Case Example 5

"Who's going to protect her now?"

Philip was thirty-nine when he was arrested for domestic violence toward his wife, Doris. The couple had three children, ranging in age from six to seventeen. Philip was a trained plumber who operated his own plumbing business and home heating oil delivery business. Philip was convicted of one count of domestic violence and sentenced to a probation term of one year. Two conditions of Philip's probation were that he obey the protective order that forbade any contact with his wife and that he attend a forty-week BIP. During his first group session, Philip admitted that he had pushed and grabbed Doris in a restaurant during the incident that led to his arrest. When asked about prior incidents, he estimated that there had been at least twenty. Included in these had been several threats to kill Doris. In response to a question about suicide threats and attempts on the intake form, Philip wrote that he had cut his wrists six weeks earlier. Philip had been seeing a psychiatrist since the incident and had been prescribed one medication for anxiety and another for depression.

Shortly after Philip started attending the BIP, his group leaders learned from Doris that he had violated the terms of his protective order by entering her home and had committed a new act of violence toward her. This consisted of throwing a knife at her. The knife had narrowly missed her head, lodging in the wall. Doris went on to describe past incidents of violence on Philip's part that far exceeded his own accounts. During a prior period of separation, Philip had threatened and assaulted her sister and punched Doris in the jaw when she came to her sister's defense. Doris said that Philip was extremely jealous and would continually accuse her of having affairs. One time, after accusing her of having a romantic interest in a neighbor, Philip had taken out a knife and attempted to bind Doris' hands and feet with duct tape. When the knife grazed her and she began to bleed, Philip began to cry and plead with her not to call the police. His pleas were accompanied by Philip's threats to kill Doris, the children and himself.

Doris said that Philip had frequently threatened to kill himself in the past and even kept a packet of Exacto blades in his pants pocket. He would sometimes take a blade out while they were sitting together on the couch and begin to cut his wrists. Doris also reported that Philip had continued to drink even after beginning his medications for depression and anxiety. Doris said that when she attempted to discuss this with Philip's psychiatrist, he refused to believe that Philip had been physically abusive to her and urged her to accept Philip back into the house so that she could support the management of his depression.

Doris did not want the BIP staff to report Philip's new act of violence to the police or court, saying that she believed it would only put her in more danger. Doris believed that Philip would kill her and possibly the children if he were arrested. She said that when Philip had been arrested in the past, he had used his mental illness as a reason to avoid jail. Philip's group leaders respected Doris's wishes but advised her to begin seeing a battered women's advocate so that she could strategize about her children's and her own safety. Doris agreed to do this. Because Philip had disclosed to his group leaders that he had continued to drink, they were able to speak with his probation officer, who agreed to arrange for random alcohol and drug testing during the duration of his probation. The probation officer also agreed to begin seeing Philip on a weekly basis to monitor his progress. Meanwhile, the batterer intervention program continued to provide monthly reports to the court that documented the indicators of dangerousness that were present in Philip's situation. None of these oral or written communications included any references to the new act of violence that Doris had reported, however.

During his group sessions, Philip was asked to talk about his feelings of depression and jealousy. His group leaders and fellow group members pointed out to Philip that he had an important role to play with his seventeen-year-old son who was now living and working with him. The son, Robert, had a serious drinking problem and had been arrested several times for drunk driving, disturbing the peace, and vandalism. The group encouraged Philip to set a good example for his son by maintaining his own sobriety and nonviolence. Philip began to attend several AA meetings with his son. Robert also attended a parent-teacher meeting with Robert to discuss his problems at school. Over time, this new focus appeared to help Philip become less focused on the status of his relationship with Doris, though he continued to hope for reconciliation with her. Because of his continuing feelings of jealousy, Philip's group leaders recommended that he continue in the BIP for additional time beyond the forty weeks that were minimally required, and Philip agreed to do so.

Philip eventually left the program after two years. Though they could not prevent Philip from leaving the program at this point, his group leaders continued to worry that Philip had still not abandoned his hopes of reuniting with Doris. Most troubling, when asked if he accepted the divorce, Philip said that he mostly accepted it but asked rhetorically, "Who's going to protect her now?" At this point, according to Doris, Philip was continuing to violate her protective order by showing up at her house about once a month but that he had avoided any new acts of physical or verbal violence toward her. She said that the two daughters who remained with her had become progressively less anxious and fearful during this time. She also confirmed that Robert had maintained his sobriety, had graduated high school, and was doing well at his new job.

The BIP staff have spoken with Doris periodically over the six years since Philip completed the program. At last report, she and the children were continuing to do well. She reported that for the most part, Philip had adjusted to their divorce and had remained nonviolent. She added that he would still show up "unannounced" at her house once or twice a year, usually offering to repair something. Doris said that she felt she had escaped what she had once felt would be certain death at Philip's hands. She continued to worry that if she should begin a new relationship, Philip would become threatening again, but said that she was not looking for a new relationship and just felt lucky to be alive and free of "the daily terror" that she and her children had once faced.[35]

Career Criminal Type

Perhaps the most easily identifiable type of killer and would-be killer that we investigated was the career criminal. One-fifth of the killers fit this profile while one-fourth of the perpetrators of attempted homicide did. This represents a combined proportion of 21% of the offenders. The criteria we used for classifying a perpetrator into this group included whether he had been incarcerated four or more times as an adult, whether he had five or more prior convictions for felonies, and whether he derived at least half of his income from criminal activities. To qualify as a career criminal, the perpetrator had to have met at least one of these conditions. Table 3.6 compares the proportions of career criminals who met each criterion with the other perpetrators.

Table 3.6: Prior criminal activities of killers and would-be killers (by percentage)

Criminal record	Career criminals	Others
Was incarcerated 4 or more times as an adult	54	0
Was convicted of 5 or more felonies as an adult	45	2
Derived at least half of his income from criminal activities	100	0
	N=11	N=40

Prior Incarceration

Just over half of the career criminals qualified on the grounds of having served four or more prison terms or having been convicted of five or more felonies. Only one additional man in this group had served a prison sentence; the rest had avoided convictions for their crimes or eluded arrest altogether. By comparison, none of the other perpetrators had been incarcerated as many as four times. In fact, only twelve percent of these men had been incarcerated at all. Mostly, their prior incarcerations had been for domestic violence crimes. Overwhelmingly, the prison time served by the career criminals had been for other crimes such as breaking and entering, assault and battery, assault and battery with a weapon, drug possession, drug sales, or probation or parole violation. However, two of the career criminals had also served time for past domestic violence crimes. One example was James, previously described as the man who had smothered his partner, Corinne, to death with a pillow. Two of James's six prison terms had been for domestic violence toward Corinne. The other four had been for larceny, possession of a Class D drug, assault and battery, and assault and battery with a dangerous weapon. Both of these last two crimes had been committed against strangers. Prior to killing Corinne, James had appeared in court forty-eight times to face ninety-one charges. The five years of combined prison time that James had served were but a small fraction of what he would have served had it not for his many suspended sentences and reductions in prison time for "good behavior."

Three of the career criminals had served at least half of their adult lives behind bars prior to killing their partners. One of these was Gerald, the man who shot his partner Cynthia in the face with a sawed-off shotgun. Prior to meeting Cynthia, Gerald had spent twelve years—nearly three-fourths of his adult life—behind bars. The longest of these sentences had been five years for three armed robberies. During the entire fourteen months of their relationship, Gerald had been "on the lam" for having violated the terms of his parole. Facing a warrant for his arrest, Gerald had lived in hiding with Cynthia while continuing to support himself via robbery and larceny. On the day he killed Cynthia, they had argued over her refusal to let him use her car to commit a robbery.

Prior Convictions

Career criminals who kill their partners distinguish themselves from the other killers not only in the sheer volume of their past crimes but in their crime versatility. For the non-career criminals, the vast majority of their prior convictions had been for domestic violence, non-felony motor vehicular infractions, such as driving without insurance, or alcohol-related ones such as disturbing the peace or drunk driving. The career criminals had committed many of these same crimes as well, but their criminal activity extended far beyond these realms. They had committed many more violent crimes against people other than their intimate partners, including rape and other assaults on strangers or acquaintances. They had many non-violent felony convictions, such as for fraud, grand theft, home invasions, drug possession and sales, and burglary. The sheer volume and variety of their crimes reveal these men as chronic and pervasive violators of social conventions and authority.

Criminal Lifestyle

Some of the career criminals we interviewed would not have qualified as such based strictly on prior convictions or prison terms. Two of the qualifying killers and three of the would-be killers had had no prison records and few felony convictions. They qualified as career criminals because most of their income as adults was derived from criminal enterprises. There were subtypes of these men: those who were members of organized crime and those who appeared to be "solo operators." Of the first group, two of the men were longtime "bikers," according to the women whom they had attempted to kill, while the third was evidently a member of a more established crime syndicate, akin to the Mafia. All three of these men were perpetrators of attempted homicide. Their victims declined to discuss the details of these men's criminal activities for fear of retribution from them or from their crime associates. Some of the career criminals that I interviewed confirmed that they had warned their partners not to disclose their criminal activities, and two men said that they had specifically threatened to have their partner harmed by others if she disclosed their crimes. One victim of attempted homicide reported that her partner had repeatedly said that he had "put a contract out on her" after his arrest for selling drugs. These threats continued from prison. This woman added that "he was so paranoid towards the end, he thought it was me, even though that was the last thing I would have done."

All three of this latter group of men—those who appeared not to be members of organized crime—were men who had killed their partners. Despite their not being part of a formal network, each of these men admitted that most of his friends and peers were also involved in criminal activities. One of these men, Donlon, characterized himself as a fulltime "dealer and stealer" who also took part-time legitimate jobs "when business was slow." Donlon denied having any formal criminal partners but said that he relied upon his network of friends to conduct and protect his drug sales. This depiction is similar to that of another killer, Everett, to whom I asked whether his friends supported his criminal activities. Everett responded, "They was all doing the same thing" but also denied having any formal crime partners. Both Donlon and Everett reported that their fathers had extensive criminal records. Everett's father had been incarcerated for killing a girlfriend ten years prior to Everett's murder of his partner. Everett said his father had taught him "how to survive on the streets" and that they had committed many crimes together when he still lived with his father. Interestingly, most of the career criminals I interviewed said that they were closer with their fathers than their mothers. This was the only group of killers in which the majority said this.

Donlon and Everett are typical of the other career criminals in that their criminal lifestyle appeared to be one that they learned from their fathers as well as from other adult figures during their upbringings. Once established, this lifestyle was actively abetted and refined by their respective peer networks. This kind of intergenerational and peer support for antisocial behavior is reminiscent of that reported by the substance-abusing type of killer. This is not coincidental given the large overlap that appears to exist between these two groups. Nine of the eleven men that we characterized as career criminals were also substance abusers. Compared to the other three types of killers, men in these two groups were far more likely to report having five or more male friends, and to say that they saw their friends at least twice per week. Their friendships appear to have provided a powerful form of peer support for these men to engage in drinking, drugging, violent and in many cases, criminal behavior. For the most part, the substance-abusing men had attempted to induct their partners into this network. This was somewhat less true for the career criminals, who tended to keep their peers somewhat separate from their partners. In any event, the existence of such a strong peer network for these men surely poses a daunting challenge for a female partner who seeks to complain about, or leave, her abusive partner. The victims of attempted homicide whose partners were substance abusers or career criminals were least likely to say that they could turn to mutual friends for support or help. As one woman put it, "They were all doing the same thing," referring both to their drinking and violence. Another woman, Anita, said that she would routinely see her boyfriend's friends "slapping their girlfriends around," adding, "it was like a big joke [to them]."

Abused women whose partners are involved in crime appear to be especially vulnerable. Not only do they have fewer mutual friends to whom they can turn for help, but also fewer of their own friends as well. Most of the victims whose partners were involved in criminal activity said that they feared disclosing this information to their friends and family for fear of jeopardizing them. Not coincidentally, these women seemed the most isolated. One woman, Angela, said that her parents knew about her partner's criminal activities and feared for her life. "But what could they do?" she asked. "They knew what he was capable of." Angela went on to describe how her partner had repeatedly threatened to kill her father.

Triggers for Homicide

The career criminals identified many of the same triggers that the substance abusers did. For some men, killing their partners appeared to arise out of mundane arguments. One example was Vincent, already profiled in the previous section, who had killed Carol by backhanding her to the face after she had complained that he'd stopped up the toilet. Similar to this was James, who smothered Corinne after she had complained about his breaking a flowerpot. In other cases, the triggers for murder are more similar to those described in the section about materially motivated killers, reflecting another overlap in style. Many of the career criminals appeared to have contempt for their partners, which seemed to be fueled by long-standing grievances against them. This was evidenced by Gerald, the man who killed Cynthia after she refused to let him use her car because he had been drinking. Gerald's fury about this fit with his intolerance for any past complaints or defiance by Cynthia. This same contempt was manifested by Everett, who shot his estranged girlfriend when she showed up at his house to demand that he return some jewelry that he had taken. Another example was provided by Reagan, who killed his girlfriend, Crystal, after she refused to have sex with him. Gerald, Everett, and Reagan are examples of highly vindictive men with very little emotional attachment to their partners. All three men appeared primarily to expect money and sex from their partners. Each would frequently come and go with little accounting of their activities to their partners. Each admitted to having had frequent sex with other women. At the same time, they were intolerant of any expectations or complaints from their partners. Gerald and Everett both talked of frequently having been "bothered" by their respective partners, such as their complaints about the other women or the lack of time spent together. Each had a prior history of other financially exploitative relationships with women. None of these men seemed upset about having killed his partner. Similar to the materially motivated type of killer, each appeared to blame the deceased for the legal consequences that had ensued.

Murder appears to be the result of the killer's immediate triggers and the evolving situational factors, as well as his longer-term traits and grievances. Of all the types of killers we interviewed, the career criminals seemed most predisposed to kill. Similar to the materially motivated men, the career criminals held overwhelmingly negative views of women. They appear to view women as a somewhat necessary nuisance: useful for sex and a place to stay but "nothing but trouble" in other regards. Not only did they continue to demonize the deceased but most of their past partners as well. Five of the six career criminal killers admitted to violence toward at least one past partner. By comparison, less than one-fourth of the other killers admitted violence toward a past partner. It is likely that a much higher proportion of the other killers had actually committed violence in their past relationships but were unwilling to admit it. It is revealing that the career criminals had no such qualms about disclosing such ill treatment of women. For them, it appeared to be a point of pride. Donlon talked of vandalizing an ex-partner's apartment and car and stealing money from her after she had kicked him out of her apartment. In disclosing this, Donlon explained, "I had to show her that I don't take that kind of crap from a woman."

Based on their relationship histories and criminal records, as well as their lack of remorse about the murders they committed, these men seem most similar to how criminologists often portray murderers in general. Many if not most chronically violent offenders are thought to have anti-social personality disorder. Though I did not administer any tests to assess for these traits, I suspect that most if not all of these men would score high on psychopathy scales that are designed to measure features of anti-social personality disorder. People with these features were previously referred to as "psychopaths." According to criminologist Robert Hare, the most common traits found in psychopaths include the following:[36]

Emotional/Interpersonal Realm	Social Deviance
Glib and superficial attachments to others	Impulsive
Egocentric and grandiose	Poor behavior controls
Lack of remorse	Need for excitement
Lack of empathy	Lack of responsibility
Deceit and manipulation	Early behavior problems
Shallow emotions	Adult antisocial behavior

Though many of these features are present to some degree in most men who kill their partners, career criminals stood out in seeming to have many of these features. For these men, women are objectified as disposable and interchangeable commodities. This is evidenced not only in their lack of remorse for their deceased partners but for their overall pattern of exploiting women. With this set of expectations, it seems inevitable that each woman soon outlives her usefulness. In fact, these men's relationships with the deceased were more short-lived on average than those of any other of the killer types. Their relationships averaged twenty-nine months compared to ninety-two months for the other killers.

Potential Deterrents

For most of the career criminals, the most obvious deterrent to killing or trying to kill their partners would have been serving a jail sentence for domestic violence or other crimes so that they would not have had access to their victims. None of the victims of attempted homicide whose abusers were career criminals had called the police due to a prior act of domestic violence. In the few times the police were involved, witnesses had called them. Even when they had been arrested, none of these men had been convicted of prior domestic violence, since their victims had refused to testify. In two of the five cases, the perpetrators even avoided prosecution for the final act of attempted homicide due to their victim's reluctance to testify. In both of these cases, however, the men received substantial prison sentences for subsequent convictions for drug-related crimes. A third perpetrator, who had bludgeoned his victim unconscious with his motorcycle helmet, agreed to plead guilty to assault and battery in exchange for having charges of assault with intent to murder dropped. This perpetrator received only a prison suspended prison sentence of six months, with one year of probation to follow. The two career criminals who were convicted of assault with intent to murder were prosecuted because of "no drop" charges on the part of the district attorney. In both cases, these cases were prosecuted without the testimony of the victims and the perpetrators received prison sentences of eight to ten years.

Similarly, only two of the six career criminal killers that I interviewed had previously been arrested for domestic violence. In both of these cases, the violence occurred in public, and bystanders—not the victim—had summoned the police. Though there was strong evidence of prior domestic violence by the other three career criminals, it appeared that their victims might have been too fearful to call the police. Despite this, two of the career criminals had active warrants against them at the time that they committed murder. One of these was Gerald, who had been "on the lam" the previous fourteen months for parole violations. The other was Vincent, who had an outstanding warrant for violation of the terms of his probation at the time that he killed Carol. Following his three-month jail term for assaulting Carol, he had violated probation by not checking in with his probation officer. Had he been picked up by police for his warrant, Vincent would likely have received an additional jail sentence because of his long criminal record. In both Vincent's and Gerald's cases, long prison sentences might well have provided their respective victims with the opportunity to end the relationships. For his part, Gerald said that he likely would not have resumed his relationship with Pamela if he had been incarcerated for violating his parole since he "didn't want her to begin with." Gerald went on to explain that his primary interest in Pamela had been that she provided a place for him to stay while avoiding the law.

Only one of the career criminal killers who had served jail time had attended a batterer intervention program while in prison. At the time that some of these murders were committed, no such programs existed in most prisons or jails in Massachusetts. Currently, nearly all the state's county jails have such programs. Since 2000, many states have begun to shift toward more of an emphasis on rehabilitative programming in their prison systems, especially for prisoners with histories of violence and other crimes against persons. This has been prompted by the many studies that have shown that the vast majority of prisoners with violent records re-offend within one year of their release from prison. Further, most prisoners are released without parole, probation, or any level of community supervision. This means that convicted batterers who serve prison sentences do not attend batterer intervention programs upon their release unless attending such a program was made a condition of their original sentence. Even batterers who received a prison sentence for violating the conditions of their probation by failing to attend a batterer intervention program are often not required to attend such a program once they wrap up their sentences. I have known some batterers who have chosen to serve a relatively short prison sentence, say of one to three months, rather than attend a forty-week batterer intervention program. In choosing this option, they sometimes are able to avoid any kind of rehabilitative programming altogether.

With a new emphasis on prisoner re-entry programs, however, an increasing number of batterers are being required to attend batterer intervention programs either during or following their prison sentences. This makes sense for a variety of reasons. One is that there is strong evidence that most batterers refrain from abuse while attending batterer intervention programs. Further, those who complete their programs are two to four times less likely to re-offend than those who don't complete one.[37] Batterer intervention programs in most states are required to notify courts promptly in cases when a batterer has dropped out of his program or otherwise not complied with program requirements, such as to consistently attend, actively participate, refrain from abuse, and follow program recommendations. Further, programs are required to provide the court with written documentation of the perpetrator's noncompliance. This notification to the courts serves as an early notice to courts that an offender is at increased odds to re-offend. In many jurisdictions, the probationer's failure to fulfill program requirements results in a probation revocation hearing, where he is subject to being incarcerated for violating the terms of his probation.

Too often, however, batterers who fail to attend or to complete their batterer intervention programs are simply allowed to attend a less rigorous program of their own choosing. In many cases, convicted batterers are able to avoid a certified batterer intervention program altogether by agreeing to plead guilty to domestic assault in exchange for being sentenced to a shorter program, such as an anger management program, a substance abuse program, or a private therapist. One study has shown that convicted batterers who attend anger management or substance abuse programs are significantly more likely to re-offend than those who attend state-certified batterer intervention programs.[38] Certified batterer intervention programs, unlike anger management programs, are required to provide information to victims such as the whether the batterer has enrolled in the program, dropped out, or failed to complete the program. These programs provide both victims and referring courts with written documentation about the batterer's potential to commit serious acts of violence, including homicide and suicide. This information is often instrumental to the victim's decision-making about her own safety, and also is useful to judges in their sentencing decisions.[39]

Several outcome studies of domestic violence offenders referred to batterer intervention programs have shown that program completion rates are improved and recidivism is reduced when the courts strictly monitor attendance in such programs.[40] In some jurisdictions, dedicated domestic violence courts provide the structure for such enhanced monitoring. Typically, in such systems, offenders attending batterer intervention programs must go before a judge every thirty days for reviews of their progress. This review not only includes whether they have refrained from violence and respected protective orders but also whether they have actively and positively participated in their batterer intervention program.[41] Positive participation generally entails a willingness to discuss openly one's own past violence without blaming the victim, an ability to grasp the concepts of the program, and a demonstrated willingness to use nonabusive and noncoercive ways of communicating with others.

Comparing Killers to Would-Be Killers

The most obvious difference between the men who killed their partners and those who attempted to do so was the ineptness of the latter group's efforts. For many, the problem did not seem to be in their lack of effort but rather in poor execution. One strong factor in their lack of success was that far fewer of these men used guns. A comparison of the methods used in the killers' and the would-be killers' final assaults on their victims is provided in Table 3.7. While nearly half of the killers used guns to kill their partners, only one of the would-be killers used one. This was Mark, the man described at the beginning of this book, who had fired seven shots into his estranged wife's car, missing each time.

Why didn't more of the perpetrators of attempted homicide use guns? One reason may be that they apparently had less access to guns than did the killers who succeeded. While 58% of the killers said that they had had easy access to guns when they committed their crimes, this was true for only 40% of the would-be killers.

Of course, this does not tell the whole story. I mentioned previously that three of the killers went out to get guns specifically for the purpose of killing their partners. Therefore, a more likely explanation for the killers' greater success was that a higher proportion of them carefully planned their fatal attacks. Two-thirds of them, after all, were convicted of murder in the first or second degree, meaning that there had been irrefutable evidence of premeditation. By contrast, far fewer of the would-be killers showed strong evidence of such careful calculation. Only about half of these men were prosecuted for attempted murder. The major reason for this low prosecution rate appeared to be that fearful victims were reluc-

Table 3.7: Methods used by killers and would-be killers during their final assaults on their victims (in percentages)

Method Used	Killers	Would-be killers
Shooting with gun	45	5
Stabbing	16	35
Strangling with hands	16	5
Bludgeoning/Beating	10	40
Asphyxiating/Smothering	6	0
Stabbing and bludgeoning	3	5
Strangling and beating	0	5
Sabotaging victim's car	0	5
Strangling and running over with car	3	0
	N=31	N=20

tant to testify against their assailants. In some cases, this was additionally prompted by hearing that the offender would agree to plead guilty to a lesser charge such as assault and battery with a dangerous weapon, kidnapping, rape, or just assault and battery.

Two of the perpetrators weren't charged with any crime, however, due to insufficient evidence. This was because the victims did not file a police report. Both women said their partners were members of organized crime and that they were too fearful to call the police.

Judging from the victims' accounts, about one-third of the perpetrators (35%) had engaged in some form of planning for their final assaults on the victims. Here is a sampling of these cases.

1) Reggie's wife, Anna, had left him three years earlier and was living with another man when he tried to kill her. Having just found out that he was dying of liver disease, Reggie called Anna and asked her to meet him at a subway discussion so they could discuss their children. When she arrived, Reggie took out a knife and stabbed her in the stomach. "He didn't say a word before he stabbed me," Anna recounted. "After he stabbed me he didn't say anything either. It was weird; he just stood there and waited for the police to arrive."

2) After his wife, Sylvie, moved out of their home, Edgar began sneaking into her apartment to spy on her from a hidden crawl space that he had enlarged underneath the stairway. Once he overheard her telling a friend that she never intended to return to him. The next evening, he knocked on the door and when she opened it, he stabbed her five times in the head while their two-year-old daughter sat on the floor crying.

3) Shortly after Lisa tried to have her estranged husband, Alex, committed to a detox center, he broke into her house at midnight, bound her wrists and feet as she lay naked in bed, and began bludgeoning her and stabbing her with a screwdriver. Lisa was able to break free at one point and dove headfirst through the closed second-story window, but Alex caught her by the feet and pulled her naked body back through the broken glass of the window. He then rebound her and resumed his attack. Lisa broke free a second time and leaped out the window, crashing onto the driveway below. She then ran to a neighbor's house and had them summon the police. Lisa sustained multiple lacerations, penetration wounds, and broken bones.

In contrast to these attacks, however, the majority of victims believed that the near-fatal assaults on them had been less calculated. Most believed that their partners' decisions to kill had been made "on the spot" or immediately before an attack in reaction to something said or done. Often, the attack had occurred within the context of a heated exchange between them. This is somewhat misleading, however, since it also appears that many of the men had initiated the interactions with the intention to kill their partners. In fact, it seemed to some victims that the verbal attacks had been simply the first part of the murder attempts. Many of these victims said that the attacks began with the assailants loudly accusing them of something, swearing at them and threatening to kill them. In many cases, the assailant appeared to have been ruminating about the victim's presumed affair or plans to end the relationship. One woman said it seemed he had been "working himself up to it more and more." Another said, "I could see he was kind of psyching himself up for whatever." A third woman said, "I could tell he was hurting and just wanted to end it all. I should have known he wanted to end me!"

While most of the killers were more calculating than this, a substantial number of them were similar to the attempted killers in their apparent lack of planning. This seemed particularly true of the killers who bludgeoned or strangled their victims. I have previously mentioned Vincent, for instance, the man who had punched his partner, Carol, in the head after she had complained about his stopping up the toilet with macaroni. Carol died two weeks later of a brain aneurism. Vincent was one of the ten killers who were convicted of manslaughter.

Aside from being less calculating and adept at killing, how else did the attempted killers differ from those who succeeded? Demographically, they were remarkably similar. Table 3.8 summarizes the demographic traits of both groups of men. They were nearly identical in age, class background, employment status, and marital status. One significant difference is that a somewhat higher proportion of the killers were Caucasian, and while an equal proportion of each group was African American, none of the killers were Latinos. In contrast, four of the would-be killers were Latino men. The racial breakdown of all fifty-one of the perpetrators collectively, however, is similar to that found among men who kill their partners in this country, though our study had fewer African American victims. While 20% of the victims in this study were African American, just under 30% of American women killed by their intimate partners in 1998 were African American. The rate of Latina victims during this same year is unknown since Hispanic victims of crime are classified as of "White" or of "Other Race" by the National Institute of Justice in Uniform Crime Reports. However, Peace At Home, a victim advocacy group that tracks intimate partner homicides in Massachusetts, found that of 149 women killed from 1991–1995, 9.4 percent were Hispanic.[42] This same study found that 65% of the victims were Caucasian, 21% were African American, 2.7% were Asian, and 2% were classified as "Race Unknown." The previously cited Campbell study of 445 homicides and attempted homicides of women in eleven American cities found that 24% of the women were of Hispanic backgrounds.[43]

One other substantial difference between the killers and the would-be killers was that a higher proportion of the former group had failed to complete high school. Despite this, equal proportions had attended college. Overall, the perpetrators were significantly less educated than the general population of men, though their collective level of education is some-

Table 3.8: Comparison of demographic characteristics and circumstances of killers and would-be killers

Characteristic	Killers	Would-be killers
Mean age	33	34
Mean grade completed	11	12
Had completed high school	48%	70%
Had attended some college	22%	20%
Had married the victim	45%	45%
Had children with victim	61%	80%*
Caucasian	81%	60%
African American	19%	20%
Latino	0%	20%
Had blue-collar occupation	87%	85%
Had white-collar occupation	13%	15%
Unemployed at time of final assault	29%	25%
Estranged at time of final assault	48%	50%
Victim was planning to separate or end relationship at the time	16%	10%
Estranged at time or planned estrangement	64%	60%
	N=31	N=20

* This includes all children, whether biological or step-children, who lived in the same household with the couple.

what consistent with the lower economic backgrounds of their families of origin. The class background and occupational status of the perpetrators matches those found among perpetrators of domestic homicide in larger research studies.

Nearly equal proportions of both groups of perpetrators were unemployed at the time that they committed their final assaults. Looking at the context of these cases, however, I found that unemployment was not always coincidental to the murder or attempted murder. Some of the unemployed men had quit their jobs in order to have more time to monitor their partner's activities. A few others had been fired from their jobs because they were missing so many days from work in order to conduct surveillance. Examples of these cases are given in the later section about stalking.

Another similarity between the two groups of perpetrators was that the majority of each group were estranged from their victims, or about to become estranged, at the time of the fatal or near-fatal assaults. Many research studies have previously identified estrangement as a strong factor in domestic homicides.[44] For this reason, estrangement is one of the risk markers included on nearly all formal tools to assess danger and potential lethality in domestic violence cases. Only recently, however, has this factor been broadened to include planned estrangement by the victim. In my interviews with the killers as well as the victims of attempted homicide, I found that the victims' plans to separate or to end the relationships were just as likely to be cited as triggering factors for the perpetrators as cases where the victims had already left. As can be seen from Table 3.8, imminent estrangement was a condition in about one-eighth of the cases. In conducting threat assessments, it therefore makes sense to include whether the victim is making plans to separate from her abuser and whether he knows about those plans.

Beyond the demographic and relationship status similarities in the homicide and attempted homicide groups, I found that the would-be killers could be classified according to the same types that I had profiled among the killers. Further, in determining which type each of these perpetrators fit, I found that there was a similar proportional spread across all five of the killer types. This is summarized in Table 3.9.

Double and Triple Threats

Most of the killers and would-be killers could be called multiple threats in that they had characteristics of more than one type. In fact, this was true of nearly two-thirds of the men. Table 3.10 provides a breakdown of this. A somewhat higher proportion of the perpetrators of attempted homicide (70%) qualified as multiple threats than the killers (58%). This may reflect the greater likelihood that victims, relative to perpetrators, would identify key perpetrator behaviors such as jealousy and substance abuse.

Jealous Substance Abusers

The most common type of double threat was the jealous substance abuser. The overlap between these two types of killers is considerable. Two-thirds

Table 3.9: Breakdown of perpetrator types (in percentages)*

Perpetrator type	Killers	Would-be killers	Overall
Jealous	71	80	75
Substance abusing	61	75	67
Materially motivated	19	15	18
Career criminal	19	25	22
Suicidal	9	10	10**
	N=31	N=20	N=51

* Totals exceed 100% since many perpetrators were classified as more than one type.

** Due to the exclusion from this study of actual suicide cases, this undoubtedly undercounts the true proportion of suicidal perpetrators. From larger research studies of femicides that include murder-suicides, the proportion of murder-suicides ranges from 25% to 30%.

Table 3.10: Breakdown of killers and would-be killers according to number of membership types they fit

Number of killer types the perpetrator fit	Number/proportion of perpetrators
One type only	19 (37%)
Two types	22 (43%)
Three types	10 (20%)
N=51	

of the substance-abusing killers also qualified as jealous types. Just over half of the jealous killers were also substance abusers. Jealousy and substance abuse appear to be particularly deadly combinations. In some cases, it is possible that one factor without the other would not have been enough to trigger murder. A number of the jealous killers, for instance, said that their drinking had exacerbated their jealousy. Asked what had made him jealous, James said, "To be honest, I'm not that jealous. I guess if I was drinking, that would make me more so. You know, the insecurity would kick in and then I'd be talking some real shit to her [Corrine]."

Interviewer:	Are you saying that when you were drinking that you would think things that you normally wouldn't think?
James:	You can say that! I'd be thinking a lot of things, yes. Sick shit.
Interviewer:	Like what?
James:	Like her and her father.
Interviewer:	You mean, you'd think Corrine was sexually involved with her father?
James:	I might have accused her of that a couple of times when I had alcohol in me.
Interviewer:	Did you really believe that?
James:	Nah! Not regularly no. But again, if I'd been drinking, yes.

Several victims of attempted homicide similarly noted that their abusers' jealous threats would become worse with their drinking and/or drug use. Commenting on her partner's changes before his near-fatal assault on her, Lydia said, "He seemed more paranoid. I think it was the drugs."

Interviewer:	What do you mean by paranoid?
Lydia:	He'd always be thinking people was out to get him. He'd say people was coming into the house and stealing his money. He'd accuse me of crazy things.
Interviewer:	Like what?
Lydia:	Hiding things from him. He'd accuse me of taking his clothes if he couldn't find them.
Interviewer:	Was his jealousy worse?
Lydia:	Oh God, yes! It was always bad but then he'd think I had something going on with every person I'd meet.

Other women did not believe that their abusive partners were necessarily more jealous when they had been drinking or using drugs but that their jealous threats and violence would be more severe. As one woman said, "That [jealous suspicions] was always in his head but when he was drinking he'd really let me have it. He wouldn't hold back as much." Asked to explain the connection between her abuser's use of alcohol and his jealousy, another woman said, "I'd say it just enhanced his insecurities."

We classified just over half of the perpetrators of attempted homicide as both substance-abusing and jealous types. From the victims' accounts, it was clear that both substance abuse and jealousy had been longstanding features of their relationships with their assailants. In most cases, both appeared to play prominent roles in the final near-fatal assault. Over 90% of these women said that their partners' jealous behavior had escalated in the six months leading up to the assaults. Two-thirds of the women said that their partners' drinking and/or drug use had also escalated. Was one of these factors more critical to the assault than the other? Asked which factor—jealousy or substance abuse—had played the biggest role in the final assault, most of the women said they believed it had been their partner's jealousy. All but one of the women (92%) said that their partners had made jealous accusations or threats on the day of the assault. By comparison, only two-thirds of the victims said that their partners were drunk or high on the day of the assault. Jealous accusations and threats seemed an inimical part of the physical assaults. Lynette reported that her estranged husband, William, kept demanding to know, "Who are you sleeping with?" as he bludgeoned her over the head with a baseball bat. Though his drinking and drug use had increased in the three months leading up to this attack, Lynette said she believed that "he would have done it [the attack] regardless." In fact, only two women said that they believed that their partner would not have attacked her had he not been drinking or using drugs. One of these was Amanda, whose husband, Ernesto, struck her repeatedly over the head with a wrench after overhearing her reveal his recent drug use to her mother. Though conceding that Ernesto was "very jealous" in general, Amanda said that jealousy played no role in this attack. The other woman was Sylvie, whose husband, Edgar, stabbed her in the head. Asked what prompted this attack, she said, "I think he had to get messed up [with alcohol] to give him the courage."

For the majority of jealous drunks or jealous drug abusers, it appeared that jealousy provided the motive for their attacks while alcohol or drugs were merely facilitating factors. In some cases, alcohol or drug use also was used to camouflage premeditation. Alcohol and drug impairment are commonly cited grounds for diminished capacity during murder trials, and in fact, many of the killers cited their alcohol or drug use on the day of the murder as evidence that the murders were not premeditated. This was true even for two killers who were found to have no alcohol or drugs in

Table 3.11: Comparison of crimes for which jealous and non-jealous Substance Abusers were convicted (in percentages)

	Jealous substance abusers	Non-jealous substance abusers
First degree murder	54	17
Second degree murder	15	33
Manslaughter	31	50
	N=13	N=6

their systems when apprehended immediately following the murders they committed.

One distinguishing feature of jealous substance abusers, compared to non-jealous ones, was that the former group was more likely to have planned their crimes. The jealous substance abusers were more likely to be convicted of first degree murder compared to those who were substance abusers only. Conversely, the non-jealous substance abusers were more likely to be convicted of manslaughter, suggesting a much lower level of premeditation. Summaries of these findings are provided in Table 3.11. The level of premeditation shown by the jealous substance abusers mirrored that shown by the other jealous killers who had no history of substance abuse.

Case Example 6

"I wanted to destroy all reminders of him."

James was a slightly built man who cried nearly continuously during my interview with him. James said that he met Corrine in the fall of 1993 and moved in with her within a week. Both were thirty-six. Corrine's daughter, Mary, was two years old. Shortly before James moved in, Corrine had quit her job as a legal secretary and sold her condominium. The couple then lived off the proceeds of that sale. During their first month together, Corrine confided to James that she had been the victim of an incestuous rape by her uncle. Though James was initially sympathetic, he began to blame Corrine for what had happened and to accuse her of being in love with the uncle. In November, Corrine came home to find that James had torn up a picture of the uncle that he'd found in her family scrapbook. When Corrine complained, James backhanded her in the face. Corrine obtained a restraining order the next day.

The following April, James broke into Corrine's place, burned all of her pictures, and tore up all her clothes. He also destroyed many of her other belongings. In explaining this to me, James said, "I wanted to destroy any reminders of her uncle." James was convicted of breaking and entering, violating a restraining order, and making threats, for which he received a two-year prison sentence. During the one year he spent in prison, Corrine visited James every week. James completed an alcohol education program in prison and was promising never to drink again. James Jr. was born before his father was released.

Within two months of James's release, James and Corinne had an argument outside a supermarket after he had refused to buy something that Mary wanted. James kicked Corinne in the shin and headbutted her. A bystander called the police and James was arrested. This time, he received a two-and-a-half year sentence for assault and battery and violation of probation. All but six months of this time was suspended. Corrine had initially decided to end her relationship with James but he convinced her to give him another try by agreeing to attend a batterer intervention program in prison. Corinne and the children visited every weekend.

Shortly after James's discharge in June 1993, James Jr. fell out of his high chair onto his face, according to James. Corinne called the police and the police filed a report of child abuse. The following day, James and Corrine were arguing in the car about what had happened. Corrine got out of the car and ran to her mother's house. When James pursued her, the police were called. After the police arrived, Mary began crying and James yelled, "Shut the little bitch up!" He was arrested and the police filed a second child abuse report. Following a child abuse investigation, the state removed both children and placed them into foster care. James received a five-year term of probation with the condition that he maintain sobriety and see his probation officer every two weeks.

In August, Corinne went to court to charge James with violation of her restraining order, saying that he had threatened to "knock [me] out." He was arrested and released after posting bail of $200. James continued to see Corrine outside of her house, despite the conditions of the restraining order which forbade such contact. On August 20, James and Corrine fought after she accused him of talking about her to friends. James went to a bar and began drinking. He called Corinne from the bar to demand that she take his name off their phone bill. James says that, while at the bar, he consumed ten to twelve beers and two shots of Jack Daniels. He called Corinne four more times but she did not answer the phone. James took a cab to Corinne's house, arriving at 11:00 p.m. When Corinne let him in, James told her the place was a mess and ordered her to get rid of a particular houseplant. When she refused, James knocked it over, breaking the pot. Corinne began to scream at him to leave. James put his hands over her mouth to prevent her from yelling. They struggled and fell down several times, ending up near the couch. James was continuing to hold Corinne by the mouth when he noticed she was no longer breathing. He was giving her mouth-to-mouth resuscitation when the police arrived, having been called by Corinne's neighbor. The police tried but failed to revive Corinne. Their report indicated that Corinne had been suffocated, citing that there was a pillow impression on her face. James pled guilty to murder in the second degree and received a sentence of twenty years to life.

Jealous and Suicidal

While suicidal types of killers and would-be killers were clearly under-represented in this study, their ranks among killers are substantial and therefore warrant inclusion in this analysis. Nearly one-third of American women's murders by their intimate partners are followed by the suicides of the killers. As already noted, jealousy, combined with estrangement or pending estrangement, appears to be the leading trigger for murder among this type of killer. In many, and perhaps most of these cases, the man's jealousy was not only an immediate trigger to murder-suicide but also a long-term factor in the relationship. As was the case with Allen, who was profiled in the section about suicidal type of killer, this jealousy is accompanied and perhaps fueled by depression. Depression may lead this type of man to become extremely dependent on his partner for emotional support and caretaking. Allen's depression and dependency on Andrea appeared to have been major factors in her desire to end the relationship, which in turn only made Allen feel more jealous and depressed.

The picture that emerges from many other accounts of murder-suicide is one of a depressed husband who becomes increasingly jealous and desperate as his partner seeks to end the relationship. Due to his depression and extreme dependency on his partner, he sees no life for himself beyond the end of the relationship. His sense of ownership over his partner also leads him to want to ensure that his wife will have no life beyond the end of the relationship. In more rare cases, jealous suicidal men seek to end their children's lives as well. Besides indicating depression and jealousy, the idea that no part of one's family shall continue to exist beyond oneself reflects a profound self-centeredness and sense of ownership. Otherwise, why not just kill yourself?

Carmen (later profiled in the chapter about child abuse) tried to kill himself as well as his two children with carbon monoxide shortly after stabbing his former wife, Amy. This occurred after Amy and the children had moved into a new apartment and Amy had started a relationship with another man. Reflecting back, Amy said that Carmen had been depressed throughout their three-year relationship. He had repeatedly threatened to kill her and the children along with himself whenever she spoke of divorce. According to Amy, Carmen's depression and suicidal behavior preceded their relationship. He told her that he had once attempted to kill himself at age fourteen. Amy said that Carmen had become increasingly depressed and dependent upon her during their relationship. Though she had encouraged him to get help for his depression, he'd refused to do so. Only after his incarceration for attempted homicide of her and the children was Carmen psychologically evaluated and diagnosed with bipolar disorder. This fit Amy's perception of Carmen as being extremely moody. Regardless of whether he was depressed or manic, said Amy, Carmen was "always jealous." She reported that his first act of violent jealousy had occurred two months after they began dating when they were playing golf with mutual friends. "Out of the blue," said Amy, "Carmen accused me of wanting to have sex with one of our friends." In a jealous rage, Carmen banged Amy's head against the side of the car. Amy went on to say that Carmen would make jealous accusations virtually "every time we went out socially, or any time I changed my routine a little."

Jealous and Suicidal Substance Abusers

Also a substance abuser, Carmen qualified as a triple threat. While Amy did not believe that alcohol or drugs played any role in Carmen's attempt to kill her and the children, she said that he had been a habitual user of marijuana. Carmen's marijuana use might have contributed to his depression, according to Amy. Other researchers have found that suicidal killers are more likely than other types of killers to abuse alcohol or drugs. In many cases, substance use may be an attempt by the perpetrator to "self-medicate" his depression. Since alcohol is a depressant, however, it often has the effect of making the individual more depressed. As was the case with Allen, profiled in the section about suicidal killers, alcohol also counteracts the effects of anti-depressant medications. Many other kinds of drugs, including marijuana, function as depressants. Substance use, depression, and jealousy become a very deadly combination for some abusive men. Each condition often exacerbates the other two, leading to an escalating spiral of depression, substance use, and jealous behavior. Feeling the increasing danger, some victims of these men actively seek help for their partners. One victim of attempted homicide, Lisa, had sought to involuntarily commit her estranged husband to a detox program. Unfortunately, this attempt backfired when he sought retribution by trying to stab her to death shortly after the judge refused to commit him. Though severely injured, Lisa survived the attack. Other victims were not so lucky.

Karen Trudeau was killed by her husband, Henry, on May 31, 2002. Three months earlier, Karen had filed for divorce, alleging longstanding physical abuse, and was awarded temporary custody of the couple's two children. In mid-March, however, Karen filed a criminal complaint, reporting that Henry had violated her protective order twice within four days. Henry was arrested and held over the weekend. On March 25, Karen and Henry's family sought to have Henry committed to an in-patient substance abuse program for thirty days, citing evidence that his suicidal behavior and his drinking had escalated. He had twice been hospitalized for depression and attempted suicide. Several months previously, Henry had punched Karen in the back, destroyed her belongings, and threatened to kill her. Despite this, the court denied the petition to commit Henry, and he was released from custody with the conditions that he submit to random drug and alcohol screenings, report to probation, and comply with the protective order. A review hearing was scheduled for May 23. In early May, Karen applied for three additional criminal complaints, alleging that Henry had followed her around town, shouted obscenities at her, and driven by her house. Though the court held a new hearing on May 14, Henry's conditions of release were not revoked, and a pre-trial hearing was scheduled for June 6 when all pending charges would be handled. Henry stabbed Karen to death on May 31 and then committed suicide.[45]

Substance-Abusing Career Criminals

Five out of the six career criminals were substance abusers. All five of the perpetrators of attempted homicide who qualified as career criminals were also substance abusers. This connection makes sense given that most of the career criminals were traffickers of illegal drugs. Their use of drugs extended far beyond product sampling however; most were daily users of drugs as well as of alcohol. Compared to the other perpetrators, these men were also more likely to pressure or compel their partners to use alcohol and drugs. The four victims of attempted homicide who reported that they abused alcohol or drugs were partners of substance-abusing career criminals. Being the victim's supplier appeared to serve two functions for this type of perpetrator. First, he could more effectively control his partner by making her dependent upon drugs and then threatening to cut her off. Secondly, he could threaten to reveal her drug use as a way of keeping her quiet about his criminal enterprise. Said one victim, "He wanted me hooked [on drugs] 'cause he could always use that against me if I was to ever go to the police. After we was separated, he was always threatening to report me to DSS [the child protection agency in Massachusetts]."

Beyond being their partners' drug suppliers, two of the perpetrators also were their pimps. In both cases, the perpetrator had inducted his victim into prostitution. Neither woman had been a prostitute prior to her relationship with her abuser. Prostituted women are known to be at high risk for domestic violence.[46] Many have said that they are forced into this lifestyle by an abusive partner who also acts as their pimp or trafficker. Abuser-pimps often utilize a combination of violence, induced drug dependency, control over wages, and social isolation to control their victims. The social stigma that these women experience becomes an additional means of entrapment within their relationships. Prostituted women with children often fear that their arrest for prostitution might result in the child welfare system stepping in to remove their children. One victim of attempted homicide said, "That was my constant fear, that I was going to lose my babies."

4 | The Killers' Upbringings

Upon hearing the title of my book, several colleagues have asked, "What about their upbringings?" This question implies that the seeds to murder are to be found in the childhoods of the killers. I must confess that, in plumbing their upbringings, I had also hoped to find a "smoking gun" of some kind. But, as a psychologist, I've found that many human problems are overdetermined, meaning that they don't have a single cause but many interconnected ones. The list of contributing factors to family violence is very long, with many competing theories about which are most important. Sociologists often point to larger social factors such as social isolation, poverty, sexism, and conformity to peer or subgroup norms and peer groups that support violence.[1] Psychologists and other kinds of therapists are more apt to cite a wide variety of problems within individuals and families. These include rigidity, competitiveness, distrust of others, low self-esteem, self-centeredness, fear of intimacy, substance abuse, and mental illness. Therapists also identify dysfunctional interactions within families that hinder the learning of nonviolent ways of resolving conflicts. Individuals with such features may be predisposed to react to stress and interpersonal grievances with violence. I have wondered whether there were common factors in the killer's childhoods that predisposed them to commit murder.

In my interviews with the killers, I employed two strategies to investigate this. One was to ask the men directly what problems from their childhoods, if any, had contributed to their violence, or to their killing of their partner. The exact question I asked was, "Thinking back, do you see anything in your upbringing that might have contributed to your violence or to the murder you committed?" This question was intentionally open-ended and ambiguous. The men were free to provide explanations for their violence or just for the murder they had committed. In their actual responses, some focused on the former, some on the latter, and many focused on both parts of the question. My other approach was to ask the men more specific questions about family and childhood factors that are already known to contribute to domestic violence. For instance, many studies have found that one of the strongest predictors of domestic violence among men is their having been exposed to family violence as children. Interestingly, a male child's past exposure to domestic violence is a stronger predictor that he will become a batterer than if he was abused as a child.[2] One national survey of domestic violence in the United States found that men who were exposed to domestic violence as children were three times more likely to grow up to become wife beaters.[3] These researchers also found that when children witness severe abuse between parents, the odds become exponentially greater. Sons who witnessed severe abuse of their mothers by their fathers had spouse-abusing rates that were one hundred times greater than sons who not been exposed to spouse abuse.

This is not to say that child abuse does not also increase the odds for future battering behavior. Abused children are more likely to grow up to become perpetrators of domestic violence. This is not surprising given the high overlap between domestic violence and child abuse. An investigation of child abuse and neglect cases in Massachusetts, for instance, found evidence of domestic violence in just under half of these cases.[4] In most instances, the father was the perpetrator of domestic violence as well as the primary perpetrator of child abuse. Some studies have also found, however, that child abuse and neglect is more common among battered women. Some researchers have attributed this to the increased stress faced by battered women, which in turn often impedes their ability to parent effectively.

In investigating the potential childhood etiologies to murder, I asked each killer twenty-five to thirty questions about his family of origin and overall upbringing. These questions included detailed inquiries about his parents and other adult guardians, as well as his siblings and influential peers. I specifically asked about child abuse and neglect, exposure to domestic violence, child sexual abuse, and whether there were any crimes committed by immediate family members. I asked each man to characterize and rate how each parent and guardian had treated him overall.

Each man was asked how his parents and other guardians had interacted with each other. Specifically, I asked how they communicated affection as well as criticism, whether they had been abusive to each other, and if so, what this had consisted of as well as how often it occurred. Further, I inquired about other significant events in his upbringing such as the death of a loved one, health problems, mental illness, divorce or separation, and relocation.

To provide a point of comparison to this information from the killers, I also asked each victim of attempted homicide a similar series of questions about the upbringing of the man who tried to kill her. About one-fifth said that they did not know enough about their ex-partners' upbringings to answer the questions. The rest were able to provide substantial information based on what they had heard directly from their ex-partners or from their friends and family members. Their responses provided a fascinatingly different perspective about the upbringings of serious offenders than what was provided by the killers. Table 4.1 provides a summary of the men's and women's responses regarding child and spouse abuse in the perpetrators' upbringings.

Table 4.1: Perpetrators' upbringings according to the killers themselves and the victims of attempted homicide (in percentages)

	Killers	Victims of attempted homicide
He had been exposed to spouse abuse as a child	55	94
He had been physically abused by one or more of his parents	48	93
His father abused his mother	48	87
He had been abused by his father	42	64
He had been abused by his mother	16	57
He had been sexually abused as a child	6*	14*
His mother abused his father	6	19
	N=31	N=16

* In all cases cited, the perpetrator was the child's father or stepfather.

Did Their Parents Abuse Them?

Half of the killers said they had been victims of child abuse by one or more parents. According to the victims of attempted homicide, however, nearly all the men who tried to kill them had been abused as children. Even without the extraordinarily high rate of child abuse reported by the women, the proportion of killers who said they had been victims of child abuse is high. This far exceeds the rate of child abuse experienced by the general public but also somewhat exceeds the rate generally reported by men who batter. Surveys of battering men have found child victimization rates that range from 25%–75%, depending on how child victimization is defined as well as the specific populations of batterers being surveyed. One study of 177 incarcerated spouse and child abusers found that 41% had been abused or neglected as children.[5] A Canadian national study of prisoners with histories of spouse abuse found that 46% had either experienced or witnessed abuse in their families of origin.[6] Comparing abusive husbands to nonabusive ones, the authors of a national survey of family violence in the United States found that 39% of the abusive men said they had been abused as children, compared to 11% of the nonabusive husbands.[7]

High as the rate of child abuse reported by the killers is, how do we explain the even higher rate of victims of attempted homicide who said that their ex-partners had been abused? It is possible that this simply reflects natural differences between two relatively small groups of research subjects. Another possibility is that this reflects differences in how men and women define child abuse. In my work with men who abuse their partners and children, I've often noted that many of these men have a high threshold for what counts as child abuse. They commonly characterize parental actions such as slapping a child in the face or hitting a child with a stick as acceptable "child discipline" while other people might characterize these actions as abusive. Child abusers in general tend to rationalize abusive behavior on the grounds that it is well-intended. For instance, one man who I counseled justified slapping his three-year-old son in the face for crying by saying, "He needs to learn to wait for things . . . and you don't always get what you want." This reflects the notion that violence toward a child is not abusive when it is not malevolently intended. It also reveals a very rigid set of expectations about acceptable child behavior.

Additional evidence of minimizing child abuse came from the killers themselves. Besides the sixteen men who said they had been physically abused by a parent, three additional men talked of rather harsh "physical discipline" from their fathers, although they refused to characterize such treatment as abusive. Asked for examples, one man said that his father had beaten him with a strap after he had come home drunk. Another man said that his father had beaten him with a board after he had "talked back to my mother." Both of these men thought their fathers' actions to be a warranted response to misbehavior on their parts.

Vincent, the man whose father had beaten him with a strap, said, "How else could he have kept me in line?" adding, "I really would have been out of control if he hadn't have done that." Despite this, it is hard to believe that Vincent could have been more out of control. He admitted that he had begun to drink and to use drugs every day at age twelve. During his teens, Vincent had been arrested dozens of times for stealing cars, breaking into homes, vandalizing property. When Vincent was in his late twenties, several child abuse reports had been filed against him. One of these was filed by his five-year-old son's pediatrician, who had found numerous welt marks on the child's legs and behind. Though admitting that he had used a strap to hit his son, Vincent vehemently denied that this constituted abuse and insisted on his right to "discipline" his son.

Vincent exemplifies abusive fathers raised by abusive fathers who have internalized violence as a normal and legitimate means of enforcing parental rules and expectations. Over one-quarter of the killers had engaged in behavior toward their own children that many people would characterize as child abuse, but only two of these men (6%) thought that their behavior qualified as child abuse. In contrast, 63% of the victims of attempted homicide said that their ex-partners had been abusive to their children.

For the killers who acknowledged that they had been abused as children, the abusers had been overwhelmingly their fathers or stepfathers, and not their mothers. Moreover, the only two men who reported that they had been sexually abused by a parent or guardian said that the assailant had been their father. Both men attributed their violence toward their partners to their childhood victimization.

Edward said, "I've had a warped sense of what love is. Where's the line between violence and love? I felt cheated, like I never had a real father and mother. Life was survival. I had to protect myself." Edward had previously talked about also having to repeatedly protect his mother from his father's brutal assaults on her. "He said he'd kill us both if we didn't do what he said. I'd hide the shovel he said he was going to use to bury us with. He'd retrieve it every day."

Asked what from his childhood might have contributed to his domestic violence or to the murder he committed, Reagan said, "All of it. Being assaulted, sexually abused . . . the drugs and alcohol. I started smoking pot and using mescaline and drinking when I was ten or eleven. My older brothers were negative influences. Being taken out of my home at an early age." Reagan's parents divorced when he was seven. Reagan lived in a series of foster homes after this but also spent considerable time in juvenile detention centers starting at age sixteen. His first sentence was for raping a fifteen-year-old girl. Reagan went on to spend most of his adult life behind bars for a long series of crimes, culminating in the murder of his girlfriend when he was twenty-five.

Almost three times as many killers said that the parent who abused them as a child had been their father or stepfather as opposed to their mother or stepmother. Interestingly, a much higher proportion of victims of attempted homicide reported that their ex-partners had been physically abused by their mothers, though abusive fathers were still in the majority. The high proportion of child abuse committed by fathers compared to mothers deviates from what is found among the general population of victims of child abuse. Mothers usually more often commit child abuse, according to most studies. Some researchers have argued that women are more often the abusers partly because they are more often the primary or sole caretakers of children. Some studies have shown that the frequency of child abuse committed by fathers is much closer to that of mothers, and may even exceed it, in two-parent families headed by a heterosexual couple.

Not surprisingly, the killers who said they had been physically abused by their fathers and not their mothers said that they had felt much closer to their mothers. I quantified this by asking the men to rate how closely they felt to each parent during their growing-up period. The men made these ratings on a scale of 1–10, with 10 representing the highest possible degree of closeness and 1 representing the lowest. A summary of these findings is given in Table 4.2.

Table 4.2: Ratings of how close killers felt to each parent during their childhoods*

	Closeness to mother	Closeness to father
Men abused by father and not mother	8.5	4.5
Men abused by mother only or both parents	1	5
Men abused by neither parent	9	7.5

* Mean scores on a scale of 1–10, with 10 meaning the highest degree of closeness and 1 meaning the lowest.

More than twice as many of the killers overall (55% versus 26%) said that, during their childhoods, they had been closer to their mothers than to their fathers. The only group of men who appeared to have preferred their fathers was those who had been physically abused by their mothers or by both parents. It appeared that child abuse committed by mothers counted more against the mothers than that committed by fathers. All three of the men who had been abused by both parents said they had felt closer to their fathers. This was despite the fact that all three said that their father had been the more frequent and severe child abuser! Those men who had been abused by the mothers expressed great contempt for their mothers, and judging from their ratings of closeness felt toward their mothers (with a lowest possible mean score of 1), they had no affection whatsoever for their mothers. In several cases, this contempt for their mothers appeared to extend to all women, including and perhaps especially to those with whom they were involved.

When asked if he could think of anything from his upbringing that might have contributed to his violence toward the woman he killed, Elliot said, "My friends say that I had a thing against women, maybe because of my weird relationship with my mother [referencing her physical and verbal abuse of him]. I verbally castrated [sic] my best friend's wife once. . . . I think I was 27 at the time . . . when she didn't let him buy a boat with me." Elliot ultimately stabbed his girlfriend shortly after she broke off their relationship.

When asked the same question, Lee said, "My mother, her attitude. No matter what I did wasn't good enough. I don't do well with being slapped or having stuff thrown at me. I reach my limit sooner." Lee is the man who killed his girlfriend with a punch to the throat after she threw a cup of hot tea in his face.

Explaining his violence toward women, Calvin said, "I'd always say that to hit a woman was wrong but I always did it. Once, I slapped this chick on the playground when I was young, like seven or so, after she said something smart." Calvin ultimately shot his girlfriend to death after she ended their relationship.

Fear Turns to Respect

Over half of the killers said that they had grown up in homes where one parent abused the other. By comparison, 94% of the victims of attempted homicide said this was true of the men who tried to kill them. According to both sources of information, the perpetrators of domestic violence were overwhelmingly the men's fathers or stepfathers. Only two of the thirty-one killers said that their mothers had been abusive to their fathers, while fifteen said that their fathers or stepfathers had beaten their mothers. Men who had witnessed their mothers' abuse reported a wide range of effects. Many said that they were fearful of their fathers. Just as many said that they felt angry. A number of men said they grew up with no guidance on how to have successful relationships. While some attributed this to the negative example set by their fathers, others said it was because of their fathers' absence from the home following divorce or parental separation. Altogether, one-third of the killers said that they had grown up without a father or father figure for five or more years of their childhood.

Matthew attributed his abuse and stalking of women to the absence of his father, whom his mother had divorced due to his infidelity and domestic violence. Asked how this specifically contributed to his violence, Matthew said, "I think just not having a father teach me about life. Nobody ever taught me how to deal with rejection. It led to a dependency on women for love to fill that void." Matthew went on to explain that he started having sex with many different girls when he was thirteen. "Some girls might have felt I was obsessed with sex. The problem wasn't sex so much as letting go." At age twenty-one, Matthew killed his twenty-year-old ex-girlfriend, Allie, several months after she had broken off their relationship. Convinced that the break-up only reflected Allie's parents' wishes, Matthew hitchhiked down to her house to talk with her directly on the night that he shot her in her car. Matthew had previously been arrested for stalking or harassing two other young women who had rejected his advances.

Louis is the killer cited in the section on short courtships who asphyxiated his girlfriend, Pamela, by forcing his hand down her throat. Asked what from his childhood had made him violent, he said, "Maybe not having my father there at key times of going from boy to man. My mother is small and couldn't control three boys. I always pretty much got my way. I started drinking when I was thirteen on account of all my friends was doing it too. I probably would have done it regardless. If I hadn't gotten my way so much throughout my life I wouldn't have committed this crime as far as having my way. What I want I always get. I didn't want anyone telling me, 'No, you can't have that.'"

A number of men said that, while once fearful of fathers who abused their mothers, they had learned to emulate them in their treatment of partners. There appeared to be two aspects of this emulation. One was developing a general dislike or antipathy towards women. The other was developing a tough and sometimes hypermasculine exterior. Some of these men talked of having shifted from defending their abused mothers to adopting more of their fathers' attitudes and behaviors. Some experts who work with children who are abused say that this reflects the need of some children, particularly male ones, to identify with the more powerful parent. This also appears to be a common solution for children who feel vulnerable or unsafe because of an abusive parent. By adopting the abusive parent's attributes, the child sheds feelings of vulnerability and anxiety. For boys, it is simultaneously a way of resolving conflicts about male identity. Many of the once-fearful killers came to appreciate their abusive fathers; one man gave his father credit for helping to "toughen me up." It appeared that these men gradually came to equate fear with respect and ultimately with love. Their motto seemed to be "those we fear are those that we love." Of course, the logical extension of this philosophy is "those who fear us are those who [should] respect and love us."

When his parents were still living together, Everett had always defended his mother against his father's attacks. He continued to live with his mother for several years after his parents' divorce and had very little contact with his father. After a visit from his father when he was fifteen, Everett decided to live with his father in another city, where his father inducted him into a life a crime. Asked what had influenced him to make this decision, Everett said, "I was attracted to my father's philosophy which was to do unto others before they do unto you. I was just tired of being scared. Together, we was strong and nobody could beat us. Living in the ghetto, I had to fight every day and it kept me on the offensive." While Everett was serving time for killing his girlfriend, his father was convicted for killing a woman that he had dated.

Explaining how his upbringing had influenced him, Emmit said, "Maybe because of my father, we was so scared and mentally beaten [referring to his mother, sisters and himself]. The turning point came when I was fifteen. My brother, Elroy, used to beat on me real bad every single day. He would degrade me in front of my friends and shit but I couldn't do anything 'cause he was my father's favorite. Then one day, I beat him bad and after that he never touched me again. And I was my father's favorite after that!"

Rough Neighborhoods and Other Reasons

About one-third of the men could think of no factors from their upbringings that might have contributed to their violence or to the murder they committed. Most of these men claimed no abusive behavior in their families and said that they had been close to both parents. A major contributing factor cited by these men, as well as a number of the other men, was growing up in a rough neighborhood. Perhaps directly related to this, some men also attributed the murders they committed to their alcohol or drug abuse, which had generally begun in their early to middle teens. For these young men, drinking and fighting in the neighborhood usually went hand in hand.

Kevin, the youngest of the killers that I interviewed, was twenty-one when he killed his nineteen-year-old girlfriend, Rebecca. Asked if there was anything from his upbringing that had contributed to his violence, he said, "Nothing. Just alcohol. Nothing from my home." Kevin went on to say that he had begun to drink heavily with his friends in the neighborhood from age fourteen, claiming, "I was wrecked every day after that. Me and my friends would be partying day and night. And Rebecca was one of them." Asked if there had been violence in some of the other relationships, Kevin replied, "All of them! Me and Rebecca was in a car one night with two of our buddies, they was another couple, and a fight broke out in the back seat and he hauled off and whacked her. She was crying and screaming for me to let her out of the car but two minutes later they was laughing and making out. We all went to a keg party after that."

Vincent said, "The neighborhood was tough. People made me violent. I've been in a thousand battles. People would want to fight. The police would fight me. We moved around a lot." (He listed nine different towns in Massachusetts where his family had lived.) "I had to make new friends. People would want to pick on me when I moved to a new town. I felt I had to be a tough guy to survive."

Douglas said that his neighborhood wasn't violent per se, but intolerant of him because of his different cultural and lower economic background. "I was Polish and was made fun of by the other kids which made me mad at people. I couldn't fight them 'cause there was always five of them. We weren't as well off as other kids in the neighborhood." Douglas killed his young girlfriend after she had broken up with him by strangling her and running her over with his car in their suburban neighborhood.

It is hard to know what to make of some of these explanations for violence and for murder. Some men were clearly grasping at straws, perhaps with no real idea of what the real factors might have been. For instance, one man's response to my question about childhood factors was, "I don't know. TV? Cops shows? My parents didn't go to my games. My father worked, came home and watched TV." Other men seemed more circumspect about what they revealed about their upbringings, preferring to stick to the immediate circumstances that preceded the killings. Those who claimed self-defense or temporary insanity, for instance, seemed eager to deny any violent behavior that might make their crimes look more premeditated. In some cases, this included minimizing any violence that might have existed in their childhoods.

Michael steadfastly denied committing any prior violence toward his wife, Connie, prior to shooting her to death shortly after she'd filed for divorce. Michael's defense at his trial was that Connie had been involved with another man and that he had killed her in a steroid-induced rage. Michael claimed to abuse steroids that he had used as a competitive bodybuilder. Asked what from his childhood might have contributed to his crime, Michael said, "Nothing about my parents or George [his stepfather]. My mother thought my father was cheating on her and that bothered me when she threw him out. Maybe I'm more suspicious because of my mother."

Another killer, Milton, said, "I'm not a violent person. The only thing that might have contributed to my crime was my being so trusting toward my mother. I was naïve. She was a church going woman and would be against infidelity." Milton's defense at his trial for murdering his wife was that he had been "temporarily insane" from discovering that she had been romantically involved with another man.

Learning Violence

The killers' accounts of their upbringings provide fairly clear pictures of their parents, and especially their fathers, as their original teachers of violence and control. A summary of the men's accounts of their mothers and fathers is presented in Table 4.3. From this, it appears that the men acquired much more of their bad behaviors from their fathers than from their mothers, though there was a small subset of men with abusive mothers. Nearly three times as many of their fathers as their mothers abused them as children. Moreover, their fathers were seven times more often the perpetrators of spouse abuse, and while the victims of attempted homicide reported higher rates of domestic violence among their abusive partners' parents, the proportion relative to male and female offenders was even more tipped toward men as the abusers.

Several men acknowledged the bad examples set by their fathers but said that, as young adults, they had unsuccessfully tried not to emulate them. This is a common sentiment expressed by men who batter. Even when they recognize their problem, it is difficult for many to change. Outcome research on batterer intervention programs has shown that while the results are generally positive, approximately half of the participants fail to complete their programs. Even more troublingly, the vast majority of batterers do not voluntarily seek help. Many batterers deny their problem, and this seemed to be the case with the vast majority of the killers. Only one man had ever sought help for his domestic violence, and this was only because it had been a condition of his incarceration. Several of the killers said that they now wish they had sought help for their violence, and had they done so, they would not have committed murder. One said, "I just didn't think it was me with the problem. I blamed her for everything."

Table 4.3: Comparison of parental behavior as reported by killers (by percentages)*

Behaviors	Father	Mother
Was frequently affectionate	52	77
Was frequently critical of him	52	29
One parent was violent to the other parent	48	6
Parent abused alcohol or drugs	48	19
Physically abused him	42	16
Was very protective	39	58
Was cold or distant	39	13
Was never there	35	10
Spoiled him (gave whatever he wanted)	22	22
Parent was treated for a mental illness	19	22
Sexually abused him	6	0
N=31		

* The term "mother" and "father" connotes the primary female and male caretakers of the child respectively. In some cases, these were stepfathers or stepmothers. In one case, the grandmother served as the primary female guardian for the child, and in another, the grandfather served as the primary male guardian. In each of these cases, the man was asked to evaluate his actual caretaker (rather than the biological parent who had played little or no role in his upbringing).

One thing that stands out in analyzing the killers' feelings for their fathers is the co-existence of fear and love, and of fear and respect in others. Despite their fathers' often brutal violence toward them and others in their family, many of the men did not appear to hold it against them. A great number of the men appeared to have resolved their fear of their fathers by emulating their behavior. More than merely mimicking their behavior, these men had internalized their fathers' values. Though none of the men said this, many appeared to be proponents of the philosophy that "what doesn't kill you only makes you stronger."

While, as a group, the killers' fathers stood out as much more violent than their mothers, there was a substantial subgroup of abusive mothers. Just less than one-fifth of the men said that their mothers had been abusive to them and/or their fathers. However, the victims of attempted homicide reported a much higher proportion. Over half of the women

(57%) said that their abusive partners had been abused as children by their mothers. What are we to make of this discrepancy between the men's and the women's reports? It is possible that the killers under-reported child abuse committed by their mothers. It is also possible that the victims of attempted homicide had a skewed picture of their abusive partners' up-bringings based on what they had been told by their partners. It is not uncommon in my experience with abusive men for them to exaggerate the extent of past child abuse in order to gain sympathy or to excuse their own abusive behavior. It is also possible that some of the women might have simply assumed that their abusers had been abused by their mothers, since they themselves were being mistreated. One of the women told me that she strongly suspected that her ex-husband had been abused by his mother "because of the way he treated me." She theorized that this must have been the original source for his "hatred of women."

Regardless of the actual proportion of child abuse committed by the killers' mothers, it was clear that those who had been abused by their mothers had learned some of the same lessons as those who were abused by their fathers. Several of these men talked of continually confusing love with violence. Several also talked of feeling insecure with women. Additionally, these men expressed some of the most overtly hostile attitudes towards women.

Asked about the possible childhood origins of his violence toward his wife, Debra, John replied, "[my] general disrespect and anger toward women because of the way my mother was. Not having a good idea of right and wrong or strong morals. It wasn't enforced, talking back to mother, shooting birds with a pellet gun. Always getting what I wanted might have given me jealousy." John had previously talked about his mother's occasional violence and frequent verbal abuse toward him. John is the man cited in Chapter 6 who carefully planned his wife's murder after becoming convinced that she had left him for another man, and who had been arrested three years earlier for poisoning 10,000 migratory birds on Cape Cod.

These findings about the killers' upbringings lend additional support to the notion that there is a "double whammy" effect when children are exposed to both child abuse and spouse abuse, and that perhaps neither single factor can be singled out as primary. One set of researchers has argued that children exposed to family violence are also more likely to be exposed to other "adverse childhood events," which have more familiarly come to be known by health care professionals as ACEs.[8] ACE factors include parental mental illness, substance abuse, discord, and physical and emotional neglect of children. It is believed that these factors are cumulatively damaging to children's ability to form healthy relationships. Their retrospective study of over 16,000 adults found that "the prevalence of each ACE factor tended to increase as the frequency of maternal battering increased."

It's Not Always About the Parents

As abusive as many of the killers' parents had been, it is important to note that nearly one-third of the killers claimed to have no violence in their families of origin. This mirrors findings about the family backgrounds of abusive men in general. If not from their parents, where then did the killers learn to be violent? These men provided three different and somewhat overlapping explanations to this. The most common was that their violence toward the women they killed was not part of a pattern but in response to the women's violence toward them. Usually, they claimed, their violence had been in self-defense or in response to other "provocative" behavior on the woman's part. It bears noting, however, that there was a rehearsed quality to many of these accounts. Most of these men had used self-defense, or the notion that they were dealing with a violent and vindictive partner, as the basis of their legal defense during their murder trials. In reading through the trial transcripts, the evidence they presented for violence on the deceased's part was often specious and contradicted by other witnesses.

A second explanation offered by men with no violence in their families of origin was that they had learned to be violent from their peers. All told, about one-third of the killers said that most of their friends as teenagers had had violent and otherwise reckless tendencies. From their depictions of their friends, many of their peers would fit profiles of juvenile delinquency. Asked what had attracted them to this element, some of the men said that it had been the only option available in their neighborhoods. Others said their attraction to a violent, reckless crowd had been due to insufficient limits set by their parents. One man said, "My parents was working nights and I just always wanted to get high with my friends. Part of it was that they was drinking with their friends, too."

Drinking and drug use by one or more parents was the third explanation for violence offered by men who did not grow up with violence in their homes. In the majority of cases where the parents had abused alcohol or drugs, there had also been domestic violence in the home. Just under half of the killers with an alcohol or drug-abusing parent claimed that there had been no violence. This did not mean that there had been no problems, however. In four of these cases, the killer's parents had divorced or separated when he was quite young. Two of these men had lived with their mothers exclusively after this, while the other two had lived with neither parent but with other relatives. One common theme expressed by these men was that they had lacked the security of living in a "normal family," as one man put it. Another theme was that they had lacked sufficient supervision and guidance that would have come from a more stable family.

Donlon's parents had split up before he was born. With his mother psychiatrically institutionalized and a father whose whereabouts were unknown, his maternal grandmother and a series of her boyfriends raised Donlon. Asked what might have contributed to his domestic violence as an adult, Donlon said,

> The lack of structure, without a doubt. I was free to roam all over, man. I hitched to California with this older dude when I was thirteen, I think. When my grandma died, I was just trying to find someone to fill her shoes, and that's when I met Frida. She was always there cooking for me and seeing to my grandma when she was still in the hospital. See, I never had a girl and I never had someone who looked after me. For a while I even gave up the drugs when she was pregnant. 'Course that didn't last. I just couldn't escape the drugs, man. This all might be an excuse but it played a part.

Shortly after Frida broke up with him, Donlon broke into her apartment and stabbed her sixty-eight times. She was two months pregnant with his child at the time.

What to Make of This?

Clearly, there is no single factor from these men's upbringings that sufficiently explains these men's murderous actions. I believe that no amount of information from a person's childhood would be sufficient to explain a single action such as murder. In this book, I will argue that our understanding of domestic murders is incomplete without also including an analysis of the killers' patterns of behavior as adults. I will also attempt to show that murder is the end result of an interactive pattern between the killer and his victim, one that involves a continuous struggle of control, resistance, and escalation. Domestic violence is a strong pattern that emerges from examining the killers' adult lives. While examining their childhoods does not tell us why they became killers, I think it does help to shed light on their long-term patterns of control and abuse within their adult relationships.

Most experts on domestic violence view battering as learned behavior. According to social learning theory, behavior is learned in two ways. One way is behavior, such as violence, modeled by one's parents and peers. As mentioned previously, research has overwhelmingly shown that children's exposure to domestic violence, particularly for boys, vastly increases the odds that they will learn to become abusive in their adult relationships. Of course, whether the child becomes an abuser is mediated by many other influences and experiences in his life. These include peer influences as well as a wide array of other kinds of interpersonal and social influence. The second way that behavior is socially learned is through positive reinforcement. Positive reinforcement occurs when a person engages in a behavior, such as violence, which results in a positive outcome for him. Proponents of spanking children, for instance, often claim that it is the "only thing that works" to change their child's undesirable behavior. Once satisfied that it works, they are more likely to repeat this behavior. There is often a self-reinforcing aspect to this. The more the person sticks to the chosen behavior, such as spanking, the less he or she is inclined to use other behaviors that might work just as well or even better. In claiming successful results, people who use violence often cite the immediate impact of their actions, such as the child's compliance and immediate cessation of the problem behavior. They sometimes ignore longer-term side effects, such as the child's learning to engage in the problem behavior covertly so as to avoid future punishment. Men who engage in domestic violence similarly claim that it is the only thing that works for them. Numerous abusive men have told me "she won't listen to me unless I yell at her." Other men have learned that violence is an effective way of getting their partners to "shut up" or to otherwise comply with their wishes. For some of these men, their partners' complaints about mistreatment actually reinforce the men's views that their partners deserve to be beaten.

5 | **Short Courtships**

One of the unanticipated findings of this study was that a high proportion of the relationships that ended in murder or attempted murder had very fast beginnings. I further found that the relationships that began with short courtships had much faster demises than those with longer courtship periods. Since length of courtship has not previously been identified as a potential risk factor for femicide, it therefore warrants further investigation. Courtship is defined as the period of time from the beginning of a dating relationship to the start of the couple living together. Both the perpetrators and the victims of abuse were asked how long they had dated or were "involved as a couple" prior to living together. Subjects were asked not only to estimate the number of weeks or months of the courtship period but also to give approximate dates for when they first met, when the relationship began, when they began living together, when and if they got married, and when each child was born. To give meaning and context to the answers, the subjects were also asked to say where they had been living as well as what they were doing work and school-wise during these periods.

Table 5.1 shows courtship data derived from the twenty-six killers who had lived with their victims. Startlingly, half of these relationships (thirteen) had had courtships or three months or less, while nearly a third (eight) had had courtships of one month or less! Three of these relationships had had whirlwind "courtships" of one or two days. These were cases in which two strangers had met and almost immediately begun living together.

The remaining five killers never lived with their victims, and therefore had courtship durations that could not be objectively measured or meaningfully compared to those couples that had cohabitated. In four of these cases, the relationship had begun when the victim was a teen or preteen

Table 5.1: Length of courtships among killers before onset of living together

Length of courtship	Number (percentage) of killers
6 months or more	12 (46)
6 months or less	14 (54)
Breakdown of those with short courtship:	
3 months or less	13 (50)
2 months or less	12 (46)
1 month or less	8 (31)
1 or two days	3 (12)

N=26 (this excludes 5 killers who never lived with the deceased partner)

and was still living with her parents. All four of these young women were still living with their parents when they were killed. These non-cohabitating couples most closely resembled those cohabitating couples with short courtships.

Though killers with quick beginnings to their relationships were somewhat more likely also to be substance abusers, this connection wasn't strong enough to characterize them primarily as alcoholics or drug abusers. In fact, these men were amply represented among all five of the killer types that I've previously profiled. For this reason, it made sense to analyze how these men and their relationships compared to the rest of the men. I found that relationships with shorter courtships differed in many ways from those with longer ones, and generally seemed to unfold at a much faster pace. Their median courtship duration was forty-five days, compared to 345 days for those relationships with courtships that exceeded six months. Not only was the courtship period shorter in these relationships but also the entire relationship, as measured from the onset of living together to the murder of the victim. As seen in Table 5.2, victims in relationships with shorter courtships were killed more than seven years sooner, on average, than those in relationships with slower beginnings. Only those victims who never lived with their killers died younger and sooner.

Besides beginning and ending more quickly, relationships with shorter courtships appeared to be less stable, faster-paced, and possibly more violent. It is worth highlighting the unique features in these relationships

Table 5.2: Period of time between onset of living together and the woman's murder

Length of courtship	Average period	Median period
6 months or longer (N=12)	11 ¾ years	6 years, 8 months
6 months or shorter (N=14)	4 ¼ years	3 years, 10 months
Never cohabitated (N=5)	1 ½ years	9 months

since this may help us to identify more specific violence and homicide prevention strategies.

Alcohol and Drug Use

Many of the relationships with short courtships seemed to revolve around alcohol and/or drugs. In ten of these fourteen relationships (71%), the perpetrator had abused alcohol, drugs, or both. In at least five of these cases, the victim had also abused alcohol or drugs. Often this mutual substance abuse had begun as soon as the relationship did and steadily escalated until the woman's murder. Killers in these relationships were also more likely to report that they had been intoxicated or high on the day of the murder. Seventy-one percent of these men said they had been drunk, high, or both, compared to 42% of the men in relationships with longer courtships. A summary of these findings is presented in Table 5.3.

Frequent Sex

The faster pace of relationships with shorter courtships was also reflected in the frequency of sex. Killers in these relationships were twice as likely to report that they had had sex on at least a daily basis with their partners. Several of these men claimed that they had been having sex multiple times per day. Daily sex was an immediate feature of these relationships, often beginning on the day the two people first met or had their first date. Sex in these relationships was often accompanied by mutual alcohol or drug use.

None of the thirty-one killers admitted ever to raping his partner or forcing her to have sex, and only four even admitted to using any kind of pressure or coercion to obtain sex. Several admitted pressuring their partners to use alcohol or drugs during sex, though none thought that this constituted sexual coercion. This information from killers about sexual

Table 5.3: Number (percentage) of couples experiencing alcohol and drug abuse

	Couples with longer courtships	Couples with short courtships	Couples who never cohabitated
Perpetrator abused alcohol	5 (42)	6 (43)	2 (40)
He abused drugs	5 (42)	7 (50)	6 (60)
He abused both alcohol and drugs	2 (17)	3 (21)	2 (40)
Both victim and perpetrator abused alcohol and/or drugs	2 (17)	5 (36)	2 (40)
Killer said he was drunk or high on the day of the murder	5 (42)	10 (71)	3 (60)

coercion contrasts radically with information obtained from the victims of attempted murder. Nearly three-fourths of these women reported having been raped by their partners.

Frequent Violence

As mentioned earlier, killers seemed most dishonest when asked about the frequency and severity of their past violence toward their partners. Many claimed not to have been violent at all prior to killing their partners, even when court or police records indicated otherwise. Thirty-eight percent of the killers denied any prior acts of physical violence against their partners, and several others claimed only rare and minimal acts of violence. Only three men, all in relationships with shorter courtships, admitted weekly acts of physical violence. The only four men who admitted breaking bones in their victims came from these relationships. Men in relationships with shorter courtships were also more likely to say that their violence had occurred when they were using alcohol or drugs.

Age Differences

Perpetrators in relationships with shorter courtships were significantly older than the other men, with a median age of thirty-one at the beginning of the relationship compared to a median age of 21.5 for those men in relationships with longer courtships. This age difference at the relation-

Table 5.4: Age of perpetrators

	Longer courtships	Short courtships	Non-cohabitating
Man's median age at beginning of relationship	21.5	31	25.5
Man's median age at time of murder	33.5	33.5	27

ship outset disappeared by the time the murders occurred since the shorter courtship men killed their partners much sooner than their counterparts with longer courtships. The median age for each set of perpetrators at the time of the murder was 33.5. (See Table 5.4)

Not only were these men older but also they were more likely to be significantly older or younger than their partners, compared to three (25%) of the other men. Five of these seven men had been five or more years older than their victims while the other two had been significantly younger. The biggest age differences were in two relationships in which the man had been ten years older. While such an age difference may not be unusual, it seems significant when one considers the short courtship periods of these relationships. For instance, Cole was nineteen and Christine was fourteen when they began their relationship. Two months later, they began living together. In another relationship with a courtship of two months, Eliot at age thirty-four was ten years older than Jill when they began living together. In these cases, the fact that the man was significantly older may have been a factor in the woman's attraction to him.

Instability

Couples with short courtships appeared less stable in a number of ways than the couples with slower beginnings. They were less likely to be married. Only five of these couples (36%) were married compared to eight (67%) of those with longer courtships. They were much less likely to have children together (25% compared to 64%). However, men in these relationships were more likely to have had children in prior relationships. Five of these men (36%) had biological children with ex-partners while only two of the other men (17%) had children from past relationships. Only one of the men with children from past relationships had maintained contact with these children.

Another indicator of instability among the couples with abbreviated courtships was that they were more likely to be estranged just prior to the homicide. Eight of these fourteen victims had separated from their partner while at least one additional woman had been planning to leave. In the relationships with longer courtships, five women had departed and two additional women had been planning to do so.

The men with short relationships also appeared to be less economically stable than the other two men. They were much less likely to own their own homes. Only two of these men owned homes (14%), compared to six of the men in longer relationships (50%). One couple from the short courtship group was homeless. Men from this group were somewhat less likely to have completed high school: 43% compared to 58% of the men with longer courtships.

Just over half of the killers met the criteria for indigence, with annual incomes of $15,000 or less. While the short courtship killers were no more likely to be indigent than those with longer courtships, they were more apt to be unemployed or underemployed (57%). Six of these men were unemployed and two others worked less than half time. By contrast, only two of the men in relationships with longer courtships (17%) were unemployed or underemployed. Men in the short courtship group were also more likely to say that they supported themselves primarily through illegal enterprises. Four of these men, compared to none of the longer courtship killers, admitted that their primary means of support had been theft and/or drug sales. As one of these men put it, "My whole life was just stealing and dealing."

Hidden Pasts

Four of the men with shorter courtship periods had been incarcerated prior to committing their murders. In comparison, two men with longer courtships and one of the non-cohabiting men had previously served time in prison. Over half of the short courtship men (57%) had been convicted of a previous crime, compared to 33% of those with longer courtships. Two of the five men (40%) who'd never lived with their victims had been previously convicted. Four of the five killers that we classified as career criminals were from the short courtship group while the fifth was from the non-cohabiting group.

Women in relationships with short courtships undoubtedly had less time to learn about their new partners' past histories before they made the commitment to live together. Our research into these men's lives suggests that there had been much to learn about their pasts. And since these men were ten years older, on average, than men in relationships with lengthier courtships, they had much more life history at the outset of their relationships with their victims. According to the men we interviewed, much of the less savory aspects of their past histories had been unknown to the women they killed. Several of the men said that they had avoided telling their partners about their criminal records, as well as their violence toward past partners, for fear that the women would leave them or hold it against them. For some of the women, by the time they did learn about their partners' past violence, they may have felt too committed to the relationships or entrapped by them to leave. The majority of the women in these relationships did leave shortly before their deaths, and their decisions to leave may have been partly prompted by leaning more about the perpetrators' pasts. Some of the men who had been engaged in illegal practices said that they had feared their partners might report their crimes to the authorities once the relationships had ended. One man who had had an open warrant against him due to parole violations said that he had feared his partner might turn him in to the authorities.

"Rescuing" the Woman

Several killers, particularly those with short courtships, said that they had felt they were "rescuing" their new partners from bad situations, such as homelessness, poverty, drug abuse, violence in a previous relationship, or from abusive parents. Citing his partner's past alcohol and drug use, one man said, "I guess I felt I was picking her up from the gutter." Several men said they had felt they were saving their partners from bad situations with her parents, usually citing sexual or physical abuse by their partners' fathers or stepfathers. For the women in these relationships, being "rescued" by an abusive man must have felt like a double-edged sword. Many of the men we interviewed conveyed the idea that their partners had been "damaged goods" and that this had made them more legitimate targets for abuse. Some men said that they had used their partners' pasts against them. For example, one man whose partner had been sexually abused by her uncle said he would "always throw this in her face," and would sometimes accuse her of having had "an affair" with her uncle.

Case Example 7

"I loved her very much but nobody fucks with me."

Louis Nelson and Pamela Beltron met on a bus where they immediately struck up a conversation. They seemed to have a lot in common. Both had recently lost their driver's licenses due to drunk driving. They were also close in age: Louis was thirty-one and Pamela was twenty-eight. Neither had been married or had children. Louis and Pamela had their first drinks together the next day, and afterwards they had sex.

Pamela revealed that she was living with a boyfriend of ten days but was not happy. She was planning to leave that relationship but had no place to go, and her job as a home health aide did not provide enough income for her to get a place of her own. A few days later, Louis invited Pamela to move into his two-room apartment with him. Two weeks after meeting Louis, Pamela packed up her belongings at her boyfriend's house and moved in with Louis.

Louis worked as a school custodian, a position he'd had for five years. Louis hadn't been in a relationship in five years. His longest relationship of seven years, with Jenny, had started when he was in high school. Following high school, they had lived together for three years before Jenny left Louis due to his repeated violence toward her. The last incident had resulted in Jenny going to the hospital with a broken nose, a cut lip, a swollen face, and two black eyes. Louis had repeatedly punched her in the face following an argument in a restaurant. Louis had been charged with assault and battery; the case had been continued without a finding after Jenny declined to testify. Louis's next relationship, with Diane, had lasted six months, including three months of living together. This relationship had also ended due to Louis's violence. His most serious incident included punching Diane in the face two or three times, leaving her with a black eye and a swollen face. The assault and battery charges against Louis had been dismissed when Diane did not appear for the court hearing.

Pamela knew nothing about Louis's past arrests for domestic violence. She also did not know that Louis had once served time in prison for operating under the influence and had appeared in court twelve times to face eighteen charges, including breaking and entering, assault and battery with a dangerous weapon, and an act of violence that had been directed against another man. For this last crime, Louis had been sentenced to probation for one year. Over time, Pamela did come to learn that Louis had been in a detox center for his drinking problem, which had started when he was fifteen.

Shortly after moving in with Louis, Pamela received a $7,000 insurance settlement due to her injuries from a car accident. They began to drink and to smoke marijuana on a daily basis. Sex was very frequent—usually one to three times per day. Louis's violence toward Pamela had started before they began living together. One night, Louis had punched Pamela in the face while they were sleeping together. When Pamela complained about it the next morning, Louis said he didn't remember doing it due to his drinking.

Louis's most serious act of violence toward Pamela occurred three months before her murder. Louis brought Pamela to the school where he worked during a bingo night. With the bingo game going on in the hall over them, Louis and Pamela sat in the basement, drinking beers and smoking pot. When Pamela accused Louis of being interested in a particular student at the school whom he had spoken with earlier that evening, Louis began to beat Pamela. The beating lasted thirty to forty-five minutes and consisted of Louis punching Pamela repeatedly in the face and body, and then hitting her about the head and body with a lead pipe. When Pamela became unconscious, Louis called the ambulance and followed her to the hospital. Pamela told the doctors that she had fallen down some stairs. Not believing her, the medical staff wanted to call the police but she convinced them not to. After receiving multiple stitches and staples for her lacerations, Pamela was released that evening and Louis drove her home.

Over the next couple of months, the couple continued to drink over a case of beer each night and usually a substantial amount of rum. They fought nearly every day. Ten days before her murder, Pamela went to the mother's house and called the police after Louis punched her in the face and gave her a bloody nose. Louis was arrested and released on $50 bail. The next day, Louis alleged that Pamela had also hit him and obtained a temporary restraining order against her. He agreed to vacate the order the following day when Pamela returned.

Louis's arraignment for the recent assault and battery was still pending when he killed Pamela on November 1, 1992. When Pamela returned home from work that evening, they immediately began to argue, and Louis kept telling Pamela to keep her voice down since the landlord had recently complained about their loud arguments. Louis began to push, grab, and punch Pamela. When she screamed, he knocked her to the floor and held her. When she continued to scream, he placed his hand over her face. When Pamela began biting Louis's hand, he forced his fingers deeper into her mouth while pinning her by the throat with his other forearm. He kept holding her like this until she lost consciousness. When the police arrived, they found Pamela dead and Louis passed out on the floor. The medical examiner ruled that Pamela's cause of death was asphyxiation. According to the police report, Louis had a high amount of alcohol but no drugs in his system when he was arrested. Louis claimed to have taken large amounts of Pamela's prescribed medications (Valium, Darvocet, Elavil) as well as aspirin in an attempt to kill himself after Pamela's death. Police found a message that Louis had scrawled on a chalkboard that read:

> Pamela, I hope you are not mad at me. I don't want you to be. I love you and want things to be good between us, I mean it. We can work things out, I know it.
> Love, Louis.

Police also found a note that Louis had written to his mother that read:

> I'm sorry I killed Pamela but she wouldn't listen to me. I didn't want to hurt her but it became apparent that she was going to hurt me and I could not stand that. I loved her very much but nobody fucks with me. So it ends. Mama, please leave everything I own to John [his brother]. Tell him I love him as I do all of you, but . . .

6 | **Child Abuse**

In my investigation of the perpetrators' treatment of their children, radically different accounts were provided by the victims of attempted homicide than those offered by the killers. I asked the members of each group of perpetrators over twenty-five open-ended questions about their relationships with any and all of the children they had shared with their victims. Additional questions sought to ascertain whether there had been conflict between each perpetrator and victim over the handling of the children. For instance, question #179 for the killers was, "Did your treatment of the children change in any way in the days or weeks leading up your partner's death? If yes, how?" For the victims of attempted homicide, this question was, "Did you notice any changes in how your partner treated the children in the days or weeks leading up to his final assault of you? If yes, in what ways?" I additionally had each participant fill out a thirty-item checklist of abusive or controlling behaviors toward children. The women were three times more likely than the killers to report at least one act of child abuse by the perpetrators.

Victims' Accounts

Sixteen of the twenty (80%) victims of attempted homicide had children with their abusive partners. Ten of these women (63%) said that their partner had physically or psychologically abused the children. The following is a brief description of the child abuse in these cases.

1) On numerous occasions, the perpetrator put Tabasco sauce on his toddler son's tongue or made him brush his teeth with soap on his

toothbrush. Other times, the son would be yanked up by his arms or made to stand alone in a dark room for long periods. These behaviors were usually "punishments" in response to the boy singing or talking.

2) The father would slap his four-year-old son in the face and yell and "growl" at him, according to the mother.

3) Several times, a teenage girl was slapped or punched in the face and thrown against a wall. When she was seventeen, this girl took out a restraining order against her father.

4) A six-year-old girl was repeatedly "smacked really hard" in the face or on her hands by her father.

5) A two-year-old son was grabbed by the arms and thrown on a couch by his father.

6) One father would frequently scream at his three young children, to the point where they would be "cowering in the corner."

7) One father, William, once grabbed and held a gun to his three-year-old son.

8) Jacob would make his three-year-old daughter "bend down" so he could "paddle her."

9) One father would frequently grab, hit, or "beat up" all four of his children.

10) Edgardo, age four, would often "hide in the fields" to escape his father's physical and sexual abuse.

As can be seen, children of all ages were subjected to abuse by the perpetrators. That most child victims were in their pre-teen years reflects that few of the perpetrators had children who were teens or older. Only three of the perpetrators of attempted homicide had biological or stepchildren who were thirteen or older. In two of these cases, the perpetrator had been physically and emotionally abusive to at least one of his teenage children. The third father had never been physically abusive to his children, according to his partner.

Killers' Accounts

Nineteen of the thirty-one killers (61%) had biological children and one additional man had only stepchildren with the woman he killed. Seven of the men had biological children with previous partners. Few of the killers admitted to having physically abused their children, and we did not have adequate sources of information by which to assess their rates of child abuse. Only four of the nineteen men (21%) with biological or stepchildren acknowledged any physical child abuse, and the level of violence reported was mild in comparison that which was reported by the victims of attempted homicide. All four of these men claimed only to have occasionally grabbed or slapped one of their children. A fifth man, James, admitted verbal abuse of one child but denied any physical violence. While reporting that police had filed a child abuse report against him and physical abuse of his infant son was substantiated by the Massachusetts Department of Social Services, James claimed that his son's injuries had resulted from a fall from his highchair. James did admit to yelling and swearing frequently at his two-year-old stepdaughter, Mary, in response to her crying. There was strong evidence of physical abuse of children by three additional killers. Two of these men had been convicted or charged with child sexual abuse. In the third case, testimony of past child abuse was offered by the man's teenage stepson at the killer's murder trial.

Threats Against the Children

In two cases, the perpetrator appeared intent on killing the children when he tried to kill his partner. Police rescued the children in both instances. One of these men, William, ambushed his estranged wife, Lynette, and their two children at her mother's house. William struck Lynette repeatedly over the head with a baseball bat until she lost consciousness. When she came to, Lynette found that her hands and mouth had been taped and William was pacing the room and threatening to kill her and the children, aged eight and three. At one point, Lynette broke free and called the police. William stayed in the house with the children for twenty minutes while a police SWAT team negotiated with him. When the police broke in, William was standing over the children with the baseball bat. When she was interviewed eight years after this attack, Lynette said that both children were still having nightmares, anxiety, and other signs of trauma.

Case Example 8

"I can't believe he tried to kill my babies."

Amy had been separated from Carmen for two and a half years when he tried to kill her and their two children who were aged five and four at the time. Amy had been living with her mother and was making plans to move into her own apartment with the children. She had also begun to date a man named Frank who worked at the racetrack where she was employed as a horse trainer. Also employed at the track, Carmen had become increasingly jealous over this relationship and was following Amy and Frank around when they were together at work.

On a day in January, Carmen followed Amy when she went to Frank's house for lunch. On the way there, Amy dropped the children off at daycare. Ten minutes after her arrival at Frank's house, Carmen knocked on the door. When Frank answered the door, Carmen said he just wanted to talk with Amy. Frank agreed as long as he could sit in. Shortly after all three sat at the kitchen table, Carmen began calling Amy names and threw some orange juice in her face. Before Frank could intervene, Carmen grabbed Amy and began to strangle her. When Frank tried to pull Carmen away, Carmen picked up a kitchen knife from a counter and attempted to stab Amy in the chest. Amy put up her hand to ward off the blow and was stabbed in the hand. She ran out of the house as Carmen and Frank were struggling with the knife. Carmen broke away from Frank and ran out of the house to get into his car. Carmen then drove to the children's daycare center and convinced the staff to release the children to him. This was contrary to the explicit instructions that Amy, as the custodial parent, had left with the daycare center. Carmen drove the children to his house where he attempted to poison himself and the children with carbon monoxide by attaching a hose from his tailpipe to the inside of his car. The police rescued all three.

Carmen had made three prior attempts to injure Amy seriously, all when they were still living together. During two of these incidents, he had tried to strangle her. During the last incident, he had tried to run her off the road with his car. During their six-year relationship, Amy had grown increasingly worried about Carmen's treatment of the children, Andy and Lurina. One of the scariest moments had occurred when Andy was two.

In response to Andy's crying, Carmen had grabbed him and run down the stairs to the living room where he had thrown Andy onto the couch. Amy said that Carmen had always been "easier" on Lurina and was much more patient and loving toward her. Carmen seemed more cold and angry to Andy and would often become intolerant when Andy cried or whined. Shortly before separating from Amy, Carmen began telling her that he would kill the children and himself if she left him. Though Amy had sole physical and legal custody of the children, Carmen had not paid any child support during the 2 ½ years of legal separation. Amy had not pushed this issue for fear that Carmen might do something to harm the children. Perhaps still in shock, Amy said, "I always knew he might come after me but I can't believe he tried to kill my babies."

Amy and Lynette were among five of the victims of attempted homicide who said that the perpetrators had previously threatened to kill the children. In all cases, these threats had been made when the couple was estranged or when the mother was making plans to end the relationship. In all five of these cases, the perpetrator had previously abused the children.

Parenting Styles

Most of the killers characterized themselves as affectionate and good parents. By contrast, most of the victims of attempted homicide portrayed their abusive partners as overly strict, distant, or abusive parents. Table 6.1 provides a summary of how the killers and the victims rated the perpetrators' parenting styles.

Twelve of the sixteen victims who had kids with their perpetrators rated their husbands or boyfriends as emotionally abusive to the children. The most commonly cited forms of emotional abuse were yelling at the children, criticizing or calling them names, and swearing at them. Nine of the twelve mothers said that their abusive partners did at least one of these things to a child on a monthly basis. Four said it occurred on a weekly or daily basis.

In terms of parenting styles, just over half of the victims characterized their partners as strict, and half said they were authoritarian or bossy. Despite this, two-thirds judged their partners to be "loving" toward the children while just one-quarter thought them to be "cold or distant." From these ratings, as well as from the women's descriptions, the predominant

Table 6.1: Perpetrators' and victims' ratings of the perpetrators' parenting styles

Parenting trait	Percentage of killers claiming parenting trait	Percentage of victims who say their partners exhibited trait
Loving	100	68
Patient	93	31
Understanding	100	37
A push-over	75	37
Easy-going	93	37
Strict	25	56
Authoritarian or bossy	25	50
Cold or distant	6	25
Never there	50	25
Disciplinarian	25	37
Emotionally abusive	6	75
Physically abusive	22	62
	N=16	N=16

parenting style that emerges is that of men who are strict and intolerant of children's emotional expressions and needs. While most of the women believed that their partners loved the children, they also rated them low in patience, understanding, and consistency. On the other hand, few of the victims rated these fathers as "never there." Most of the women said that their husbands were highly inconsistent in the quality of attention and affection that they gave to their children. Many also found their partners to be inconsistent in how and when they disciplined the children. One woman said, "What he'd get upset about seemed to depend on his mood more than anything."

Another woman, Isa, attributed her husband's inconsistency to his drinking. This woman said that, when he was not drinking, her husband, Melvin, would commonly "sit down and talk to Malcolm [their eleven-year-old son] and tell him how much he loved him." She added that her husband would also spend hours helping Malcolm with homework and help him to maintain a special diet. When Melvin had been drinking, however, Isa said that he would get "overly upset at Malcolm" and discipline him by making him "sit for hours on the couch."

Six of the mothers said that their partners were often intolerant of their young children's crying. Five of these women said that their partner would frequently respond to this by spanking or yelling at the child. Two women said that their husbands were particularly intolerant of crying by their sons. Both fathers would frequently call their sons a "sissy" or a "mommy's boy." One of these fathers, Carl, is the one who would put Tabasco sauce on his son's tongue or make him brush his teeth with soap. Carl's wife, Monica, said Carl had never done these things to his daughter. She added that Carl seemed "obsessed" with "toughening [his son] up" and "making him a man." Not all the fathers disproportionately targeted their sons for abuse, however. Two mothers said that their daughters were the more frequent targets of violence and derision. In one of these cases, the mother said her husband would frequently accuse his fifteen-year-old stepdaughter of "trying to come between us." She added that he came to see this girl as "evil personified" and would often accuse her of "being a slut." This mother attributed her daughter's obesity and depression to being treated in such a manner.

All four of the women who said that their husbands had never abused the children rated their husbands as good parents. One of these women said, "He would always take his anger out on me." While judging their ex-abusers to be good parents, however, three of these four women acknowledged that their children had been exposed to their partners' violence toward them. The fourth woman insisted that the children were unaware of their father's violence toward her except for the final act of attempted homicide.

How Are the Children Affected?

Ninety percent of the victims who had children with their perpetrators said that their children had witnessed them being physically and emotionally abused. They reported that the children had not only witnessed abuse but had been exposed to its immediate and long-term aftermath. Part of this aftermath is the ways that the mothers themselves were adversely affected by the abuse. Most of the mothers said that they had been depressed for significant periods during their relationship with their abuser. Three of the mothers said that they had attempted suicide at least once. It was unclear whether their children knew of these attempts. Regardless of whether they experienced depression, most of the mothers said that living with abuse had detracted from their availability or responsiveness to their children.

We asked each mother to describe how her children had been affected by their exposure to violence in the home and its aftermath. Many of these mothers said it was difficult for them to separate the effects of their child's witnessing abuse from those from being directly abused themselves. Ten of the sixteen mothers said that one or more of their children had experienced nightmares or difficulties sleeping. One quarter said their children had exhibited difficulties with eating. Half talked about difficulties their children had with school. The most commonly cited of these was frequently missing school due to being anxious or sick, poor academic performance, and having behavior problems at school. In almost all of these cases, the mothers said that these problems had lessened or alleviated over the months and years since the ending of their relationships with the abusers.

Two-thirds of the mothers talked of negative emotional effects on the part of one or more children. The most commonly cited of these were depression and anxiety. Three-quarters of the women said that their children were fearful of their fathers or stepfathers. Nearly all the women said that their children were also fearful for their mother's safety. One woman said that her three children would always be "on edge" whenever their father came home, and would "hover around me whenever he [her husband] was in the same room [with her]." Another woman said that her children were extremely fearful of getting into the car with their father. She attributed this to the many times he had screamed at her or become physically abusive while driving. Not all the children were fearful of their fathers, however. One twelve-year-old girl, Michelle, had adopted a tough demeanor in regard to her stepfather and had often come to her mother's defense when he was yelling at her. Following the homicide attempt against her mother, Michelle attempted to rally her mother and sister to look forward, telling them, "There are more important things to be afraid of than a man."

Another common emotional response to abuse for children was anger. One-third of the victims said that one or more of their children had expressed strong anger or hatred toward their father or stepfather. An equal number of women said that their children expressed anger toward them. These mothers cited three different reasons for their children's anger. Some children directed anger toward them for remaining with their abuser. One woman said that her eight-year-old once screamed at her, "Why do you put up with it?" Some children were angrier with their mothers for their failure to protect them. One four-year-old boy told his mother, "Daddy is going to kill us." Lastly, some children were angry at their mothers for taking steps to curtail their father's contact with them. In four cases, the mother had taken steps to legally stop or limit the father's contact with the children. The father was banned from having any contact with his children in two of these cases while he was only allowed supervised visitations in the other two. Practitioners who work with children exposed to domestic violence say that many children continue to love their fathers despite the abuse of their mothers. For some children, their exposure to violence in the home may not be as upsetting as the loss or potential loss of contact with their fathers. Children may be angrier with the mother for taking steps to end the relationship than at the father for his violence. Experts who work with children exposed to domestic violence say that it is often easier for children to be angry with the nonviolent and more emotionally available parent. In some cases, children adopt the abusive father's perspective in blaming the mother for the violence or for other problems in the relationship. One four-year-old son of a man attending a batterer intervention program would sometimes advise his mother, "Don't make daddy mad." In another case, a sixteen-year-old son told his mother "Dad's right, you are a bitch" after she had refused to let him drive the family car. The mother had just recently filed for divorce and obtained a protective order that required the boy's father to vacate the home.

Perhaps the most extreme trauma for children is witnessing their mother's murder. In three of the eighteen murders where a child lived in home, at least one child witnessed the killing. One four-year-old boy, Jose, also witnessed the murder of his grandmother as well as the attempted murder of his aunt. Having already killed Jose's mother, his father then patted Jose on the head before turning the gun on the boy's grandmother, while shouting "Die, bitch. You've robbed me of my son and my wife." Besides the three murders that were witnessed by children, there were six additional murders that occurred in close proximity to the deceased's children. I have already described John, who placed his two young daughters in the car before killing their mother. Also previously cited was Anthony, who killed his wife in the bathroom while their three children waited for her in the car; Robin had already packed the car and was in the process of fleeing Anthony on that early morning. In another case, the murderer awoke his three-year-old son to tell him, "Something has happened to mommy" shortly after shooting the boy's mother. His twelve-year-old stepson was also woken and called the police. In two other cases, teen stepchildren were in their bedrooms when their mother was killed. These children later became witnesses in their stepfathers' murder trials. In his victim impact statement, seventeen-year-old Robert wrote that his mother would never "see me graduate from high school."

Child Sexual Abuse

Three of the victims of attempted homicide said that they strongly suspected that their partner had sexually abused one of the children. All three cases involved three-year-old children: two boys and one girl.

Mary said that her boyfriend, Terrence, would often punish their daughter by making her bend over in a corner without her clothing on and remain in that position for several minutes. Mary's suspicions grew when her daughter would scream while she bathed her. Mary had herself been repeatedly sexually abused by Terrence. On several occasions, Terrence had come into her bedroom, nailed her door shut, and raped her for hours. When she had once threatened to leave him, Terrence had torn her daughter out of her arms and driven off with her for several hours. At the time Terrence tried to kill Mary, she and her daughter had been in hiding from him for three months.

In the other cases of suspected child sexual abuse, the mother had left the perpetrator prior to the near-fatal attack. In one of these cases, the couple had been separated for nearly three years when the perpetrator attacked the victim and her new partner as they lay in bed by bludgeoning them with a motorcycle helmet. In the other case, the couple had been divorced for one year when the perpetrator attacked his partner.

One of the killers had been previously convicted of sexual abuse of a child. This man had served a one-year prison sentence after sexually abusing the twelve-year-old daughter of a previous partner. When he was arrested for killing his next partner, police found a stash of child pornography in his apartment. Another killer, Donlon, had been accused of sexually abusing his three-year-old son. In response to this alleged incident, relatives of the mother attacked Donlon with a crowbar on the street shortly before he killed her. Shortly before stabbing his wife to death, Donlon had pleaded with her to drop the charges.

Child Abduction

Mary was not the only woman whose abusive partner had abducted or otherwise taken the children without her permission. All told, half of the mothers said that their partners had threatened to take the children, and 38% said that their partners had illegally taken them. The periods of child abduction ranged in length from one hour to five months.

Five years before attempting to kill Annabel, Wilberto took their two-year-old daughter, Michelle, to Mexico to stay with his aunt. Michelle is the girl who later told her mother, "There are more important things to be afraid of than a man." As an undocumented immigrant, Annabel lacked the financial resources and knowledge to seek legal intervention. Eventually, she convinced Wilberto to bring Michelle home by offering to pay for their plane fare.

The shortest child abduction lasted one hour. Supported by legal and physical custody of her two-year-old son, Abigail called the police when her estranged husband took him. The police returned the boy to Abigail and arrested her husband. Charges were later dropped. Another victim, Mindy, reported that her estranged husband had once grabbed her infant son out of her arms in front of the police who had responded to a domestic violence call. The police threatened to arrest Mindy's husband. The husband's attempt to kill Mindy occurred three years later when she filed for sole custody of her son.

Some victims said that their abusive partners' threats to take the children had been accompanied by threats to kill them. Lori reported that her husband had repeatedly threatened to do both to their three young children. Sometimes these threats were ambiguous ones, such as when he would tell her, "You will never see them again." In two of the cases, the abuser had threatened to abduct the children and subsequently tried to kill them or threatened to do so during their homicide attempts on the mother.

Red Flags

Past child abductions or threats to do so are warning signs for homicides of women and their children. Threats to kill the children are also warning signs. Of the sixteen perpetrators of attempted homicide who had children with their victims, just over half had done at least one of these things prior to the murder attempt on the mother. Such behavior is also known to precede cases of familicide in which the perpetrator kills both his partner and one or more of their children. Familicide is exceedingly rare even in comparison to domestic homicides of women only. Though statistics about the frequency of familicide are not available in the United States, one team of researchers in Canada found that approximately four percent of femicides also include the killing of at least one of the mother's children.[1] These same researchers found the rate of familicide relative to femicide in Great Britain to be about 3.5 percent.

Do killers exhibit other behaviors toward the children that could be seen as predictors of homicide? Some research has shown that men who kill women are more likely to have engaged in extreme child abuse. The Campbell study that compared homicides to other cases of domestic violence found evidence of this link. This research team found that the perpetrators of homicide and attempted homicide were three times more likely to have been reported for child abuse than the batterers in the comparison group.[2]

To identify other potential warning signs of murders concerning children, I asked each of the fathers who had killed his partner whether his treatment of the children had changed in any way in the days or weeks leading up to the murder. Thirty-eight percent of the fathers said that they had been denied contact with their children by a protective order. In all of these cases, the protective orders had also forbidden them from having contact with the mother of the children. One of these men was Henry, who killed his wife and mother-in-law in the presence of his son. Formal child abuse charges had been filed against two of these fathers, and in one case, the children had been placed in the custody of the Department of Social Services. This father, James, was profiled in the section about killers who qualify as "double threats." All six of the killers who had had either restraining orders forbidding contact with their children or supervised visits only with them said that they blamed their partners for such orders. This was true even for the two men against whom the child abuse reports had been filed by police and not their partners. As James said, "If she hadn't called the police to begin with, this [losing custody of his children] would never have happened. The other man said, "She didn't realize how important this was to me. . . . It wasn't right for her to take my children away from me." A third man, Anthony, said that he had chillingly told his partner, "I will kill for my children."

Sixteen percent of the killers had been embroiled in legal custody or child visitation disputes with their partners when the murders occurred. One-quarter of the victims of attempted homicide who had children with their perpetrators similarly reported that legal custody or visitation issues had been pending when the near-fatal assaults occurred. All four of these women had reported serious physical or sexual child abuse on the part of their partners. Some of these women talked of the agonizing choice that they had been forced to make in protecting their children while at the same time not further antagonizing their abuser. One woman said, "I didn't know what was right. . . . He was threatening to kill us all." This woman's partner had been threatening to kill her on at least a weekly basis even before she had obtained a restraining order. For many of the women, there had seemed to be no safe course of action. To take no legal steps to protect themselves and their children meant that their abuser's severe abuse would continue, yet to file legal actions might "send him over the edge," as one mother put it.

Having less or no contact with their children just prior to the murder was not the only change that killers reported in how they related to their children. Five men said that they had had more contact with their children. Two of these men attributed this increased contact to the fact that they had quit or been fired from their jobs and therefore spent more time at home. The other three men said that they had actually spent more time with their children after their partners had separated from them. One of these men, Michael, admitted that he had spent very little time with his young son prior to the separation. He admitted that his decision to had been partially prompted by advice from his sister and brother, who had told him that if he didn't keep his scheduled visits with his son, the judge who was to rule on child custody arrangements might think "you don't care about your son."

For the men who were still living with their children when they killed their partners, the most commonly cited change in their treatment of the children was that they had become more depressed or agitated. Francis said that he had become more depressed because he was "ruminating" about his wife's suspected affair with another man. Francis had also been out of work on disability for more than a year when the murder occurred. He said that during the last two to three months, he would "not even get up from the couch" during his days alone with his three-year-old son. Like Francis, Emmit attributed his increased depression and "agitation" around his children to his jealous ruminations about his wife. Another jealous husband, Duane, said that he had been yelling and criticizing his children more often just prior to killing his wife. About half of the victims of attempted homicide who were mothers had noted similar escalations of anger toward the children on their abusers' parts. Most attributed this to their husbands' jealous ruminations. One woman said that her husband would make jealous accusations about her to the children or ask them, "Do you know your mother is having sex with other men?" Another woman said her husband would put all three young children in the car and drive around the neighborhood with them, telling them they were helping to find "mommy's boyfriend."

Violence During Pregnancy

Several research studies have found battered women to be at increased risk for violence during pregnancy.[3] It appears that the frequency of violence during pregnancy is even greater in the more serious cases of abuse. According to one large study, perpetrators of homicide and attempted homicide were four times more likely than the control group of abusive men to have beaten their victims when the victims were pregnant.[4] The impact on both mother and child is often devastating. Studies have found that battered pregnant women are at a much greater risk to miscarry their children.[5] Just under two-thirds of the victims of attempted homicide that we interviewed said that their partners had beaten them at least once while they were pregnant. Most of these women said that the frequency and severity of violence that they experienced during pregnancy was either the same or less than when they were not pregnant. Only two victims said that their partners' violence escalated during pregnancy.

Angela said that her boyfriend, Robert, seemed to become more agitated and "bothered" when she was pregnant. Angela was sixteen and six months pregnant when Robert became enraged when she showed up late to an outdoor party. In front of more than fifteen mutual friends, Robert punched Angela several times in the face and body. Robert then dragged Angela by the hair into his car where he stabbed her five or six times in the leg and the pelvis. Robert then drove Angela to the hospital, yelling at her the whole way. Angela remembers hearing "You're going to get killed if you don't do what I say" before she passed out. Angela required about 120 sutures to close her stab wounds and miscarried her child. Robert showed up at the hospital at 7:00 the next morning, ripped out her IV lines, and drove her over 400 miles to stay with his grandmother for four months. Five years later, Angela miscarried a second child shortly after being severely beaten by Robert. This occurred two months before Robert's second act of attempted homicide on Angela.

When asked why he had been bothered, Angela said she felt that Robert had been upset that she was "not as focused on him" when she was bearing a child. Other victims articulated similar perspectives. Selma, for example, speculated that her partner had been bothered because she had stopped drinking during her two pregnancies. Selma and Angela were also the only victims who said that their partners had refused to let them eat at times during their pregnancies. Given this prior ill treatment while they were pregnant, it seems no coincidence that Selma and Angela were the only two victims who reported having miscarriages during their relationships with their abusers.

Only one of the killers, Donlon, admitted assaulting his partner when she was pregnant. This violence occurred when he killed his estranged partner, Frida. I've previously cited Donlon as one of the alleged perpetrators of child sexual abuse. Donlon said he was embittered about Frida having recently alleged that he had sexually abused their three-year-old son, resulting in a restraining order that forbade him from having any contact with the boy. Two days later, Donlon broke into Frida's apartment and stabbed her sixty-eight times. Frida was two months pregnant at the time. Asked his motive for killing Frida, Donlon said he wanted to punish her "for taking my son away from me."

7 | Patterns of Possession and Punishment

Victims and perpetrators often have opposing perceptions about violence and control. For the most part, abusers minimize their violence and disavow any intent to control their partners. Compared to other abusers, it appears that severe abusers are even more likely to do so. The killers I interviewed admitted far less violence than those I regularly counsel in a batterer treatment program. Is this because they are less violent? Or is it that they have more to hide? Judging from the evidence, the latter explanation is far more likely. Less than one-tenth of the killers admitted making any death threats prior to the murder, and only one-third admitted any past acts of violence towards the deceased.

A more accurate picture emerges from their past police reports and criminal records. From these sources of information, there is strong evidence that nearly all the killers had committed past physical and verbal assaults toward the women they murdered. Further clues to the killers' violence were provided by information about their relationships with prior partners. Some of this information was contained in past domestic violence incident reports by police. More detailed information was obtained by conducting a relationship history with each killer. In my work with men who batter, I'd conducted hundreds of such histories. I've found that men often unwittingly reveal much information about past abusive or controlling behavior when asked such questions as, "How did you meet this ex-partner?" "What first attracted you to her?" "What did you argue about?" "What were her biggest complaints about you?" and "How did the relationship end?" From the men's responses to these questions, strong patterns emerge of how they begin, maintain, and end relationships. These patterns include short courtships, social isolation, jealousy and possessiveness, infidelity and overlapping relationships with women, financial control or exploitation of women, and relationships that revolve around substance use and/or sex. From such histories, it often emerges that the men's controlling and abusive behaviors toward their partners tended to escalate over time. In this sense, many abusive men are serial batterers.

Further evidence for this was provided by the Massachusetts Department of Probation, which investigated civil restraining orders taken out against men and women in Massachusetts in 1992. Over 85% of these defendants were male.[1] The department tracked the records of the 730 defendants for a six-year period ending in 1998 in order to determine whether they had been served with additional protective orders. They found that almost one-quarter of the defendants were serial batterers. A serial batterer was defined as someone who had been the recipient of a protective order taken out by at least two different intimate partners. Serial batterers had as many as eight different victims over the six-year period. Compared to the other batterers, serial batterers were more likely to have a prior criminal record (91% compared to 68%) and to have a history of alcohol or drug use (60% compared to 36%). Serial batterers were also found to be younger than "nonserial batterers." The term "serial batterer" is somewhat misleading in that it is sometimes confused with "repeat batterers." The Massachusetts Department of Probation's study was not intended as a measure of recidivism—only of the issuance of additional protective orders to new victims. Many batterers re-offend without having a new protective order taken out against them. It is generally acknowledged that only a fraction of batterers have protective orders issued against them. Also, most recidivists would not have qualified as "serial batterers" simply because they stayed with the same victim during the designated tracking period, which in this case was six years. With a longer tracking period, say of twenty years, a much higher proportion of abusers would undoubtedly qualify.

Just over one-third of the killers admitted violence in relationships that preceded their involvement with the woman they murdered. However, only three men (10% of the total) had been convicted for such violence. One man had been arrested for stalking two different women. Another was still on probation for violating the restraining order of his ex-wife when he killed his next partner. A third killer had been convicted for raping his former partner's daughter. Though never prosecuted for these crimes, a fourth man had punched and threatened to kill one ex-partner and had broken the nose of another. A fifth had threatened a former partner, torn up her clothing, and stolen money from her when she broke up with him. This man stabbed his subsequent partner to death after she'd ended their relationship. According to these killers, none of their murder victims had known about their past violence toward women.

Possessive Beliefs

Men's killings of their intimate partners are best understood as extreme manifestations of their attempts to maintain proprietary control over women, according to Wilson and Daly.[2] They point to historical and cross-cultural norms that have supported men's rights to control women's sexual and reproductive capacities. In many nations, for instance, double standards still exist in laws pertaining to adultery. When a wife commits adultery, the aggrieved husband is often legally entitled to monetary damages, and sometimes even violent revenge. And while adultery laws in many Westernized nations have become more equalitarian, violent revenge by aggrieved husbands has often been viewed as more legitimate, and sometimes results in more lenient legal penalties than that which is meted out to vengeful wives. For men who kill their wives, alleged adultery by their wives is often been seen as grounds for reducing murder charges to manslaughter. Such killings are sometimes socially sanctioned as "honor killings." By contrast, women who kill their husbands are often subjected to harsher penalties, even when it can be shown that the men they murdered had been battering them.

Barbara Hart has argued that violence in intimate relationships serves to establish rules of control and ownership.[3] Once introduced, violence further serves to reinforce and clarify rules that have already been established. Examples of such clarifications include "You can have friends but not ones that I dislike," or "You can be upset about my going out but you may not question me about my whereabouts." Rules are not always expressly stated in words but are more often conveyed in abusive actions, as tacit punishments, in response to rule infractions. Perhaps the most obvious example of this is the abuser's jealous behavior. The other realms in which rules of dominance can be played out are in sexual relations, child rearing and custody, handling of finances, and decisions about the relationship status.

In many ways, killing one's partner is the ultimate act of possessive control. Analyzing eighty-six cases of men who had killed female sexual partners in Australia, for instance, one researcher found strong themes of "masculine possession" and "sexual ownership" among most of these killers.[4] One presumptive right of ownership in the case of a material possession is the right to destroy it when it no longer meets our needs. And while ownership also confers the right simply to get rid of something—say, a television or an old computer—by donating or selling it, no one denies the owner's prerogative to junk it or destroy it so long as waste disposal laws are obeyed. To a far lesser extent, the same rights exist with our ownership of pets. We have the legal right to "put down" a pet when it is sick or even when we no longer want it. Motives for killing animals do matter, though, and someone who kills or hurts one in a fit of rage would be subject to prosecution for animal abuse. No such rights exist for the killing of people, however, except in the contexts of self-defense, war, or capital punishment.

Possessiveness and jealousy are normal (and some say even healthy) emotions for most people. In an intimate relationship, a certain level of possessiveness is desirable as it signifies one's investment in the relationship and in the other person. There is something comforting and reassuring about being referred to as "my husband," "my wife," "my partner," or "my dear." Similarly, jealous feelings are normal and reassuring in many intimate relationships. When not accompanied by coercive behavior, jealous feelings can help to set boundaries in an intimate relationship by communicating each partner's comfort level about time spent and degrees of intimacy with others. Articulation of jealous feelings can also lead couples to clarify issues of trust in a relationship. Expressions like "If I can't have you, nobody can," "You have no right to leave me," and "I own you" represent the far extremes of the continuum of jealous and possessive behavior. Clearly, these kinds of expressions communicate attitudes of possessive control rather than of love and reassurance. They are frightening rather than comforting, and for good reason. All are threats of violence, and possibly of murder.

Case Example 9

"I wanted [the other man] to know
I was the last to have her."

John Perkins was twenty-nine when he killed his wife, Debra. Debra had reluctantly agreed to invite John over to see their daughters, aged six and two, on that evening in early December 1993. She felt somewhat reassured when her brother agreed to stay at home that evening, though for the most part he remained in his room. John and Debra had dinner with the girls, watched a video together, and put the girls to bed at about 8:00 p.m. John said that he then convinced Debra to have sex, and afterwards they watched a video, *Body of Evidence*. During this time, he served Debra two rum and cokes, knowing from past experience that the alcohol would make her sleepy. When Debra fell asleep at midnight, John took his daughters out of their beds and put them in the car. John then had a few more drinks "to psych myself up" for what he knew he wanted to do. It was about 2:30 a.m. when John picked up a baseball bat, went into the bedroom where Debra was sleeping and struck her in the head four or five times. To ensure Debra's death, he then stabbed her in the neck with a large hunting knife. John then got in his car with the girls, and drove around for several hours before breaking into a vacation cottage to spend the rest of the night. John turned himself into the police in the early afternoon. He pled guilty to murder in the first degree and is serving a life sentence.

Four months prior to her murder, Debra had left John and was living in another state. Shortly later, she had agreed to let John see the children at her parents' house. During this visit, John had put his hands around Debra's neck and begun to strangle her. He had stopped only after Debra agreed to return to him. Debra had later called the police and John was arraigned for domestic assault and battery. His trial for this had been pending when he killed Debra.

Explaining his decision to kill Debra in her sleep, John said he was determined "this time not to let Debra talk me out of killing her." John said that he'd told Debra before they were married that he would kill her if she ever left him or became involved with another man. He added that he had often reminded Debra of this, particularly after she left him and began seeing an ex-boyfriend. "The idea that I could always kill her," said John, "was just a comforting thing for me to say to myself; kind of like a safety valve." John stressed that no one could have talked him out of this since "I was convinced and felt morally in the right. And I'd gone to great lengths to explain the situation to Debra. That's why there's no feelings of guilt or remorse or anything." Asked why others didn't try to talk him out of it, John said, "I was tremendously obsessed, every waking moment . . . but on the outside I was very calm and cool."

John said it was important for him to kill Debra in their home after making love to her since "it was a way of preserving us as a couple forever." He said that he had also wanted Debra's new boyfriend to find out from the police report that John's sperm was inside her and therefore to know that John had been "the last to have her."

John's chilling words and actions communicate beliefs about ownership in their most extreme form. In essence, he is saying that he believes that Debra had no right to exist independently of him. Though he had not been involved in any church or organized religion, John partly justifies this belief on moral grounds by saying that he did not feel any guilt or remorse since he felt "morally in the right." When asked to clarify this, John said that this was not based on any religious convictions so much as his own belief in the sanctity of promises made. This attitude was later repeated when John was asked to fill out a questionnaire that measures one's beliefs about domestic violence. The first item on this scale is the following: "A husband has no right to beat his wife even if she breaks agreements she has made with him." John hesitated at this item, and then asked the examiner, "What if you don't believe in beating your wife but in killing her?" When asked the significance of this distinction, John said that he hadn't wanted to hurt Debra, adding "that's why I waited for her to fall asleep before killing her. Beating is like a form of punishment," he went on to explain, "but killing is like a way of straightening out the situation." John later said that he felt Debra was responsible for her own death since he'd warned her many times that he would kill her if she left him. He professed to being perplexed that Debra would have defied him "knowing what would happen." Repeating his belief in the importance of promises made, John said that it was important that he follow through on his promise to kill her if she left him since "I keep my promises."

One other aspect of John's belief in his ownership of Debra was his treatment of her as an object of competition with her new partner. This is conveyed in his wanting the new partner to know that his sperm was inside her and that he was therefore "the last to have her." One other killer, Harold, lured his estranged partner, Jenaya, to a hotel room where he shot her in the head immediately after having sex with her. Convinced that Jenaya was involved with another man, Harold wanted to be her last sexual partner. Objectification, or the viewing of one's partner as an object, is not uncommon among men who batter, though it may be more extreme among those who kill. In its barest form, objectification means that once objectified, the individual no longer has person status but exists only to serve the objectifier's needs. This is similar to how rapists and pedophiles often objectify their victims. Demoting the victim to object status serves to remove any need for guilt or remorse over one's abusive treatment of that person.

Comparing the Killer's and Victim's Perceptions

For the most part, the killers I interviewed disavowed any beliefs about ownership of their partners. In the most direct measure of this belief, they were asked to rate the degree to which they agreed with the statement "I own you" in relation to their deceased partner. None of the men indicated that they strongly agreed with this statement and only two (6%) said that they moderately agreed. The vast majority, including John Perkins, strongly disavowed this belief. A slightly higher proportion of the killers (26%) agreed with the belief that "she should do what I say" in reference to their partner, but most of the rest mildly or strongly denied believing this. The killers' denials of attitudes that support proprietary ownership contrast sharply with how many victims appraise their abusers' attitudes. In our study of victims of serious assaults, the women were asked to rate their ex-partners' attitudes and expectations related to ownership and control. An astounding 86% of these women (thirty-one of thirty-six) said that their ex-partners strongly or moderately believed that "I own you." The same proportion of victims said that their ex-partners held the expectation that "you should do what I say." An even higher proportion of the women (89%) felt that their ex-partners believed that "if I can't have you, nobody can." Just under half of these women said that their ex-partners had explicitly stated this to them. Table 7.1 summarizes these ratings. The victims were asked to rate their former partners' attitudes while the killers were asked to rate their own.

Table 7.1: Ratings of perpetrators' attitudes about possessive control (in percentages)

Attitude	Percentage of perpetrators who strongly or moderately agree to possessing attitude.	Percentage of victims observing attitudes in their abusive partners
I own you.	7	86
You should do what I say.	26	83
You have no right to disobey me.	3	81
It's your duty to serve me.	7	78
You have no right to say no to sex when I want it.	0	72
When you do things for yourself, you are being selfish.	13	72
If I can't have you, nobody else can.	3	89
If you leave me, you don't deserve to live.	3	72
	N=31	N=20

The divergence of perception about the men's attitudes is not surprising given their different experiences and perspectives. I believe that the victims' ratings were closer to the truth than those of the perpetrators. Many of the killers appeared intent on creating as positive an impression of themselves as possible. Killers are not unusual in their wish to disguise anti-social or unpopular attitudes. Research in social psychology has shown that many individuals are averse to admitting certain attitudes or beliefs that might be deemed socially undesirable. Such has been found to be the case with regard to beliefs about racial inferiority or stereotypes, for instance. Investigations of beliefs about gender roles and attitudes towards women has suggested that our collective social consciousness about women's rights over the past thirty years has led to real shifts in attitudes, but also has created a new self-consciousness about more traditional beliefs. This has created a "social desirability factor" that leads people to disguise beliefs or expectations that might be considered "sexist." The social desirability factor has led some researchers to construct more discreet measures of attitudes in which the "socially correct" response is less obvious.

Another approach has been to examine people's behavior as a gauge of their attitudes. The assumption here is that certain beliefs and expectations, particularly those that run counter to perceived conventional norms, are best identified by people's behavior than by their stated beliefs. Hochschild found that couples engage in "family myths" about gender equality by overstating their commitment to equality of gender roles.[5] Her research found that, in reality, men contributed considerably less time to housework and childcare than what they or their wives believed that they contributed. Couples believed that there was an equal division of labor in their relationship because they *wanted to believe* this more than it reflected the reality.

Another study conducted by Dobash and Dobash examined sequences of abusive behavior among battering men as a means of examining the underlying logic to the men's violence.

> The altercations relate primarily to the husband's expectations regarding his wife's domestic work, his possessiveness and sexual jealousy, and the allotment of family resources. . . . When a husband attacks his wife he is either chastising her for challenging his authority or failing to live up to his expectations or attempting to discourage future unacceptable behavior.[6]

For their part, batterers generally deny any possessive beliefs, as well as any explicit intentions to control their partners. In fact, many abusers are successful in presenting their abusive behavior as spontaneous, irrational, or caused by substance abuse. In my work with batterers, I have witnessed how batterers frequently attempt to avoid responsibility and accountability for their violence by claiming that they "lost control" and therefore did not intend to hurt their partners. Most therapists who work with batterers view these claims with skepticism, deeming them excuses for abuse. A closer examination of the batterer's actions reveals that his "loss of control" is rather selective, as exemplified by the following account:

Counselor:	Can you describe what you did in your most recent incident of violence?
Abuser:	We were arguing about something, and one thing led to another and I just snapped.
Counselor:	I see from the police report that you punched her.
Abuser:	I didn't *punch* her. I would never hit her like a man. I slapped her.
Counselor:	I see. But her nose was broken so you must have hit her pretty hard. Let me ask you this: Why didn't you stab her?
Abuser:	She's my wife; I would never stab her.
Counselor:	I thought you said you lost control. If you lost control, anything could have happened, right?
Abuser:	Well, I lost control but I didn't *lose* control.[7]

The abuser's violence is selective on several accounts; first in what he chooses to do and not to do, and secondly in whom he targets for his violence and whom he doesn't. The majority of batterers, for instance, do not lash out at friends, co-workers, police officers, or others who provoke them. This selectivity of targets may hold less true for those batterers who kill their partners, though it appears that a substantial proportion of wife killers have only been violent to their partners. In this study, 42% of the killers admitted to having been violent toward other adults besides their intimate partners. We also asked each victim of attempted homicide if she knew whether her abusive partner had been violent toward other adults, excluding any of his past intimate partners. Forty-five percent of these women said "yes" to this. Even among the most lethal abusers, it appears that many are highly discriminating in who they assault.

Sexual Violence

There was no greater divergence in what victims and perpetrators reported than in the area of sexual violence. If we are to believe the killers, none of them had ever been sexually violent or even coercive to the women they killed. Only nineteen percent of the killers admitted to having used any kind of pressure for sex. Even those who admitted this insisted that their pressure tactics had consisted of only mild measures such as repeatedly asking for sex or sulking when sex was denied. Only three of the killers said that such pressure had occurred on a weekly basis or more. Far from seeing themselves from sexually coercive, all the killers rated themselves as "always" or "nearly always" sensitive to their partners' sexual needs and desires.

The victims of serious abuse painted a very different picture. Nearly three-fourths of the women said their abusive partners had raped them. This proportion might well have been higher were it not for different semantic definitions of rape among the women. Besides those who said they had been raped, two additional women said that their partners had "forced" them to have sex at least once. These women did not define this as rape, even though they said that the sex had not been consensual. This illustrates the difficulty in defining rape within the context of an abusive relationship. Many battered women say that sex with their partners is frequently coerced even without the use of any physical violence or threats. One victim said, "He never raped me but I never said 'yes,' either. If I said 'no,' he made me pay in so many other ways." This woman went on to say that her husband would keep her up all night while accusing her of sexual involvement in other men. "It got to the point where it was just easier for me to go along [have sex with him]," she added. Nearly two-thirds of the victims similarly complained about having been kept up all night when they refused to have sex with their abusers. The most commonly cited forms of sexual coercion, however, were angry yelling or badgering and threats of violence. Table 7.2 lists the kinds of sexual coercion reported by the victims.

The vast majority of victims said they had been subjected to sexually violent and abusive behavior. This ranged from rape to violent or rough sex to pressure to perform sex acts that they considered degrading or insulting. Surprisingly, the victims of attempted homicide were only slightly more likely to have experienced sexual violence than the other victims of serious violence we interviewed. One such victim, Karen, said that her abuser had viciously raped her on four separate occasions during the four years they were together. These are summarized as follows in the order that they occurred.

1) David began yelling at Karen while her parents were sleeping in the next room. When Karen warned that he might be frightening

Table 7.2: Types of sexual coercion experienced by victims of serious abuse

Sexually coercive behavior	Proportion of victims who said their partners had done this when they resisted sex
Yelled or screamed at her	94
Badgered	94
Made (direct or implied threats) to kill or hurt her	92
Accused her of being involved with someone else	92
Threatened to have sex with other women	71
Threatened to withdraw financial support	64
Kept her up all night until she submitted	61
Demanded sex immediately following an incident of violence	58
Plied her with alcohol or drugs	41
Threatened to have sex with the children	10
Threatened suicide	10
N=39	

her parents, he took out a knife and raped her, while threatening to kill her father if she yelled for their help.

2) While staying at a hotel, David inserted an object into Karen while raping her. Karen passed out, only waking up the next morning.

3) When they were staying in another hotel, David bound Karen by the feet and hands with duct tape while telling her "If you don't do what I want, I'm going to throw you out the [thirteenth story] window."

4) After Karen said they should stop seeing each other, David hit her over the head with a phone, threw her against the kitchen counter, kneed her in the upper thigh, dragged her by the hair onto the couch while slamming her head into the wall, jumped on her stomach several times, and then bent her fingers back trying to break them until she agreed to submit to sex.

Like Karen, many of the victims in the control group had experienced acts of sexual degradation that mimicked those experienced by the victims of attempted homicide. It should be noted that these victims were not a representative sample of battered women. Given that they were recruited from emergency shelters for battered women, they represented victims on the more extreme end of the domestic violence continuum, similar to the victims of attempted homicide. Other researchers have recruited larger and more representative samples of battered women in order to assess base levels of sexual violence. For example, Campbell found that 15% of her randomly selected control group of battered women had experienced forced sex.[8] This compared to 57% of the murdered battered women that she investigated. In another study, Block found that 20% of the nearly 500 battered women they interviewed said that they had been subjected to forced sex by their intimate partners.[9] Table 7.3 shows our study's findings in terms of the relative proportions of victims who experienced acts of sexual violence and degradation.

Just over half of the victims said that their partner would sometimes or often become violent during sex. Most of these women said that their

Table 7.3: Proportion of victims who experienced sexual violence and degradation

	Victims of attempted homicide	Other victims of abuse
Pressured for sex on a weekly or daily basis	90	77
Forced sex	85	57
Sex was demanded immediately after she was beaten	70	68
Pressured for sex with no contraception	63	56
Rough or violent sex	65	42
Forced to have sex in front of or with others	35	10
Forced to look at or to imitate pornography during sex	35	16
Being bound during sex	25	10
	N=20	N=19

partners appeared "excited," "aroused," or "turned on" by violent or rough sex. Infliction of pain during sex appeared to be a unilateral action on the part of the abusers. No victim said that her abuser ever requested to be hit, slapped, or bound in return. One-fourth of the victims reported that their abusers would sometimes insist on having sex in the presence of their children or other people. Six victims said that their partner had demanded that they have sex with third-party adults. One victim reported, "He wanted me to do it [have sex with his friend] but then he would always throw it in my face afterwards, calling me a slut and a whore."

Sex Following Violence

A majority of victims also complained that their abusers had sometimes demanded sex immediately after a beating. Several victims said that they had found this to be particularly humiliating. One woman explained, "It was like he didn't even care what he'd just done." Another said, "It was like his way of making up but I didn't care for it. . . . It was creepy how he'd get all lovey-dovey after smacking me around." In response to the question, "Was there a pattern to his abuse?" a third victim said, "Absolutely. He would get mad, explode, calm down and then want to have sex."

Those who provide treatment to batterers have cited how serious abusers' frequent expectations of sex immediately following an act of violence reflects their "quick fix" thinking. Many batterers say that they worry that their partners will leave them following an act of violence. For some, this worrying is accompanied by closely monitoring the victim's demeanor for clues to what she might be feeling and contemplating. Some victims have characterized this close monitoring as "hovering." This period of monitoring the victim can extend for hours and even days for some batterers.

As one batterer attending a batterer intervention program put it,

> Yeah, I'd worried about what was going to happen, sure. What would bother me the most is when she wouldn't talk. I'd say I'm sorry and apologize and everything but she wouldn't say anything . . . and that would drive me crazy. I'd be afraid to leave the house on account of maybe she wouldn't be there when I got back.[10]

Sex after violence appears to serve several functions for the batterer, aside from any sexual arousal that he might experience. One is that for some abusers, sex signifies forgiveness on their victims' part. A common turning point that many victims of attempted homicide had noticed in their relationships was when their partners stopped apologizing for their abusive behavior. Nearly all the women cited such a shift. Rather than apologize, some men would "act as if nothing happened" and go about business as usual. Others would continue to blame their partners for hours or days. In both cases, sex was often expected or demanded within minutes or hours of the assault.

Citing her ex-partner's behavior toward her following an act of violence, Evie said, "Oh he'd blame me, saying if I could just act like a lady, he wouldn't have hurt me. . . . He started demanding sex all the time. That was his way of making up but he would still be rough. . . . That seemed to turn him on."

Batterers commonly point to their "make-up sex" as evidence that they have been forgiven for their violence. One batterer told his group counselors and fellow group members that he knew he was forgiven once "I was back in the big bed" with his partner. Other batterers go so far as to say that their partner could not have been frightened or bothered by their violence since "we had sex right after."

A second function of sex after violence for some abusers is that it reconfirms claims of ownership of their partners. Five different victims quoted their partners making such statements during sex that immediately followed acts of violence. These included:

"I don't care if you don't want to. You belong to me."
"If I can't have you, nobody can."
"I'm not playing games with you anymore.
    I can do anything I want to you, whenever I want to."
"You think you're done with me, bitch? You'll never be
    done with me."
"You are mine, remember that. I'll always have you."

This last comment was made to Dolores by her estranged boyfriend, Elston, while he raped her in the back seat of his car. Elston had just broken into the apartment of Dolores's friend, Brenda, where Dolores had been staying for two weeks following Elston's last act of violence toward her. In front of the couple's two-year-old son, Elston punched Brenda in the jaw, threw Dolores onto the floor, and dragged her down two flights of stairs to his car.

I found that there was a common context to the incidents of post-violence sex that the victims described. It was one in which the woman had separated from her batterer or had talked with him about doing so. Like Elston, many of the abusers responded with accusations of infidelity and demands for sex. These men appeared to be using sexual violence to reassert their claims of ownership of their partners. But there appeared to be another objective as well: to humiliate their partners for having committed real or imagined acts of rebellion so as to deter any future attempts. Some women said that they had felt so demoralized and depressed following such treatment that, in fact, they did feel discouraged from further resistance. Other women said it had been fear of continued violence that deterred them. As with terroristic threats, some abusers resort to sexual violence and humiliation when regular control tactics seem no longer to be working as deterrents to dissent on the victims' part. In this way, acts of terror and rape toward intimate partners follow a similar logic to campaigns of terror and rape within the context of war and ethnic genocide. In both cases, random acts of terror and rape are used to create fear and to suppress dissent. By committing acts of sexual degradation such as forcing objects into their partners, forcing them to imitate pornography, or offering them as sexual mates to their friends, abusive men seem to be communicating a message of, "See, it is pointless for you to resist; I can do whatever I wish with you."

For some abusive men, nothing seems to signify possession more than sex, and particularly sexual conquest. Nearly all the victims said that their partners' first act of violence did not occur until after they had first started sexual relations. Prior to this, according to most of the women, their partners had come across as fun, romantic, and sensitive to their needs and concerns. Some victims noted a rapid escalation of abuse once they began having sex or began living with their abusers. Others noted a more gradual escalation.

Annabel's depiction of her relationship with Wilberto typifies this. Annabel was seventeen and Wilberto was nineteen when they met through friends at a party. He came across as "fun-loving and gentle and shy."

Two months after they started having a sexual relationship, Annabel and Wilberto attended a party with many mutual friends. At some point in the evening, Annabel was shocked to see Wilberto fighting with another man. When she tried to intervene, Wilberto grabbed her by the shoulder and squeezed her arm, saying, "Why are you stopping me?" Over the next two years, Wilberto continued to abuse Annabel. His abuse consisted primarily of yelling, put-downs, jealous accusations, and pushing her against walls.

These gradually became more frequent but, according to Annabel, were always followed by apologies on Wilberto's part. When asked if she noted any other changes in Wilberto's abuse over time, Annabel said, "Yes, he stopped apologizing." She added that Wilberto then began to blame her for the violence and would often say things like, "See what you made me do?" Wilberto's violence became more and more frequent and severe, eventually including weekly threats, jealous accusations, and acts of violence such as slapping or punching her. The final incident of violence began when Annabel refused to have sex with Wilberto. Enraged at her defiance, Wilberto beat Annabel severely with his fists and then began hitting her over the head with a metal fan, stopping only after he felt for a pulse on her neck and could no longer feel one.

Expectations of Frequent Sex

Though we did not ask all the women specifically about this, several other women volunteered that their abusers had wanted frequent sex; often two or more times per day. I did ask the killers about frequency of their sexual relations with the partners they killed. Just over half of these men (seventeen) claimed to have had daily sex with their partners. Eight of these boasted about having had sex multiple times day. What does this suggest? I believe that for abusive men, their expectations of frequent sex convey a kind of possessive control over their victims. This is all the more so when frequent sex is accompanied by verbal and physical violence, jealous accusations, infidelity, and sexual coercion. Demands for frequent sex often come across to the less interested partner as conveying obsession or possession more than affection or love.

One rival explanation for these men's expectations of frequent sex is that it reflects sexual obsession more than possession. Are abusive men simply more sexually obsessed compared to nonabusive men? I'm not aware of any research that has shown this to be true. If the perpetrators of attempted homicide were sexually obsessed, one would expect a strong interest in pornography as well as frequent sex with their partners, but according to both the victims and the perpetrators we interviewed, this was not the case. The abusive men's use of pornographic media did not seem high in comparison to that of men in the general public. However, it did appear that their patronage of prostitutes was proportionately higher. Table 7.4 shows the abusive men's use of pornography and prostitution.

There is reason to believe that the killers' actual use of pornography and prostitutes is higher than avowed. For instance, one killer who denied any such use had been previously incarcerated for raping the twelve-year-old daughter of an ex-partner. Another killer was facing criminal charges for raping his four-year-old son at the time he killed his wife, the mother of the child. However, these were the only killers with such crimes on their records.

By and large, these perpetrators do not fit the profile of incest offenders or pedophiles. Nor do they fit the profile of sexual predators or so-called "sex addicts." Their high presumed rates of marital rape, combined with low to average rates of pornographic consumption, point to them as sexual sadists more than sex addicts per se. It could be that sexual possession and obsession amount to the same thing, especially when the object of sexual obsession is the abuser's partner. More likely, though, these men seem more obsessed with sex as a means of power and control than sex as a replacement for love and affection (the latter being a way that some nonviolent sex addicts are portrayed).

Infidelity

One other distinction between sex addicts and abusive men concerns their different motives for having sexual affairs. Sex addicts in a committed relationship generally attempt to keep their sexual relationships with other partners hidden from their primary partner, with the apparent motive of avoiding the wrath of their primary partner. This did not seem to be the case with the abusers I studied. In contrast, these men were not secretive about their sexual affairs. In fact, arousing the wrath of their primary partners seemed to be one of their main objectives. Seventy-five percent of the victims of attempted homicide and 68% of the other victims knew

Table 7.4: Proportion of abusers who use pornography and prostitutes

	Abusers convicted of and/or admitting to		
	Murder	Attempted murder	Nonlethal Domestic Violence
Looked at pornographic magazines			
Used at all	45	60	27
Used on monthly or more basis	22	45	27
Used on weekly or more basis	9	30	16
Viewed pornographic videos, DVDs or movies			
Used at all	32	55	44
Used on monthly or more basis	16	50	33
Used on weekly or more basis	3	20	11
Went to strip clubs or peep shows			
Went at all	19	35	33
Went on monthly basis or more	3	25	5
Went on weekly basis or more	0	10	0
Employed prostitutes			
Used at all	12	40	22
Used on monthly or more basis	6	30	0
Used on weekly or more basis	0	15	0
Viewed child pornography of any kind			
Used at all	6	5	0
Used on monthly or more basis	3	0	0
Used on weekly or more basis	3	0	0
	N=19	N=31	N=20

their partners to have had at least one sexual affair. Just over half of the victims said that their abusive partners had had sexual affairs that occurred on at least a monthly basis. Over one-third of the victims said that their abusers' affairs had been continual, whether with the same woman or with multiple others. Far from hiding their other sexual partners, many of the abusive men had flaunted them. Six victims talked of their abusers having sex with other women in their presence. Four victims said that their abusers had continued to live concurrently with another woman. Seven women complained that other women with whom their abusers were involved would routinely call their houses to taunt them or to have extended conversations with the abusers. Three of these women said the other women had threatened them.

Many of the victims said that their abusers would openly compare them to the other women. As Lydia stated, "He told me I didn't know how to make him feel like a man, like his other women." Another woman, Anna, said that her boyfriend would often "tell me I was heavy in comparison to Sylvia [the other woman]. . . . He would just always comment about what a perfect body she has and, you know, how beautiful she is and this and that. . . . Sometimes just out of the blue he'd say that. . . . I was kind of shocked when he brought her over one day 'cause, you know, she wasn't that beautiful."

Cheryl said that her husband, Rodney, used to regularly have long conversations with Rhonda, the other woman he was seeing. "He'd be having these long conversations with her and he'd be talking about me. One night I got up and disconnected the phone." In response, Cheryl said that Rodney had slapped her repeatedly in the head while saying, "Don't you ever disrespect me again, bitch!" Cheryl added, "It got to the point when he'd have her [Rhonda] right in our bedroom, doing crack and whatever."

For some abusive men, their other sexual partners appeared to be bargaining tools to be used against their primary partners. One woman, Wanda, said she had feared that her husband would leave her for the other woman at a time when she and her children were financially dependent upon him. "He would always complain that I didn't appreciate all he did for us, that was his big thing." A number of other victims said that they had felt insecure or inadequate as the result of their partners' involvement with other women. One woman whose partner had lived part time with another woman said, "It made me feel so low . . . and I felt desperate really for his attention. . . . Stupid me, he wasn't worth it, I can see that now but at the time I felt I was lucky to have him really." Three of the women said that their husbands had even threatened to "replace" them as mothers of their children with another woman.

After stabbing his wife, Lydia, in the shoulders, Albert left the house believing her to be dead. Finding out later she had been taken to the hospital, Albert enlisted his new partner, Emilie, to call the hospital to find out whether she had survived. Told that she was in critical condition, Albert then called his two children to tell them, "Mommy's been taken care of." He then had Emilie pick the girls up and bring them over to her house before he fled to Alabama. He was arrested two weeks later. In referring back to this, Lydia incredulously said, "I don't know what he was thinking, that he could just kill me and they [the authorities] would let this other woman just take my kids!"

As controlling as it was for some batterers, infidelity was clearly a double-edged sword for others. One woman, Amy, traced her decision to end her relationship to her husband's involvement with other women. Referring to her husband's second affair with another woman, Amy said, "For me, that was it. I told him; this ain't no pit stop."

Escalation

I examined the killers' and would-be killers' behavior within relationships for evidence of patterns of coercion. I sought to discern both long-term and short-term patterns of control and abuse by the abuser, resistance by the victim, and retaliation by the abuser. I hoped that this theoretical framework might give meaning to the men's behavior that otherwise might seem random, spontaneous, and irrational. Judging from these histories, the women's murders appeared to be the culmination of the men's attempts to control their victims via physical and psychological coercion. The killing was the final act of control by the abuser. Paradoxically, the murder may also have been the abuser's act of last resort, reflecting the *failure* of his past attempts to control the victim. Violence inevitably creates resistance on the part of the victim, and the abuser must continuously resort to escalating levels of violence in order to achieve the same results. This pattern of escalation is particularly evident in the many cases of domestic violence and stalking when the victim has left the abuser or is trying to leave him. Here, the abuser resorts to ever-increasing levels of terroristic threats and violence in order to compel the victim to return or to prevent her from leaving in the first place. Many killings of women occur following estrangement or attempted separation on the part of the victim. In these cases, the abuser who has failed to prevent the demise of the relationship may be settling for the next best thing: the demise of the woman who left him. This attitude is best summarized by "If I can't have you, nobody else will."

Stalking

In the public eye, stalking is primarily known as a crime against celebrities. Even in the legal and the mental health arenas, most of what is known about stalkers is based on those who stalk public figures. Stalking is easiest to identify and to prosecute when there is no prior relationship between the stalker and the victim. In many of these cases, the only attachment is the product of the stalker's imagination. Stalkers of celebrities and strangers often have a fantasized bond with their targets that may be based on only incidental contact with the person, such as a handshake or an autograph or even friendly banter. This is known as a "narcissistic linking fantasy."[11] In the most serious cases, the stalker becomes obsessed with the person and devotes increasing amounts of time and resources seeking contact with him or her. In the parlance of threat assessment, the stalker's attempts to physically contact the victim is called "approaching behavior" and is seen as a predictor of increased danger. Initially, much of their approaching behavior seems intended to capture the attention of the celebrity and to further the imagined romantic relationship. When his or her attempts to communicate with the celebrity are rebuffed, this adulation often turns to the hatred of a scorned lover. In its most extreme form, the stalker attempts to destroy the object of his obsession who he imagines to hold such vast power over him.

Threat assessment specialists have made great advancements in the detection, profiling, and management of those who stalk celebrities and public figures. Only recently has attention focused on those who stalk their intimate partners or ex-partners, despite the fact that this group makes up the vast majority of stalkers.[12] In response, many states have amended anti-stalking laws to address the special characteristics of these cases. Men who stalk their intimate partners or ex-partners have an advantage over those who stalk strangers: much of their stalking behavior is camouflaged by behavior that is common to intimate relationships. There is a presumed right for intimate partners to exhibit jealous and possessive behavior, such as asking jealous questions and checking up on each other. So long as no laws are broken, intimate partners, even estranged ones, are free to trespass on each other's property and monitor each other's activities.

Legal definitions of stalking vary but many define it as "a pattern of repeated willful malicious acts against another person with the intent to place that person in fear of bodily injury or death."[13] There are generally three elements to stalking, according to legal definitions:

1) a pattern of behavioral intrusions upon another person that is unwanted
2) an implicit or explicit threat that is evidenced by this pattern of behavior
3) as a result of this pattern, the person who is threatened experiences reasonable fear

For many victims of domestic violence, stalking is inseparable from the overall experience of being battered. Battering is in itself a pattern of unwanted intrusions and threats that induce "reasonable fear." For these victims, stalking behavior is accompanied by verbal and physical assaults, economic threats, and social isolation, making it just one of many threats to their safety and well-being. This may be one reason that so few stalking charges, relatively speaking, are brought against perpetrators of domestic violence. Another reason is that intimate partner stalking cases are notoriously difficult to prove for prosecutors. Most successful cases are those when the victim has already separated from her abuser and has obtained a protective order. But even in these cases, it may be still easier for prosecutors to establish that the protective order has been violated than to win a stalking conviction. One problem is that some state statutes pertaining to stalking require evidence that the defendant made an explicit threat to harm or to kill the victim. Another challenge is that the prosecutor must establish that the defendant has engaged in *pattern* of monitoring or following activities directed at the victim, which is usually defined as more than one or two instances. Moreover, there may not be any physical evidence to corroborate the victim's testimony. The case may rest solely on the testimony of a victim who may well be fearful of testifying due to fear of reprisals on the part of her batterer. Rather than risk losing a stalking case, many prosecutors will propose a plea bargain in which they agree to drop stalking charges in exchange for the defendant's guilty plea for domestic assault or violation of a protective order.

Virtually every victim of attempted homicide that we interviewed reported some kind of stalking behavior by her abuser prior to the final act of attempted homicide, though these women rarely defined such behavior as stalking. For instance, many used the term "checking up on me" in referring to their abusers' repeated efforts to monitor their activities. Table 7.5 shows the rate of stalking behaviors experienced by the twenty victims of attempted homicide. Three-quarters of the victims were estranged from their partners at the time of the near-fatal assault, while most of the rest said that they had been making plans to leave.

These victims of serious abuse were nearly as likely to have been stalked by their abusers prior to separation as following it. In fact, monitoring and harassing behavior are common features in many relationships in which there is domestic violence. However, it appears that such behavior is more frequent and severe in the most serious cases of domestic violence. Campbell finds that compared to less serious abusers, perpetrators of attempted homicide are almost twice as likely to have committed stalking behaviors, such as following or spying on the victim, making unwanted phone calls, and standing outside the victim's property.[14] Ac-

Table 7.5: Stalking behaviors experienced by victims of attempted homicide (by percentages)

Stalking behavior	Prior to separation	After separation
Frequent jealous questions and/or accusations	100	100
Monitoring (such as checking clothing for signs of sexual activity or car speedometer)	95	90
Threats to kill	90	100
Making unwanted phone calls	65	100
Following her	75	90
Standing outside her property	NA	80
Assaulting her in public	65	70
Destroying property	85	70
	N=20	N=10

cording to this research, such behavior occurs in 55% of relationships that end in homicide or attempted homicide, compared to 30% of the relationships in which there is less severe domestic violence. This does not tell the whole story, however. Closer examination of the cases of attempted homicide reveals that in most cases, there is a serious escalation in the most serious kinds of stalking behavior prior to the near-fatal assaults. In our study, victims reported that unwanted phone calls and threats became significantly more frequent in the three months leading up to the attempted homicide. Some reported as many as 100 unwanted phone calls a day. In most cases these were anonymous hang-up calls from a nondiscoverable number. In some cases, these anonymous calls were immediately followed by calls from their abusive partners. Other perpetrators made anonymous calls only, followed by veiled references to the victim such as, "Are you still getting those annoying phone calls?" This was apparently a covert tactic designed to ensure that the victim knew he was responsible for the calls. As one victim said, "He's smart enough not to get himself in trouble [by leaving threatening messages that she could record] but still wants me to be afraid every time I pick up the phone."

Case Example 10

"I felt so violated."

Michael Acero was eighteen when first arrested for stalking and kidnapping an intimate partner. He met Diane during his senior year in high school when she was a junior. They dated for six months before she broke it off, telling him she wasn't ready to have a serious long-term relationship. A month later, Michael went uninvited to a party that Diane was attending with about twenty-five other people. By the time he arrived, he was already intoxicated and ruminating about Diane being with another boy. After seeing Diane's new boyfriend leaving, Michael grabbed a rifle from a closet and ordered everyone out of the house. Still inside with Diane, he confronted her about her new boyfriend and pleaded with her to take him back. When she said no, he grabbed her by the hands and marched her outside to his car. He drove Diane to her mother's house where the police arrested him and charged him with assault and battery with a dangerous weapon and kidnapping.

Prior to his trial, Michael was sent for forty days of observation at the Bridgewater Hospital where he was judged not to have a major mental illness. At his trial, Michael was found not guilty of kidnapping. According to Michael, this verdict was primarily due to Diane's letters, introduced as evidence by his lawyer, which stated that she planned to run away from home. Michael was found guilty of assault and battery, however, and placed on probation. He was allowed to finish high school with the provision that he avoid any contact with Diane.

Michael continued to live with his mother for four years following his graduation. He briefly attended a junior college during the first year but dropped out due to financial hardships. Michael then worked a series of temporary jobs and continued to drink heavily every day.

In the summer of 1984, Michael met and began dating Maria. Maria broke up with Michael within four months, telling him it was because of his drinking and "being too possessive." Michael called Maria nearly every day to try to convince her to take him back. In November, he went to Maria's workplace where he was confronted by Maria's new boyfriend, Ted. Ted produced a gun and told Michael to "beat it." Michael retreated to a bar where he was kicked out for yelling and screaming to his friends about the situation with Maria and Ted. He went home, consumed more alcohol and passed out. Later on, he snorted some cocaine with his cousin.

Still enraged, Michael took his rifle and drove around town looking for Maria. He went back to her workplace and waited for her to finish her shift. Seeing Maria and Ted get in her car, Michael began to follow them in his car. When they stopped at a traffic light, he got out of his car, shattered the driver's side front window of Maria's car, and ordered both she and Ted to get out. Michael then ordered Ted to leave, telling him, "All right, tough guy, now you beat it." Ted fled the scene to call the police.

Meanwhile, Michael ordered Maria into his car and drove her to a nearby town where he planned to cash a check. On the way, the police pulled him over and arrested him. Michael was convicted of assault and battery with a dangerous weapon and kidnapping. He received a prison sentence of eight to ten years, with all but fifteen months of it suspended. With time granted for good behavior, Michael served ninety-four days of this sentence. While in prison, Michael received therapy and was diagnosed with a mood disorder for which he was prescribed a medication. He also attended AA.

Michael was released from prison in November 1986 and began working as a groundskeeper. By December, he met Connie while applying for a job as a security guard at a store where she was employed. They began dating in January 1987. Michael was twenty-three and still living with his mother. Connie was seventeen, living with her parents, and still attending high school. In June of 1988, Connie graduated and found work at a restaurant. The couple moved into an apartment together by August. Michael was employed as a construction worker and took a second job as a security guard.

In 1991, Michael took up power lifting as a competitive sport and quickly began taking steroids as a way of "bulking up." He was laid off from his construction job but continued to work nights as a security guard. Meanwhile the couple frequently fought over Connie's suspicion that he was involved with a co-worker. By 1992, Connie became concerned about Michael's increasing use of steroids as he entered more weight-lifting competitions. He had bulked up to about 280 pounds and outweighed his wife by nearly 200 pounds.

Despite their problems, the couple married in September 1992. A year later, Michael Jr. was born. Connie continued to believe that Michael was involved with another woman, and the couple continued to argue nearly every day. In early 1994, Michael worked briefly as a car salesman but was laid off by April. Strapped for cash, the couple moved in with Connie's father.

Michael began to behave more aggressively toward Connie and others. In an act of road rage, Michael assaulted another driver following a fender bender. Connie's father was more and more concerned about Michael's treatment of Connie and tried to convince her to leave Michael. Michael agreed to move out and stayed at his mother's house.

Sometime in mid-April, Michael went to Connie's house to pick up his son and became suspicious because she was "all dressed up like she's going out with someone." He grilled her about who she was seeing and insisted that he stay over that evening. Connie retreated to the bedroom and Michael slept in the den. At 2:00 the following morning, Michael woke Connie to tell her the baby was sick. The couple began to fight, and according to Michael, Connie sprayed him with mace and kicked him in the groin. Michael bit Connie on the finger, and "wildly flailing a nightstick in self-defense" twice connected with her head, causing her to briefly lose consciousness. When the police arrived, Connie told them that Michael had hit and choked her with a nightstick. The police alleged that Michael resisted arrest and subsequently smashed the squad car window with his head. Michael counter-claimed that a police officer had beaten him with a flashlight. Connie was taken to the hospital where she required stitches to close various lacerations on her head.

On April 20, Michael was arraigned for illegal possession of mace, brass knuckles, and several martial arts weapons. His other charges were assault and battery with a dangerous weapon and assault with intent to commit murder. He was jailed on $5,000 bail while awaiting trial. Michael was bailed out by a friend three days later. The friend advised Michael that there was a restraining order that barred him from having any contact with Connie or his son. He spent the next few days sleeping on the floor of the bar where he was employed.

Abetted by his sister, Michael managed an illegal visit with his eight-month-old son at her house on April 24. Michael said that this visit only increased his rumination about being apart from Connie, and his rage at her and her family for depriving him of contact with Michael Jr. That same day, Michael drove to Maine where he purchased a Civil War-era sidearm and black powder from an antique dealer. (During his interview, Michael said that his intention in buying the gun had been to put it to his head in front of Connie and force her to talk to him.)

On May 5, Michael rented a van with the intention of moving his possessions from Connie's father's house. That evening, he slept in the van. The next day, Michael attended the child custody hearing where he sought full custody of Michael Jr. The family service department of the court recommended that Michael have supervised visitations only, while Connie opposed visits of any kind. The judge ordered that Michael have unsupervised visits, with the condition that he have a third party pick up and drop off Michael Jr.

That evening, Connie told her sister that she feared that Michael would kill her and said she planned to flee to Oklahoma with Michael Jr. Meanwhile, Michael was depressed and obsessed with Connie. At some point that evening, he put his gun in his mouth and tried to "psych [him]self up" to kill himself but couldn't bring himself to do it. Later that evening, he went over to his sister's house and told her, "If I can't have them [Connie and Michael Jr.], nobody else can."

On May 6, Michael went over to Connie's house at 9:00 a.m. to see if she was there. After seeing her car, he returned to his brother's house. At 10:30, Michael parked outside Connie's sister's house, waiting for Connie to drop Michael Jr. off for a scheduled visitation. Seeing Michael, Connie became terrified and yelled to her sister that Michael was there. Michael walked up to Connie, telling her that he just wanted to talk. Connie kept yelling for her sister and warning Michael, "Get away from me." When Michael put his hand on her shoulder, she pushed him away and ran to the side of the house. Chasing after her, Michael had to stop because the gun he was carrying in his waistband kept slipping down the back of his pants. When Connie tripped on some yard debris, Michael grabbed her by the hair and took out his gun. He yelled at her, "Why didn't you tell me there was someone else?" while punching her in the mouth. (According to three witnesses, Connie was pleading for Michael not to kill her.) Michael says he cannot remember shooting Connie five times in the back and head.

According to testimony at his trial, Michael pushed Connie on the ground several times and then yanked her up by the hair before shooting her twice in the back, rendering her paralyzed and unable to move. As she lay on her back, Michael straddled her and, while she was still pleading for him not to kill her, shot her three more times in the head. After this, Michael got in his van and fled to New Jersey. Police apprehended him that day after he collided with another car.

At his trial for first degree murder, Michael claimed his heavy use of steroids had made him delusional and suicidally depressed, rendering him unable to form the intent to commit murder. He further claimed that his wife had been having an affair and had physically attacked him two weeks earlier by spraying mace in his face and by kicking him in the groin. "I felt so violated," he testified. Michael Acero was convicted of first degree murder for which he received a sentence of imprisonment for life.

Contrary to his claims to have never assaulted Connie except in self-defense, Connie's family testified that she had frequently been fearful of his jealous rages. Connie's brother testified that when his sister was in high school, Michael had even offered him five dollars to tell him every time he saw Connie speaking with another boy. Family members said that until Michael's arrest for assaulting Connie with the nightstick, she'd known nothing about Michael's past incarceration for threatening and kidnapping his ex-partner.

Surveillance

For the batterer, stalking appears to serve two primary functions: surveillance and intimidation. I examined both of these aspects of stalking in more detail in order to learn more about how they relate to patterns of control, resistance and punishment.

Domestic stalkers have one major advantage over those who stalk celebrities or other strangers; they know much more about their victims. While the celebrity stalker seeks to learn *anything* that might help him connect with his victim, the domestic stalker already has much information at his disposal. This information about the partner or ex-partner typically includes:

- her daily activities, habits, and whereabouts
- her place of employment, work hours, and names of her co-workers
- detailed information about her past, including her secrets and regrets, family history, feelings about her parents, psychological trauma, former relationships, etc.
- her bank account, ATM and credit card PINs, and credit history
- the names, addresses and phone numbers of her friends and relatives
- her computer and email passwords
- feelings about herself and her insecurities
- her plans for the future
- information about her children, as well as access to them in many cases

In the hands of a domestic stalker, each piece of gathered intelligence is potentially useful in his attempts to know and control her plans and actions. Each new piece of information becomes the grounds for potential sabotage, manipulation, and blackmail.

One victim of abuse, Audrey, had always counted on her mother as a source of support throughout her seven-year relationship with Carlton. It had been difficult for Audrey to leave her mother in New Mexico when the couple made the move to Massachusetts so that he could pursue a job. Once in Massachusetts, Carlton's verbal and physical abuse of Audrey escalated. The final straw for Audrey occurred when Carlton started also to direct his abuse at her daughter, Clarissa. Audrey obtained a protective order that required Carlton to leave their house and banned him from having any contact with Clarissa or herself. Despite this, Carlton's threats and harassment toward both of them continued on a daily basis. One day, while Clarissa and she were out, a fire broke out in their home. Though there was no evidence that linked this to Carlton, Audrey was convinced he was responsible, knowing that he had once set fire to a prior partner's car following the woman's decision to end the relationship. Audrey had also nearly lost her job as a department office manager at the local university after Carlton called her boss to falsely report that she had taken pads of paper and other office supplies. On top of this, Audrey continued to receive numerous hang-up calls each day. After filing for divorce, Audrey felt terrified and isolated from her family and friends. Most hurtful was that she had stopped receiving weekly letters from her mother. Only years later did Audrey learn that her mother's letters had been intercepted by Carlton.[15]

Intercepting these letters from Audrey's mother served two purposes for Carlton. First, he was able to gain a "heads up" on Audrey's plans to file for a protective order and for divorce. This early notice enabled Carlton to line up an attorney and to prepare his legal case. Secondly, the theft of these letters cut off Audrey's communication with her mother and sabotaged what had previously been an important source of support for her. Audrey said that the major financial concessions she made during the divorce proceedings had been prompted primarily by her fear of retribution from Carlton. In retrospect, she now sees that this fear had been exacerbated by her perception of being isolated and having no sources of support who might have helped her to identify other options. One important option would have been her mother's invitation to Audrey and Clarissa to come back home to New Mexico, one that Audrey didn't learn about until long after the fact.

The vast majority of the victims of serious assaults that we interviewed (88%) said that their abusers had stalked them or otherwise monitored their activities. The victims of attempted homicide reported the same pattern of escalating surveillance by their abusers. Ninety percent of the victims said that their abusers' spying or monitoring behavior had become more frequent during the three months leading up to the incidents of attempted homicide. In most cases, the victims felt this escalation was directly attributable to their estrangement or planned estrangement from their abusers. As one victim said, "He was always paranoid and suspicious, but when I talked about leaving it pushed him over the edge."

Threats and Intimidation

The second critical element of stalking behavior is intimidation. Perhaps the most common forms of intimidation are threats to kill, maim, or otherwise injure the victim. We asked the killers as well as victims of serious abuse about the frequency, timing, and escalation of threats in order to identify whether such behavior corresponded with estrangement or planned estrangement. We also wanted to know whether other forms of victim resistance provoked increasingly serious threats by the abuser.

Research on domestic homicides has shown that past threats to kill the victim are one of the best predictors of homicide or attempted homicide.[16] In comparing murders of women by their partners to less serious cases of domestic violence, Campbell found that the murdered women were five times more likely to have been threatened by their abusers.[17] One other distinguishing feature these cases is the *frequency* of death threats. Ninety-five percent of victims of attempted homicide that we interviewed said that they had been threatened with death at least once by their abuser, while 90% had received more than one threat. In fact, half the women had been threatened on at least a monthly basis, while a quarter had received weekly threats. Another distinguishing feature of these cases was the severity of the threats. For many victims, these threats were explicit and graphic. When we asked victims to describe these threatening words and actions, it quickly became apparent that the words "threat" and "intimidation" did not do justice to what they had experienced. In most cases, verbal threats were accompanied by actions on the part of the abuser that would more accurately be characterized as "terroristic." Here is a sampling of such terroristic threats:

> Lynette: "He took out his gun and held it to his head and said he was ready to die and he pulled the trigger. . . . Then he handed the gun to me and asked if I was ready to die." Lynette's husband made her

play Russian roulette, passing the gun back and forth and pulling the trigger six times.

Lucy: "He would threaten to kill me with an ax that he kept under the bed. He would take it out to show me and to tell me it had my name on it." Lucy's husband, a business owner, eventually tried to kill Lucy by forcing her head into a crock-pot with hot liquid, grinding her head into the broken shards of glass on the floor, and banging her head repeatedly against the floor. Lucy was rescued by a neighbor who overhead the attack.

Sylvie: "Well, almost every day toward the end . . . he would threaten to kill my mother and my brother also. . . . He held a gun to my daughter's head once, telling her that he would kill us both." After Sylvie had broken up with him, Edgar broke into her apartment, and held Sylvie and their two-year-old daughter hostage at knifepoint before and after the police had been called. The police arrested Edgar after he'd stabbed Sylvie in the head repeatedly.

Carolina: "Yes. He would threaten to cut me up in little pieces, and kept saying that they would never find my body 'cause he would know where to hide them." Carolina's husband eventually was convicted of attempted homicide after hitting her repeatedly over the head with a wrench and leaving her for dead.

Monica: "He made many threats to kill me and my son, or have someone else do it. . . . He always had lots of weapons that he'd keep around . . . whips, knives, guns, pipes, and handcuffs. . . . Once he made me get down on my hands and knees and he held a knife to me and he made me beg for my life. He used to like to scare me by driving fast and pushing me out of the car. . . . When I was getting out of the shower, he'd jump out at me with a Halloween mask on. A couple of times I thought I was going to have a heart attack. . . . But he just thought it was funny." Six months after leaving her husband, Carl, Monica was seriously injured and nearly killed when the brakes on her car failed and rolled down a steep embankment. Because Carl had recently worked on the car and had it towed and demolished immediately after the accident, Monica is convinced that he had deliberately tampered with the brakes.

Lydia: "Yes, [Albert] would threaten to kill me and Mary [their oldest daughter]. . . . He would threaten to bring his new partner over and make me watch him raping her. . . . He would threaten to crash our car into a wall. . . . Many, many times he did that." Albert was eventually convicted of attempted murder after stabbing Lydia in the shoulder and legs. Even after this, he was sending threatening letters from prison.

As can be seen from these accounts, there seemed to be a sadistic component to many of the abusers' acts of threats and intimidation. Five of the victims said that their abusers appeared to take pleasure in scaring or torturing them. This may have also been true for other victims who did not think or choose to volunteer this information. For most victims, their abusers' verbal threats were inseparable from the violence and other kinds of intimidating behaviors that they also experienced. These included the displaying or brandishing of weapons, reckless driving, being followed or chased by car or on foot, and verbal or physical assaults of their children, relatives, friends, or pets. Table 7.6 provides a breakdown of the acts of intimidation that these women had experienced prior to the attempted homicides.

Most of these women said that they had been kept in a near perpetual state of fear and anxiety by their partners' violence and intimidation. Trauma experts have labeled this state of mind "hypervigilance," when the victim is constantly wary of another attack. This condition is reinforced by the seemingly random nature of the abuser's attacks, leaving the victim the sense that since they could come at any time, she must always be on guard. As painful and frightening as the physical assaults were for these women, the abusers' frequent threats and acts of intimidation served to remind them that it could always get worse. Sometimes, quite literally, the abuser was saying, "I could kill you."

Some perpetrators did not stop at threatening their partners. In at least half of the cases of homicide and attempted homicide, the perpetrator had also threatened to kill other people. These most often included the victim's

Table 7.6: Acts of intimidation experienced by victims of attempted homicide prior to the attempted homicide

Type of intimidation used	Proportion of victims who said "yes"
Monitored	95
Slapped or punched	90
Threatened	90
Followed or stalked	75
Choked (strangulation)	65
Her possessions were damaged or destroyed	65
Kicked	60
Relatives were threatened or assaulted	60
Threatened with a knife	55
Threatened with a gun	45
Friends were threatened or assaulted	45
N=20	

children, parents, siblings, and friends. For some victims, these threats to kill others were more frightening than threats of their own deaths. This may explain why some perpetrators threatened others who were near and dear to the victim. A number of victims of serious abuse said that one of the ways they coped with the constant danger they faced was to become numb to it. A quarter of the women said that death at the hands of their abusers seemed unavoidable and inevitable. When the victim no longer fears death, this takes an important bargaining tool away from the abuser, prompting him to think of additional ways of motivating the victim's compliance. As Lynette, the victim of Russian roulette, explained:

> After that [the Russian roulette incident], he seemed more and more angry and paranoid. I think it was because he knew I wasn't afraid to die. If it was just me, it wouldn't have mattered . . . but I was always afraid of him killing my babies.

Two other victims said that their abusers had threatened to make them watch as he killed the children. Children were not the only potential targets, however. A fourth victim, Wanda, said that she had constantly worried for her parents' safety due to her abuser's frequent threats to burn down their house. More than one-third of the victims said that their abusers had threatened to kill a parent or sibling. Other common targets of threats for perpetrators were friends of the victims, particularly those who offered the victims support or assistance. More than half the victims witnessed their abusers verbally or physically assaulting a friend. Sometimes, these assaults effectively sabotaged the victim's relationships with those who had been sources of help. In at least one case, the victim's friend cut off contact with her for fear of her own safety. More commonly, victims avoided future contact with friends out of concern for their friends' safety as well as their own. In effect, the abuser's threats and assaults of his victim's friends and relatives served to further isolate her and render her more vulnerable to his control. Over time, most victims said that they had fewer and fewer friends that they could turn to for help or support. Sixty-five percent of the victims said that they had progressively become more socially isolated during the year leading up to the near-fatal assault.

In order to gain further insight into perpetrators' threats, we asked both victims and perpetrators to describe these threats in as much detail as they could recall. We asked for the exact wording of the threats as well as when they occurred within the context of the relationship. Examples of the victims' threat descriptions are contained in Figure 7.1.

The picture that emerges from these accounts is that the abusers made threats in order to maintain or regain control over their partners. The threats were made to prevent the victims from taking certain actions, such as leaving the relationships, seeking custody of the children, or becoming involved with other men. Threats were also made to coerce the victim to give the abuser what he wanted, such as sex, money, or the freedom to do what he pleased, such as to see other women, or to come and go without explanation. Ironically, it appears that threats were most likely to be made when the abuser felt he was losing control over his partner's actions, after other control tactics had failed. Violence and other controlling behaviors often elicited short-term compliance from victims but also triggered long-term noncompliance and resistance. In response, it appears that many abusers "upped the ante" in order to maintain or regain the same level of control they once had. To do this, some abusers threatened actions that exceeded what they had already done. For example, some perpetrators resorted to acts of public humiliation for their victims. After his estranged wife refused to speak with him, one perpetrator dragged her by the hair along a street in front of her neighbors. Two days prior to killing his wife, whom he suspected of having an affair, one man gathered up all of her clothing, jewelry, pictures, and other personal belongings and set them ablaze in the front yard of her home. This was witnessed by one of his sons. Many victims of attempted homicide reported an escalation of the perpetrators' threats following estrangement or attempts to get help. The perpetrators' threats became more frequent and graphic. For some women, their partners' threats to kill them were replaced with terroristic threats to maim and then kill them. When this did not produce the desired result, some perpetrators also began to threaten to kill their children or other loved ones.

Victim Resistance

The victims we interviewed responded to their abusive partners in a wide variety of ways. Ultimately, most left their abusers or were attempting to do so when the near-fatal assaults occurred. Over three-quarters had previously separated from their abusers for periods that ranged from two days to several months. For most, their decision to reconcile with their abusers had more to do with their fears of retribution than beliefs that a better relationship was possible. The victims' fears seemed a rational reaction to the escalating violence and terroristic threats that they were experiencing during their periods of separation. Faced with this, most of the women decided that it was safer to return to their abusers, even if temporarily, than to remain apart. As one victim put it, "He told me that I wouldn't make it to my next birthday [if they remained apart] and I believed him." Many of the other women we interviewed said that they were wrought with uncertainty about which was the safest course: to stay or to leave. One victim compared this choice to deciding "whether to step off a cliff when being pursued by a bear," adding "only in my case, even if I survived the fall, the bear was still down there waiting for me." As this woman so eloquently attested, leaving is rarely the final resolution for victims of serious abuse. For some victims, leaving their abuser is an attempt to survive that is based only on the hope, and sometimes a prayer, that he will let them go.

Even prior to leaving, most of the victims had taken other steps to

Figure 7.1: Examples of threats reported by victims of attempted homicide

Victim's name	Specific threat	Witnesses	Situation
Anna	"I'm going to kill you"	Children and victim's mother	Anna had left abuser to stay with her mother.
	"Next time you see her, she'll be in a pine box" (said to Anna's mother)	Anna and her mother	One year later, Anna had again left abuser to stay with her mother.
Erika	"I'll kill you if you divorce me" (said while abuser held gun to her head)	Erika only	Erika had told husband she wanted a divorce.
Monica	"You are mine, remember that. I'll always have you" (said while holding knife to Monica and making her bend down on her hands and knees)	Monica only	Monica had said she wanted to end the relationship.
Carolina	"I'll kill you, you know that"	Carolina only	Carolina had left husband two days earlier.
Cheryl	"You know you can't be with anyone else in this town if you leave" (said on a near-weekly basis)	Cheryl only	Whenever Cheryl talked about leaving.

Name	Threat	Who was threatened	Context
Mindy	"If I can't have you, nobody else can. You're going to get yourself killed"	Mindy only	Mindy was living with new partner three years after her relationship with abuser ended. A month earlier, she'd filed for sole custody of their son.
Lonna	"I'm going to kill her" (said to Lonna's relatives who were restraining him)	At least twenty of Lonna's relatives	Two years following their breakup, Lonna's ex-partner showed up at her family picnic to confront her about having a new boyfriend.
Amy	"I'll kill us all, I don't care"	Kim and two children	Kim had left abuser six months earlier and was seeking sole custody of the children.
Dolores	"I'll kill you, bitch" (repeated many times, while holding knife to her head)	Dolores only	Whenever Dolores talked about ending the relationship.
Angela	"If you don't do what I say, I'll kill you" (repeated many times)	Angela and friends	When Angela talked about no longer being a prostitute. Abuser was her pimp and longtime partner.
Nilda	"My problem is that you are still alive" (repeated many times)	Nilda only	When Nilda refused sex.

resist their abusers. Most used a variety of coping strategies that ranged from actively resisting their abusers to appeasing them. Almost all of the victims reported that they had fought back in some manner against their abuser. Most found that this had led to more violent reprisals and death threats from their abusers, however, and they often found themselves backtracking.

One time when her husband, Elston, was beating her, Dolores managed to break away and grab one of the guns that he kept in an open cabinet. Dolores cocked the gun and held it to Elston's head. While he was on his knees pleading for his life, Dolores told him, "If you ever put your hands on me [again], I'll kill you." As Elston grabbed for the gun, it went off, sending a bullet into the floor between them. This roused her father, who lived in the apartment beneath them. Her father came upstairs to "calm the situation down," said Dolores. In retrospect, Dolores believes this "commotion" saved her life, as she thinks Elston would have shot and killed her on the spot if he'd been able to wrestle the gun away from her when it was still loaded. Less than a year later, Elston tried to kill Dolores by dragging her out of the house, driving her to a remote area, throwing her out of the car, and driving over her. Feigning death, Dolores remembers Elston feeling for her pulse before driving away in the middle of the night. Dolores said she had had several previous close calls with Elston in the months leading up to this incident. During one of these, Elston had pistol-whipped her in the face several times, fracturing her skull and breaking her jaw.

Another victim, Mary, said that she had threatened to kill her abusive partner, Terrence. In response, he had merely laughed and walked away. Following this, however, his violence had steadily escalated to the point that he tried to kill her three months later. Fed up, Mary had just obtained a protective order that required Terrence to move out and avoid any contact with her and their three-year-old daughter. When she responded to a knock on her door one evening, however, she found Terrence standing there with a knife. Holding the knife to Mary's neck, Terrence asked her, "Do you want this to end good or bad?" When she screamed for him to leave, he began to stab her repeatedly in the head, all while their daughter sat on the floor crying. On his way out, Terrence cut the phone lines to the house. Mary managed to get up and stagger out the door into the street where neighbors saw her and summoned an ambulance. Terrence watched the EMTs and police from across the street. He then went to a bar, where he was arrested after assaulting a stranger. Terrence received a prison term of ten years following his conviction for assault with intent to murder.

Mary and Dolores were the only two victims who had threatened to kill their abusive partners. None had attempted to do so. Though somewhat uncommon, some victims of serious abuse do kill their partners; in fact, this is considered to be the most common scenario in husband or boyfriend killings. For some battered women in these relationships, murder seems the only way of avoiding their own deaths.

Defiance

Rather than physically fighting back, most of the women we interviewed had actively resisted their abusers in other ways. Three-quarters had left their abusers at least once. Just over half of the women had obtained protective orders. More than two-thirds had called the police to report domestic violence at least once prior to homicide attempt. Forty-two percent of those who were married to their abusers had divorced them or filed for divorce. Half of the mothers had sought to limit the abusers' access to the children. From their accounts of their relationships with their abusive partners, a picture of multiple coping strategies emerges. These included periods of open rebellion as well as appeasement, and everything in between. Often, abusers would respond to the victim's defiance with increasing levels of violence. This in turn would lead some victims to use appeasement strategies or more covert forms of resistance. Despite this, most of the women said that they had become more defiant over time. Asked whether the relationship had changed in any ways during the three months prior to the homicide attempt, seventy percent of the victims said that they had been "fighting back" more, while only one woman said she had "stopped fighting back."

This woman, Angela, was previously mentioned in the section about violence during pregnancy. After losing her second baby due to Robert's violence, Angela said she had become severely depressed and had lost all energy to fight back. Still, on the day he beat her into a coma, breaking her jaw, Robert had accused Angela of defying him. He had come home to find that she had gone into the room that they had decorated for the baby that she had lost three months earlier. Asked why she thought Robert tried to kill her, Angela said, "Because I disobeyed him."

Table 7.7 shows a summary of the changes that victims had made in the three months leading up to the homicide attempt. While the overall pattern of victim actions is not one of open rebellion, neither is it one of giving up. Victims had taken a variety of actions to make themselves and their children safer without knowing whether these measures would work or backfire. In many cases, victims had taken steps to become more economically independent from their abusers. A number of women had gone back to work or increased their hours at work. About one-third had started to put money aside. More than three-quarters of the women who had left their partners were making plans to create a new life with their children, and in some cases, with a new partner. Two of these women were divorced from their abusive husband while the divorce was pending for a third woman. This woman's ex-partner was dying of liver disease when he nearly stabbed her to death in a subway station parking lot where he'd lured her by saying he needed to talk about their children. One of the divorced women had remarried and had not lived with the perpetrator for over three years. Enraged that she was attempting to limit his contact with their daughter, he attempted to kill her and her new husband by breaking into their house, and finding them asleep in their bed, bludgeoning them with his motorcycle helmet.

These findings do not support the theory that victims of serious abuse develop "learned helplessness" in response to the futility of their efforts to escape abuse. While forty-two percent of the women said they had become more depressed during the three-month period leading up to the most serious assault, higher proportions—more than three-quarters of the women—said they had become more angry and defiant. (A number of women reported having felt both more depressed and defiant.) Only one-fifth of the women said that they had felt "resigned to die." Just under half said that they had become more "numb," however. Higher proportions said that they had felt more fearful and anxious.

Anger, fear, and anxiety seemed to co-exist for the majority of these women. Anger and fear in particular appeared to serve as counterbalances for them. Their anger appeared to keep them from giving in or giving up, while their fear prompted them to think about their safety. For most

Table 7.7: Victims' actions and emotional reactions in the three months prior to the homicide attempt

Actions and emotional reactions	Percentage
Fought back more	81
Made plans to leave partner	77*
Left partner	68
Had more trouble sleeping	66
Became more socially isolated	63
Became more afraid	59
Became more angry	54
Became numb	50
Sought to limit abuser's access to children	50
Sought help from a counselor or victim advocate	45
Attempted to become more economically independent (e.g., seeking a job or promotion, going to school, saving money)	45
Went to court	45
Became more depressed	45
Thought about or tried to kill self	31
Started a sexual relationship with someone else	22
Felt resigned to die	18
Threatened him	9
Used more alcohol or drugs	9
Stopped fighting back	4
Obtained a weapon	4
N=20	

* This total includes the women who had already left their abusers, plus one additional woman who had told her partner she was leaving.

women, their responses to their abusers alternated between open rebellion, covert defiance, and strategic surrender. None of the women appeared to blame themselves for their partner's abusive behavior, though several said they had done so earlier on in their relationships. Most women had already left their abusers or were planning to do so. Those planning to leave were biding their time, waiting for opportunities when leaving would be economically feasible or when the situation might be safer.

Angela's opportunity came when her abuser was arrested for drug trafficking and received a long prison sentence. Even following Robert's attempt on her life, Angela was too fearful to call the police. Two other women whose abusive partners were career criminals similarly said that they had hoped their salvation would come when their abusers were arrested and incarcerated for other crimes. As one woman put it, "I guess I was hoping the situation would take care of itself. The police was after him. . . . I just didn't want it to come back on me." Only one of the victims said that she had no plans to leave her abusive partner. This woman, Amanda, believes that her husband only attempted to kill her because of his heavy drug use and possibly because of his involvement with another woman.

Punishment

In the vast majority of cases, the abuser's violence had escalated during the three months leading up to the act of attempted homicide. More than three-quarters of the victims said that his violence had become more severe. The same proportion said it was occurring more frequently. We also asked if the perpetrator's violence had become "more unpredictable," "scarier," or "more bizarre." Eighty-five percent of the women said that their abuser's abuse had become more unpredictable while a slightly lower proportion (77%) said that his behavior had become scarier or more bizarre.

As examples, several women said that their would-be killers had become quieter or less communicative shortly before the near-fatal assaults, something that in retrospect was like "the quiet before the storm." Mary said that Terrence would "just be sitting outside in his van" or "just be sitting for hours in the living room with no lights on." Cheryl, whose husband Rodney nearly killed her by holding a hot iron to her face, said he used to "just sit and stare in the mirror for hours . . . sometimes he'd be blasting music . . . and sometimes he'd be flexing his muscles in the mirror or doing karate kicks." Angela said that Robert "wouldn't even bother to say anything to me anymore before hitting me. He'd just haul off and slug me [in the face] without saying a word."

With less forewarning of their abusers' violence, many of the women said that they had become increasingly anxious and terrified. A number of women talked of being raped shortly before the homicide attempts.

Though rape was not unusual for many of the women, several had noted that it had been done with increased brutality. As previously mentioned in the section about sexual violence, several of the men had raped their estranged partners in the presence of the victim's friends or children. This appeared to be designed to communicate the message "I still own you" to women who had taken steps to sever the relationship.

We asked victims whether they believed their abuser had intended to kill them when he committed the most serious assault. Ninety percent of the women said "yes" while two said they were not sure. One of these women, Nilda, said, "I have no idea whether he wanted me dead or just wanted to mess me up real bad." The jury at Luis's trial believed that he had meant to kill Nilda, however, and found him guilty of assault with intent to murder. We also asked the victims what they believed their abusers' reasons were for attempting to kill them. These responses are listed in Table 7.8. Many victims listed more than one reason. The most common combinations were "to punish me," "to make me suffer," and "to win." Asked what they believed to be the "major reason," all but one of the

Table 7.8: Victims' beliefs about why their partners tried to kill them

Motive for killing (in victims' words)	Percent of victims who said "yes"
To punish me.	95
To make me suffer.	72
To win.	68
To hurt me as much as I'd hurt him.	54
If he couldn't have me, nobody else would.	54
To stop me from leaving him.	50
To make others feel sorry for him.	40
Revenge for something I did to him.	40
To stop me from doing something else.	31
To make good on a threat that he'd kill me if I left.	27
To make sure I didn't have the children.	18
To financially gain from my death.	13
To punish others.	9
N=20	

victims (95%) said it was "to punish me." When asked to identify the behaviors for which they believed they were being punished, many of the victims cited small "infractions" that had immediately preceded the homicide attempt, such as refusing sex or arguing back, but also larger issues such as their having ended the relationship or taken initial steps to do so.

On the day Nilda was nearly killed by her husband, Luis, she had picked up the three children on her way home from work and begun cooking dinner. Luis came home and immediately began arguing with her about a new dress that he'd found in her closet. He accused her of buying the dress against his wishes and demanded that she take it back. When she refused, Luis started screaming at her, calling her a "bitch" and a "slut." He pushed her to the floor and started choking her to the point where Nilda was going in and out of consciousness and "seeing black spots in front of my eyes." Nilda broke free and began to scratch at Luis's face and eyes to make him stop. Luis then grabbed a large fireplace poker and started repeatedly hitting Nilda over the head until she lost consciousness. She awoke several hours later in the hospital.

Asked why she believed Luis had attacked her on that particular day, Nilda said, "for disobeying his order to not buy that dress." Nilda added that she believed Luis was punishing her for having recently left him to stay at her mother's house. Luis had begged Nilda to return home with promises never to hit her again.

The next most frequently cited motive for attempted homicide was "to make me suffer." It is interesting to think of the differences between "to punish me" and "to make me suffer" as motives for homicide. The latter goal is only possible when the victim is being hurt or tortured before she is killed. Perhaps this is why the victims of attempted homicide were more often stabbed, bludgeoned, or strangled than the victims of homicide. A higher proportion of the killers simply shot their victims to death without inflicting injuries beforehand, other than the psychological pain of realizing one's imminent death. In contrast, most of the perpetrators of attempted homicide stabbed, strangled, or bludgeoned their partners. This suggests that they might have wished their partners to suffer.

Several of the victims of attempted homicide stressed that their abusers seemed to take sadistic delight in hurting them. Karen, for instance, said of her abuser, "He enjoyed watching me suffer." Nilda also said this of Luis. She added that, on numerous occasions prior to his final assault of her, he had put his hands around her throat and slowly squeezed, only stopping when she was about to pass out. She also said that Luis appeared to enjoy hurting her when they had sex. Their wish to make their partners suffer may be one reason why perpetrators of attempted homicide were unsuccessful killers. Toying with their victims, much as a cat does with a mouse, provides the victim additional time to escape, as well as the opportunity for others to intervene.

More than two-thirds of the victims thought that an additional motive for their assailants was "to win." Women who had already left their abusers were the most likely to say this. This mirrors a common sentiment expressed by the murderers whose partner had left them. As John put it, "I always knew in the back of her head that if I lost her, I could still kill her." John was the killer who had sex with his estranged wife, Debra, with the intention of signaling to her new partner that "I was the last to have her."

Chronologies of Abuse

I asked each victim of attempted homicide whether she had noticed any changes in her partner's abusive behavior during the course of their relationship. From these accounts, a fairly clear common pattern emerged. Nearly all of the victims had noted three turning points in their relationships with their abusers. These are summarized in Figure 7.2.

The first was when the man's abusive behavior first appeared. This was generally within the first year of the relationship and soon after the couple began living together. The first incident of abuse usually consisted of a mild to medium form of physical violence such as grabbing and shaking the woman, slapping her in the face, or pushing her against a wall. Most victims felt shocked by this violence because it was such a departure from their partners' behavior during the "honeymoon phase" of their relationships. Most victims also expressed anger about this violence to their partners, and several threatened to end the relationships. Almost without exception, the abusive partners apologized for this first act of violence and made promises that it would not happen again. Perhaps because of this, most of the women had concluded that this act of violence was an anomaly.

The second turning point was the continuation and gradual escalation of the man's abusive behavior. This usually consisted of criticisms, jealous questions and accusations, and occasional or regular violence toward the victim. For the most part, this came within months of the first act of violence but in some cases occurred as long as a year later. During this phase, victims grew increasing confused, dissatisfied, and disillusioned about the relationship. They responded to the abuse in a variety of ways that ranged from fighting back to appeasing their partners. Some victims blamed themselves for their partners' jealous accusations and began to limit their interactions with others.

Many of the victims of attempted homicide talked of a third turning point in their relationships where their partners stopped apologizing for the violence and began to consistently blame the women for it. For many women, this signified that their partner's abusive behavior was not an anomaly but a normal feature of the relationship. Most of the women said that their partners would routinely demand sex following an act of violence. Interestingly, the growing severity and regularity of their partners' violence helped many of the women to see that it was the man's problem and not something that they had caused. In fact, many women first separated from their partners at this time. Most of the women had had children with their abusers by this point and many of these women said that they felt trapped within the relationship. The main entrapping factors that victims cited were economic dependency and fear. Some women said this had been compounded by a growing depression or sense of hopelessness about seeing any viable options.

A few women said that they also still loved their abusive partners while a higher proportion said that they felt ambivalent. Despite this, most said that within the first five years of the relationship, they had begun to have persistent thoughts about ending the relationship. The women said that they had also begun to feel chronically unhappy and fearful of their partner's increasingly frequent abusive behavior. They actively and passively resisted this abuse in a variety of ways that have been previously described.

In response to their partners' growing unhappiness and resistance, the perpetrators had continued to escalate their coercive and abusive behavior. These behaviors now included frequent jealous accusations and monitoring, more frequent and severe forms of verbal and physical violence, sexual violence or coercion, infidelity, and abuse or threats to abuse the children. Over two-thirds of the victims of attempted homicide said that

Figure 7.2: Summary of turning points in the serious perpetrators' relationships with their victims

Honeymoon period:
Ranged from one day to six months.

First turning point:
Perpetrator: Commits first act of violence.
Victim: Complains about violence.
Perpetrator: Apologizes for violence and promises it won't happen again.
Victim: Sees violence as an anomaly and accepts apology.
Perpetrator: Violence reoccurs (either gradually or rapidly).

Second turning point:
Perpetrator: Begins to blame victim for violence rather than apologize for it.
Victim: Becomes increasingly unhappy, distrusting, and angry. Has thoughts of ending relationship. Resists partner in variety of active and passive ways that range from appeasement to defiance. Some victims separate for the first time, and/or seek help.
Perpetrator: Sensing victim unhappiness and resistance, further escalates his violence and seeks new ways to control her. If victim has separated from him, this often includes monitoring, stalking, threats to the victim, rape, financial manipulation, and abuse or neglect of her children.
Victim: Becomes more fearful, desperate, depressed, and angry. Usually has turned to others for help and made one or more attempts to separate from the perpetrator.

Third turning point:
Perpetrator: Increases frequency of threats/violence and often threatens/ intimidates those who try to help the victim.
Victim: Leaves or attempts to leave the relationship.
Perpetrator: Kills or tries to kill victim.

their partners had been unfaithful at least once, while half said that this had occurred on at least a monthly basis. Rather than attempting to hide their affairs, many women said that their partners had "flaunted" them. Six women recalled seeing their partners have sex with other women in their presence. At the same time, most of the abusers had become increasingly jealous with their partners. By maintaining this double standard about sexual fidelity, and by insisting on sex whenever they wanted it, the serious abusers appeared to be asserting a claim of proprietary ownership over their partners.

The presumption of ownership was also revealed in the abusers' behavior during periods of separation from their partners. More than 90% of the victims of attempted homicide reported that their partners had engaged in harassing and stalking behaviors after the women had separated from the men. Two-thirds of the women said that this had included assaults in the presence of other people.

Eighty percent of the victims said that their partners had escalated their violence within the year of the murder attempt. Three-quarters said that the men's behavior had become "scarier or more bizarre." The victims said they had felt more and more fearful and sought different ways of responding to their partners' violence. Three-quarters had temporarily or permanently left their partners. Four-fifths of the women said they had been "fighting back more." Over half said they had taken steps to make themselves more economically independent. Almost all of the women had sought some form of outside help. Seventy percent had obtained a court protective order at least once. Two-thirds had called the police and one-third had filed criminal charges.

Looking at this from the perpetrator's perspective, things hadn't gone well. His attempts to control his partner and to keep her in the relationship seemed to have backfired. Even his most severe violence and terrifying threats no longer worked. It is in this context that the murder or murder attempt can be seen as an act of last resort by the perpetrator, and the final turning point in the relationship. As Anthony said, "She left me. The only thing left was to kill her." In saying this, Anthony was simultaneously admitting defeat in his attempt to preserve his relationship with Robin but also claiming victory by having exacted the ultimate act of control by taking her life. Asked to choose from a long list of possible motivations by their partners in the attempts to kill them, all but one victim (95%) selected "to punish me," while over two-thirds said it was "to win."

Variations

If this summary of perpetrators' patterns of abuse seems overly pat, it is because I've so far omitted discussion of the significant variations among them. Each of the five types of perpetrators exhibited the same pattern of abuse that sequentially included onset of abuse, escalation, and retribution, leading to murder or attempted murder. However, each also had somewhat distinctive triggers and fluctuations to their violence. I have previously described each type of perpetrator's characteristics and motivations to kill. Here I will summarize variations in their cycles of violence.

Jealous Type

The jealous type of perpetrator is perhaps the most easily misconstrued since he seemingly fits the classic picture of a scorned husband who is driven to murderous revenge by an unfaithful partner. As I've shown earlier, however, the reality is far different from this. First, most of the victims had *not* been unfaithful. Only one-fifth of the victims of attempted homicide said that they had had a relationship with another man, and in half of these cases, the other relationship began after the woman had separated from her abusive partner. In two of the four cases, the victim had already divorced her abuser. Asked to identify their partner's primary motive in trying to kill her, just over half of the victims of attempted homicide said it was to ensure that "if I can't have you, no one else can."

Looking at the thirty-one cases of actual homicide, the small proportion of unfaithful wives was similar to that found among the victims of attempted homicide. In only two cases could I find evidence that the deceased partner had been sexually involved with another person while still involved with her abusive partner. Interestingly, half the jealous killers admitted that their partner had not been unfaithful. These men said that they had not been triggered by the existence of another man but by the fact that their partner had ended the relationship and would soon (they assumed) replace them with a new partner. The other half of the jealous killers continued to insist that their deceased partner had been romantically involved with someone else. These men continue to proclaim that their violence was a legitimate response to an unfaithful partner. One attitude measure that I administered to each killer was to ask to what degree he believed that "a woman who is unfaithful to her husband deserves to be beaten." Not surprisingly, the jealous killers were the most likely to agree with this statement.

Besides the absence of an immediate rival, jealous perpetrators deviate from the myth of the jealous rage killer in another important way. Their jealous rages at the time of committing their crimes were not new or spontaneous responses to the victims' actions. Rather, their jealous suspicions and rages were longstanding features of their relationships with the women they killed. These men had also been extremely jealous in their relationships with prior partners. If this is true, one might ask why they had not killed past partners. In most cases, the killer had simply not had serious relationships with other women prior to his relationship with the deceased, or these relationships had occurred when he was a teenager. Even despite this, however, two killers admitted that they had been extremely jealous when dating teenage partners. I have previously cited Michael, who had abducted two different ex-partners after they had broken up with him and were dating other boys. The other man, Casey, had serially stalked past teenage partners after they had broken up with him.

In three cases, the jealous killers had been previously married. In all three cases, the men admitted to past jealous behavior but none of these men killed their ex-partners. One man, Andrew had stalked and severely attacked his former wife even as he was beginning his relationship with the woman he killed, Roberta. Another man, Emmit, had been married to two previous partners. He first married very briefly as a teenager and this relationship ended, without violence, when he moved to America at his parent's insistence. Emmit left his second wife in order to be with Louise. The key element here was that Emmit, rather than his wife, ended this relationship. This important distinction is one that several victims of attempted homicide said their abusive partners had emphasized to them. Monica's husband, Carl, once told her, "I will decide when the relationship is over. Always remember that." Cheryl's husband, Lyle, would repeatedly tell her, "You don't tell me when we're done, bitch."

During their relationships with their victims, nearly all of the jealous perpetrators had exhibited the same basic pattern of slowly escalating violence leading up to the final deadly or near-deadly assault. However, the severity of their violence tended to spike both before and during separations with their partners. Violence prior to separation seemed to be prompted by jealous suspicions toward their partners. The same was true of their violence during the separation, although it also may have served to intimidate their partners into reconciling with them. While their jealous feelings and suspicions had always been present during their relationships with the deceased, over time, these suspicions had seemed to grow in intensity and duration. This may have been because they sensed, accurately, that their partners wished to end the relationships. In this sense, their jealous accusations became self-fulfilling prophecies, not in the sense that their partners were driven to become unfaithful but in the sense that their partners became more and more alienated from them and resolved about wishing to end the relationships. Victims of attempted homicide confirmed that their abusive partners' extreme jealousy was extremely alienating to them.

Substance-Abusing Type

Most of the substance-abusing killers and would-be killers also fit the jealous profile and therefore exhibited the same basic cycles of abuse. For instance, their violence tended to escalate during periods of pending or actual separation from their partners. Unique to substance abusers, however, was the more rapid onset and increased frequency of their violence. Virtually everything in these relationships unfolded more quickly. Just as these men's courtships with their partners were faster, so too was the emergence of their first violence. This generally appeared within the first days that the couple lived together or began having sex. In some cases, these events were nearly simultaneous.

Substance abusers followed the same sequence as the other perpetrators in how they reacted to the aftermath of their violence. Over time, most shifted from apologizing to their partners to blaming them. However, this shift occurred much sooner. These men generally stopped apologizing after the first or second occurrence of their violence and never looked back. From this point on, most began to blame their partners. A unique twist for many of these men, however, was that they would also ignore their violence and act as if it had never occurred. This was often abetted by their claims to have experienced "blackouts" during which they had no recall of their violence and other actions. According to this logic, if they could not recall being violent, there was no need to apologize for it. It is worth noting here that some substance abuse experts have found that battering men claim to have "blackouts" more than other substance abusers.

The substance-abusing perpetrators often demanded sex after their violence, according to their partners. Some partners also said, however, that sex was so frequently expected that it was hard to know whether it was in response to the violence or simply "business as usual." Most of the substance-abusing killers claimed to have had sex with their partners on a daily or near-daily basis. Relative to the other killer types, they also admitted much more frequent violence toward their partners. Victims of attempted homicide who had been partnered to substance abusers confirmed that sex was expected or demanded very frequently. They also reported having been subjected to more frequent and severe violence. Often, the violence and sex were co-existent.

Substance abusers exhibited a more speeded-up and condensed version of the cycle of violence during their relationships with their victims. Once established in the relationship, the violence escalated in frequency and severity very quickly. Victims reported many prior acts of severe violence that rivaled the final assault in seriousness. Victims also recalled many other dangerous or risky behaviors on their partners' part such as drunk driving, drug overdoses, and fights with other people to which they were exposed. The killers themselves reported many previous "close calls" during which their partners had been seriously injured and nearly killed. They did in fact kill their partners much sooner than the other types of killers. The time span from courtship to murder averaged seven years for these men compared to fifteen for the other killers.

Materially Motivated Type

The materially motivated killers are unique in their lack of strong jealous feelings and motivations. These men kill in revenge for being cut off from financial resources, particularly in cases of the financially exploitative subgroup. For the financially possessive subgroup, their motivation is to prevent the loss of material assets through divorce, or to punish their wives for "causing" such losses. The relationships of the first group are much shorter and less committed than those of the men in the latter group. Financially exploitative perpetrators serially exploit women for sex and money. Much of their violence revolves around being denied either of these commodities. They also tend to become violent when "bothered" by their partners, such as when the women complain about their infidelity, lack of employment, criminal behavior, or general lack of responsibility. This is the only type of killer who has shorter relationships than those of the substance abusers. Relationships are short because these men move from one relationship to the next, with no particular investment in any one woman unless for material benefits. Like the substance abusers, their cycles of violence are more rapid and condensed. Many of these men admit to stealing from ex-partners who have broken up with them. Ironically, theft may be a logical alternative to murder for these men.

In contrast, the financially possessive perpetrator has much longer and more committed relationships. Like the financially exploitative man, however, his violence tends to cycle around his financial grievances, such as spending by his partner, or by his partner's complaints about his control over the money or lack of emotional commitment. Such men also maintain secret relationships with other women, providing additional grounds for violence once these are discovered. Violence for some men in this group is infrequent and less severe and most likely to flare up during divorces or pending divorces, when they face the loss of material assets.

Suicidal Type

This type of perpetrator overlaps almost completely with the jealous type and therefore shares many of the same motivations and patterns of violence. Compared to wife-killers in general, they are older and more likely to be in long-term committed relationships. The unique element of their depression, combined with extreme dependency on their partners, often provides them with additional grounds for violence toward their partners. For these men, murder and murder-suicide appear to be prompted most often by the ending of the relationship or its threatened demise.

Not much is known about cycles of violence among this group of perpetrators due to the lack of surviving witnesses, as well as the increased social isolation of these families when they are still intact. One clue is provided by Allen, the man who made a serious attempt to kill himself immediately after stabbing his wife to death. Allen admitted that he had been violent throughout his relationship with Andrea but said there had been long periods of nonviolence during which he had been immobilized by depression. Still, Allen said that he would sometimes become violent toward Andrea in response to her attempts to get him to seek treatment for his depression or to resume taking his medication. Allen said his jealous feelings would trigger verbal and physical violence toward Andrea. This escalated as Andrea made plans to end the relationship.

Career Criminal Type

All of the career criminals were also jealous, substance-abusing, or materially motivated types of perpetrators and therefore shared many of the same patterns of abuse. This, in fact, is one of the distinguishing features of career criminals—that each poses a double or triple threat to his partner. Most of these men were also jealous substance abusers and their violence could be triggered by either of those sets of factors. Unique to career criminals, however, is the criminal subculture in which they exist and to which their partners, without choice, are exposed. These men often exert pressure on their partners to accept and adapt to this culture. As a result, their partners become progressively more isolated from their own circles of support. Some women complained that their friends and relatives had scorned them for "taking up with a criminal." Even without this scorn, most women said they felt ashamed to be somehow associated with the criminal element and therefore avoided their relatives and old friends. One victim, Angela, said that her partner had "scared off" all of her friends with his threats and reputation for violence. Several women said that they had not disclosed that they were being abused to their friends or relatives out of concern for their friends' and relatives' safety.

Similar to substance abusers, the career criminal type of perpetrator did not trouble himself for very long, if at all, with apologies for his violence. These men moved pretty quickly to blaming their partners, with the additional element of demanding that their partners apologize. Among the killers and would-be killers, career criminals were the most likely to have assaulted their partners in public. In doing so, these men appeared to be advertising their immunity from consequences to their partners and to any witnesses. As stated earlier, victims of these men were the least likely to have called the police or obtained a court protective order. One reason cited by victims was that their partners had often threatened to have others harm them should the men ever be incarcerated. Many of these men seemed intent to exploit their reputations as criminals who did not fear the criminal justice system and therefore could "do anything." Conversely, others talked of their fear of arrest as the reason to silence their victims. Other criminals tried to enlist their partners in crime so as to make them fearful of using the system. One such man who also served as his partner's pimp had repeatedly cited his partner's prostitution, albeit coerced, as a reason that she would have no credibility even if she were to call the police.

For the most part, career criminals continually escalated their abusive behavior throughout their relationships. Feeling terrified for themselves as well as for their potential allies, these women reported far fewer help-seeking steps than the other victims. They also reported more depression and had made more suicide attempts.

8 | **Victim Help-Seeking**

In the previous chapter, I discussed some of the self-help strategies that the victims had employed prior to the attempts of their lives. The vast majority of the women had also turned to many other people as well as agencies for help.[1] These included the police, courts, medical centers, counselors, battered women's programs, child protection agencies, and clergy. Nearly all the victims had also turned to friends, relatives, and neighbors for help at some point during their relationships with their abusive partners. A summary of institutions and individuals that victims turned to for help is presented in Table 8.1.

This listing provides only a partial picture of victim help-seeking since it does not include the context of how victims sought help, what they wanted from the potential helper, and what kind of help, if any, was offered. To understand more about this, we asked each victim to discuss in detail her experience with each type of potential helper. We also asked victims to talk about the impact of these helpers on them, including whether they were satisfied or dissatisfied, whether they had been encouraged or discouraged, and whether they believed the help provided had made them more safe or placed them in more danger.

Police

Four of the victims credited the police with saving their lives, and in one woman's case, the lives of her children. Some of these cases have already been described, but all four are briefly summarized here in order to show the value of rapid police responses to domestic violence situations.

Table 8.1: Victim help-seeking prior to the act of attempted homicide

Type of help	Percent of victims who sought this type of help
Sought help from her family	73
Obtained protective order	70
Sought medical treatment for domestic violence injury	68
Called police	65
Sought help from friend(s)	63
Sought help from abuser's family	40
Sought help from a therapist	40
Sought help from a battered women's program	40
Filed criminal charge	35
Received help from neighbor(s)	35
Sought help from a clergyperson	15
Received psychiatric inpatient treatment	15
N=20	

1) Erika's estranged husband, Lyle, had abducted her in his van on the night he raped her and then stabbed her in the neck. As he drove her around in his van for two hours, alternately speaking tenderly to her and threatening to kill her, Erika remained remarkably calm and resourceful in her effort to talk Lyle down and to buy additional time. Twice, she convinced Lyle to let her call home to speak with her children who, unbeknownst to him, had already called the police. With Lyle monitoring these calls, Erika was careful not to allude to the police or to say anything else that might panic him. Already having been raped and stabbed, she was in the midst of negotiating with him about what she would tell the police when three police cruisers blockaded the van and arrested Lyle at gunpoint.

2) Without saying a word in advance, Rodney punched Cheryl in the eye as she was ironing her clothes, breaking her eye socket.

He then grabbed the hot iron and pressed it repeatedly against her face. All the while, Cheryl passed in and out of consciousness. Finally, Rodney strangled Cheryl until she passed out in the bathroom. Rodney then called the police to say he'd killed his wife. By the time they arrived and were knocking on the door, Cheryl had revived. Brandishing a knife, Rodney told her, "Now I'm going to finish you off, bitch." The police found Rodney standing over Cheryl with a knife when they burst in and shouted for him to freeze.

3) Vickie confronted her husband, Paul, after coming home and finding him in bed with another woman. Later that evening, Paul came home from work and asked Vickie for $20 so he could buy some beer. When she refused, he punched her in the head, causing her to bleed profusely. Perhaps knowing that he wanted to kill her, Paul then took the two children next door to stay with a neighbor. When he returned, he took off his clothing and attempted to have sex with Vickie. When she said no, he put his hands around her throat and began to squeeze. Seeing "black spots in front of my eyes," Vickie fought for her life before passing out. The police report of this incident reads, "P/O arrived to find suspect on top of plaintiff, choking her. Performed CPR to revive plaintiff who is suspect's wife. Placed defendant under arrest."

4) When Lonna arrived home from work, she found her estranged husband, Jason, waiting for her with a baseball bat. Striking her over the head with the bat, Jason kept demanding, "Who have you been sleeping with?" When she said, "No one," he called her a liar and asked their six-year-old daughter, Abby, who told him, "Don't hurt mommy, daddy." Meanwhile, Lonna tried to distract Jason by telling him she needed to give Abby a bath. Jason struck her again over the head, knocking her out. When she came to, he was pulling her down the stairs. Lonna attempted to flee, but Jason struck her a third time with the bat, telling her he was going to kill her. As she passed in and out of consciousness, Jason ordered her to cut up pictures of her family.

When she refused, he duct-taped her hands, feet, and mouth while threatening to kill her, the children, and her mother. Lonna managed to break away and call her mother. Jason grabbed the phone, telling her mother that he had just killed Lonna and was now going to kill Abby and her infant sister before coming over to kill her. While he was talking to her mother, Lonna escaped and ran out to the street. When the police arrived, Jason kept them at bay for twenty minutes by threatening to kill the children. When they broke down the door, they found him standing over both children with the bat.

Lonna had called the police on four prior occasions. Twice within the previous month, Lonna had called the police to report that Jason had threatened to shoot her and her mother. Police had confiscated Jason's guns on the second occasion but, citing insufficient evidence, did not arrest him. Lonna followed the police officers' advice to obtain a protective order. Though the police did not arrest Jason, by confiscating his shotguns they undoubtedly denied him of a more efficient way of killing Lonna, and possibly their children, on the day that he attacked her with the bat.

Thirteen of the victims (65%) had called the police at least once prior to the act of attempted homicide. Police had been called on behalf of two additional women. For one of these women, her children had called the police, while for the other woman, it was her father who made the call.

Altogether, police had previously responded to domestic violence against three-quarters of the victims of attempted homicide. To gain more information about the impact of these prior police interventions, we asked each victim to talk about at least one of these. Detailed data was obtained for twenty-two police interventions. We asked each woman what she had wanted the police to do, what they actually did, and whether she felt this had been helpful. We also asked victims to evaluate each police intervention in terms of whether it had "made things better," "made things worse," or had "no effect." Table 8.2 summaries these findings.

It is difficult to meaningfully evaluate and compare the quality of the police responses since they were in response to different conditions, such as the amount of available evidence that an arrestable offense had been

Table 8.2: Victims' evaluations of police responses to prior cases of domestic violence.

Police response or impact	Percent of victims who said "yes"
Victim felt police were helpful	40
Police gave information to victim about services	40
Police did what victim wanted	36
Police arrested the suspect	31
Police advised victim about suspect's dangerousness	22
Victim said intervention made situation worse	50
Victim said intervention had no effect	36
Victim said intervention made situation better	13

N=20; N=22 separate police incidents

committed. Another variable is some of these police responses came prior to so-called "pro-arrest" laws or policies that were enacted in Massachusetts and in the neighboring states where these cases occurred. In Massachusetts, Chapter 209A was amended in 1995 to expand police powers of arrest.[2] Specifically, the statute specified that police "shall" make an arrest when "there is probable cause" to believe that an assault has been committed. Not coincidentally, arrests had not been made in all six of the reviewed police interventions that occurred prior to 1995. By contrast, arrests have been made in eight of the sixteen that have occurred since then. The arrest of the perpetrator did not always make things better for the victim, however. In half of the cases when arrests were made, the victim said that the perpetrator was subsequently violent to her in retribution. Still, victims whose partners had been arrested were more likely, on average, to say that their situations had improved or at least gotten no worse. The most common complaint by victims whose partners had not been arrested was, as one victim put it, "He felt immune after that." Another woman noted, "He didn't take it seriously" after the police had "just talked to him and told him to be good and not do it [hit her] again." Consistent with this, victims of perpetrators who had not been arrested were even more likely to say that the situation had "gotten worse."

Lydia's son called the police after witnessing his father, Albert, hit his mother, giving her a skull fracture. In recalling this incident, Lydia reports that when she told police she wanted her husband arrested, "They told me I could go down to the court to fill out some papers." Despite Albert's continued assaults of Lydia following this, Lydia said she did not call the police again. Asked why, she said, "They would take their time coming and when they got here they wouldn't do anything."

Dolores reported that in response to witnessing her husband, Elston, swearing at her, one of the two female police officers slapped him in the face and demanded that he apologize to Dolores. Rather than arresting Elston, the officers told him to leave. Dolores reports that Elston hid in the bushes outside the house until the officers left and then punched her in the face. After this, he kept her up all night threatening her.

Perhaps more relevant to the victims' satisfaction with police responses was not whether an arrest had been made but whether they felt they had been treated respectfully or derisively by police. Forty percent of the victims felt that the responding police officer(s) had treated them with sensitivity and respect, while an equal proportion felt that the officer(s) had been indifferent or insensitive. Not surprisingly, the victims who felt they had been treated respectfully were more likely to have subsequently called the police when attacked again. As one victim put it, "I felt that he [the officer] cared and that made a difference." Another said, "They said they couldn't arrest him but offered to send a [squad] car by to check on me, so I felt they were looking out for me." In contrast, five victims said officers had treated them insensitively or disrespectfully. Three women reported that they had been told, "Don't call us again," unless they left their abusers.

Angela is the woman who had been severely beaten because she had defied her husband's order to stay out of the room that they had decorated for the baby that she subsequently miscarried as the result of his violence. When the police arrived, Angela did not want Robert arrested because she feared that he would then kill her. Instead, she asked police if they would take her to her mother's house. According to Angela, the officers refused to do so, telling her, "We aren't a taxi service, ma'am." Angela said she never called the police after this, despite Robert's continuing violence. She remained with him until his arrest and incarceration one year later for drug trafficking and armed robbery.

Victims who said they had been treated respectfully were more likely to report that they were also offered information about victim advocacy programs and related services. All of the women who said they were "satisfied" with the police response reported that they had been offered such information.[3]

Courts

One-third of the victims had sought to have their partner prosecuted for acts of domestic violence that preceded the act of attempted homicide. Twice as many (70%) had sought orders of protection from the court. This is further evidence that victims were not passive but had taken active steps to protect themselves and their children. Only five of the victims (25%) had never previously sought help from the criminal justice system. For the women who had used the courts, there had been two, and sometimes three, professionals with whom they had interacted; the judge, the prosecutor, and a victim witness advocate if one was assigned.[4] We asked each woman about her experiences with each of these professionals within the court system.

Prosecutors and Victim Witness Advocates

Our analysis of victims' contacts with prosecutors and prosecutor-based advocates was hampered by limited data. This is because victims could sometimes not recall whether they had previously met with a prosecutor. For some, their memory of the prior contact with prosecutors was blurred into interactions they had following the act of attempted homicide. This is not surprising since many of these court cases were still pending when the final assault occurred. In three cases, the perpetrator's sentence for a prior assault was combined with his sentence for the attempted homicide.

Sufficient data was available to conduct a meaningful analysis of ten prosecutions that had occurred prior to the homicide attempts. Table 8.3 includes a summary of these findings. Altogether, victims had mixed reactions to prosecutors. They were also evenly split about the impact of these prosecutions. Four women felt that the prior prosecution made things safer for them, albeit temporarily, while three believed that it had made the situation more dangerous. The remaining three said that it had had no impact either way. Perhaps not coincidentally, all four of the victims who felt safer said that they had been assigned a victim advocate. Altogether, six of the ten women said that they had contact with an advocate assigned to the prosecutor's office. All six of these women, and none of the rest, said that they had been referred to community services, such as a battered women's program, and also had been given information about safety planning. All six said that they also had been advised about the perpetrators' dangerousness, though none could recall whether this advice had been informed by formal threat assessments.

The women who had not been assigned a victim advocate had more complaints about their prosecutors, and said they were less trusting of the courts as a result. Interestingly, this distrust seemed unrelated to whether or not their partners had been convicted. Asked what advice they had received from prosecutors, most could only recall being advised to testify against their batterers and/or to obtain a protective order. Two victims could not recall receiving any advice at all. The victims' most common complaint about prosecutors was that they felt pressured to testify or otherwise participate in the prosecution without sufficient regard to how this might antagonize the abusers. All four of the victims who were not assigned victim advocates felt this way, compared to only two of those who had advocates. Several of women said that they had felt relieved when advised by the prosecutors or the advocates that they did not have to testify against their abusers and that prosecution would proceed without their testimony.

Aside from feeling pressured to testify, the most common complaints by victims were that the prosecutors had been unavailable or provided insufficient information about the court process or the status of their cases. One victim said, "I felt completely in the dark about whether it [the case] was dropped or what," adding that the prosecutor had not returned many of her phone calls. Four of the victims complained that the prosecutors handling their cases had been indifferent or "judgmental." One victim, Amy, said of her prosecutor, "I don't think he cared one way or the other." Three additional victims said they felt that the prosecutors had been judgmental toward them.

Carolina's husband, Jesus, was being prosecuted for threatening to kill her and vandalizing her car. This case was still pending when Jesus tried to kill her by hitting her over the head with a wrench and leaving her for dead in a ditch by the road. Asked what the prosecutor had advised,

Table 8.3: Victims' evaluations of prosecutor actions in domestic violence cases that preceded the acts of attempted homicide

Prosecutor action and/or impact	Percent of victims who said "yes"
Assigned a victim witness advocate	60
Referred victim to community services	60*
Advised victim about defendant's dangerousness	60*
Helped victim with a safety plan	50*
Victim felt prosecutor was helpful	40
Victim said intervention made situation better	40
Victim said intervention made situation worse	30
Victim said intervention had no effect	30
N=10	

* In all these cases, a victim advocate assigned by the prosecutor was the primary source of assistance or advice, according to these victims.

Carolina said, "He told me I was stupid to stay with him," adding, "I feel he was very looking down on me and that bothered me tremendously."

Victims overwhelmingly felt ambivalent about the prosecution of these prior acts of domestic violence by their abusers. This is understandable given the eventual near-fatal outcomes. This does not mean that the same outcome would not have occurred without prior prosecution, however. The victims' ambivalence about prosecution was not based on feeling protective of their abusers but rather on their not knowing whether it would further antagonize them or "scare him off," as one victim put it. The vast majority of the women who had never previously used the court system believed that to do so would place them in grave danger. One of these women, Angela, said, "That would have been my death sentence." Only one of these women said she had not sought to have her abusive partner prosecuted because she did not wish to get him in trouble. This woman, Sylvie, married her abusive partner after he had been sentenced and incarcerated for attempting to kill her.

For the vast majority of victims, their ambivalence about using the courts appeared rational, given the level of danger they faced. Their reluctance to use the courts was based on practical considerations such as whether their abusers would be free awaiting trial, whether they would be convicted, and if so, whether they would receive short prison terms. Only one of the perpetrators who had been previously prosecuted for domestic violence had received a prison sentence. He was the only man who was held awaiting his trial. He was also the only man required to attend a dangerousness hearing. The nine others received minimal to moderate bail. It should be noted that in Massachusetts, as in many states, bail amounts are based primarily on the defendant's risk of flight rather than his dangerousness, unless a dangerousness hearing is held. Recently, some jurisdictions and states have required all defendants who are arraigned for domestic violence to undergo a dangerousness assessment as a first step to determining their pretrial dispositions.

In contrast to their ambivalence regarding prior prosecutions of their abusers, the victims overwhelmingly felt safer following their abusers' convictions of attempted homicide. For the most part, this was because their abusers had received prison terms that ranged from five to twenty years. Despite this, most of the victims continued to be fearful of their abusers, especially those who had received shorter prison terms. Overwhelmingly, though, victims felt that the incarcerations of their former partners had bought them the time and the space to plan for their own and their children's safety. Nearly all had filed for divorce, for instance, and had obtained permanent protective orders.

Judges

As previously mentioned, 70% of the victims had previously obtained protective orders against their abusers. For half of these women, these orders were still in place when the homicide attempts occurred. Sufficient data was available to analyze twenty-one of these occasions when victims had obtained a court protective order. Table 8.4 summarizes these findings. Similar to their perceptions about the effects of prior prosecutions, victims were divided about whether these protective orders had made things better or worse. Just under half of the women felt that the protective orders had made things worse by further antagonizing their abusers, while one-quarter felt that they had had no effect. Most of the latter group explained that their abusers were already enraged at them to begin with and the existence of the protective orders did not significantly add to that. Just under a third of the women felt that the protective orders had helped, even if only to give them more time to think about their safety outside of their abusers' daily presence. Those who said that the protective orders did not help were not so lucky. For the most part, their abusers continually violated the orders and escalated their abuse. As with their opinions of police officers and prosecutors, the victims' perceptions about judges were mixed. In all but one case, the judges issued the protective orders that the women had sought. Despite this, just over half of the victims said that the judge had not done everything that they wanted. In half these cases, what the victim wanted was something that appeared to be beyond the authority of the judge. The most common example of this was victims who wanted the judge to "lock him up," or "put him away," as stated by several of the women. Massachusetts laws do not afford judges the ability to sentence perpetrators of domestic violence during protective order hearings, since these are civil orders that do involve charges for a specific crime. Only when a defendant is found guilty of violating a protective order does a judge have the ability to sentence him. However, about half of the victims who said they did not get what they wanted from the judge complained about things that were within the power of the judge to grant. Most common among these were more specific conditions of the protective order that the judge issued.

Erika said that the judge who granted the protective order that required her husband, Lyle, to stay away from her and their daughter "was great overall" but wished that the protective order had specified that he must not come within 100 yards of her. She reported that a subsequent charge that Lyle had violated this order by being in her driveway and by showing up at her workplace was dismissed since the protective order had not given a specific distance within which Lyle was to avoid. As a result, Erika said, "Lyle felt immune."

Mindy complained that the judge did not restrict her ex-husband, Roger, from having contact with their daughter, despite the fact that he had once abducted the daughter when a previous protective order had forbidden his contact with the daughter. On another prior occasion, Roger grabbed the daughter out of her arms in front of the police after assaulting Mindy. Despite these prior infractions, the judge allowed Roger to have unsupervised visits with his daughter twice a week, and even granted that

Table 8.4: Victims' evaluations of judge actions in protective order proceedings that preceded the act of attempted homicide

Judge action and/or impact	Percent of victims who said "yes"
Granted a temporary protective order	95
Did everything the victim wanted	47
Referred victim to community services	33*
Helped victim with a safety plan	19*
Victim said intervention made situation worse	47
Victim said intervention made situation better	28
Victim said intervention had no effect	23
N=21	

* In most cases, a court or community-based victim advocate provided this assistance, according to the victims.

Roger could have telephone contact with Mindy in order to arrange these visits.

While granting her request for a protective order, Elizabeth was disappointed that the judge did not explain the specific conditions of this order to her estranged husband, Mark. Mark had continually stalked Elizabeth in the months leading up to her decision to seek this order and she had written about these specific incidents in her affidavit. Mark's stalking of Elizabeth continued after the order was granted. Elizabeth noted that Mark would "just show up everywhere I was and claim that it was an accident." She added that it would have been helpful for the judge to explain to Mark that even "accidental contact" was forbidden. Mark's stalking of Elizabeth eventually culminated in his firing seven shots into her car from his car.

Next to their issuing orders that were not specific enough, the most common complaint by victims about judges was their being rude or dismissive. Two victims complained about being "scolded" by the judge who issued their restraining orders. One of these women, Angela, said that the judge "told me this [her boyfriend's violence] wouldn't have happened if you'd go home with your family [her parents] like you're supposed to." The other woman, Amy, said that the judge told her that he would grant the order but told her, "I don't want to see you here again." She said that she took this to mean that the judge would not grant any future orders.

In contrast, almost half of the victims had no complaints about the judges who issued protective orders, and several of these women said they were "satisfied" with the judge's actions. In particular, victims praised judges who took pains to explain the specific conditions of protective orders to the defendants, as well as the consequences of violating these orders. None of the victims who said that the protective orders made their situations better had complaints about the judges who issued them. In fact, several of these women said they felt the judges showed concern for their safety and well-being. As examples of this, victims cited the following specific statements made by judges:

"I will put him away if he hurts you again."
"Please call the police if you see him, even if you think he's not intending to harass you."
"I don't think he's ever going to stop looking for you." [The victim also recalls that the judge advised her to seek emergency shelter or to leave the state.]
"He's very dangerous. I'd sleep a little better if you'd talk to Ginny [the court advocate] here."

Medical Centers

The victims of attempted homicide had sustained an alarming number of past injuries. These are summarized in Tables 8.5 and 8.6. Thirty percent of the women reported that they had sustained a broken bone. Four of these six women revealed that their abusers had broken one of their bones on at least four separate occasions.

Table 8.5: Victims' past injuries due to prior acts of domestic violence

Type of injury sustained	Percent of women who said "yes"
Broken bone	30
Concussion or being knocked out	55
Cut or contusion	80
Visible bruise	90
N=20	

Table 8.6: Frequency of victims' injuries due to prior acts of domestic violence (in percentages)

	Frequency of minor injuries (bruises)	Frequency of more serious injuries (such as broken bone or contusion)
Daily	15	0
Weekly	30	15
Monthly	40	40
Yearly	10	35
Less than yearly	5	10
N=20		

Angela reported that she had sustained ten broken bones, and had sought medical help for domestic violence-related injuries on sixty-one different occasions. Besides the broken bones, these injuries had included at least twenty contusions and lacerations that required sutures (including two stab wounds), twelve concussions, five cigarette burns, at least thirty different injuries to her genitals, and two miscarriages. On nearly every medical visit, her boyfriend and pimp, Robert, had accompanied Angela.

Nearly two-thirds of the victims had sought medical help for injuries due to domestic violence that had occurred prior to the homicide attempt. Twelve of the twenty women had seen a doctor for injuries that ranged from contusions to broken bones to concussions. However, the true proportion of women who needed medical treatment was higher than this. Three additional women said that they had sustained serious injuries for which they did not seek treatment. All three said the reason for avoiding medical care was that they assumed the clinics would call the police and that this might trigger retribution from their abusers. For example, even those who had sought treatment at least once said there were other times when they had not done so for injuries that warranted treatment. Erika told her doctor that she had broken her wrist by falling down the front steps of her home rather than reveal that this injury had been caused by her husband grabbing and twisting her arm and yanking it behind her back.

To better understand women's past experiences with health care, we asked detailed questions about particular past visits to a doctor. This data is summarized in Table 8.7.

Generally, victims said they were warned about dangerousness and referred to victim services when the doctor or nurse had been told that their injuries were caused by domestic violence. This would be in keeping with protocols maintained by most medical clinics or hospitals since the mid- to late 1980s. Prior to this, clinics had not been required to proactively screen for domestic violence among patients with suspicious injuries. In the early 1990s, the Joint Commission for the Accreditation of Health Care Organizations (JCAHCO) formulated federal guidelines that required clinics and hospitals to establish protocols for the screening of domestic violence. Not coincidentally, the victims who sought medical help during the 1990s were more likely to have been asked about domestic violence compared to those who sought treatment prior to this. Another factor that appeared to influence women's decisions to reveal the causes of their injuries was whether they had already left their abusers. In all seven instances when the couple was separated, the victim revealed the true causes of her injuries. Conversely, women who were still living with their abusers were least likely to seek medical treatment or to reveal the true causes of their injuries when they did seek treatment. Five of the women said that one reason for this was that their abusers had brought them to the clinics and remained at the facilities while treatment was being provided.

Table 8.7: Women's past experiences with health care visits (in percentages)

Victim or clinic action	Yes	No	Can't recall
Victim was asked whether her injuries were due to domestic violence	57	36	5
Victim told doctor/nurse that her injury was due to domestic violence	52*	47	0
Victim was warned about danger	52	31	17
Victim was referred to victim advocacy services	31	57	10
N=19			

* In these instances, the victim volunteered this information without being asked, or told the doctor or nurse in response to being asked.

Several of the killers that I interviewed admitted that they had monitored their partners' interactions with medical staff.

Andrew admitted that he had coached his girlfriend, Roberta, to say that her injuries were due to a car accident. Technically, Roberta told her doctor the truth since her injuries were in fact the result of a car accident. However, this was not the whole truth: Andrew had pushed her over a wall onto a highway where she had been struck by a passing car.

Another killer, Louis, said that he had once punched his girlfriend, Pamela, in the face and bludgeoned her over the head with a lead pipe until she lost consciousness. He had then called an ambulance and followed it to the hospital. After Pamela had been revived in the emergency room, Louis had warned her to tell the doctor that she had fallen down some stairs. Not believing her, the ER staff had wanted to call the police. But with Louis hovering nearby, Pamela had convinced them not to do so, saying that her parents had offered to let her stay with them. After receiving multiple stitches and staples for her lacerations, however, Pamela had been released that evening and Louis had driven her home. Less than three months later, Louis killed Pamela in a cemetery where they had been drinking by hitting her in the head with a large rock.

This incident occurred in 1994, and of course there is no way of knowing whether the ER staff in this particular rural hospital would have responded differently had it occurred more recently. Other than requiring hospitals and clinics to establish safety measures for victims of domestic violence, JCAHCO guidelines do not specify best practices for protecting victims of abuse from their suspected abusers. Some clinics require suspected abusers to remain outside of the ER, for instance, but this is not routinely done, especially if the victim does not explicitly object to his presence.[5] As mentioned earlier, one reason that victims gave for not disclosing the true causes of the injuries to their doctors was their assumption that such disclosures would automatically result in the police being summoned. In fact, there is no requirement that clinics notify police to report domestic violence, unless the violence is occurring on the institutional premises or the suspected abuser is otherwise being disruptive. Larger medical clinics have domestic violence specialists on staff with whom doctors and nurses can consult about suspected domestic violence cases. These specialists are available to meet with victims to identify their safety concerns, provide short-term advocacy and counseling, and refer them to community services such as shelters for battered women, support groups, legal advocacy, and counseling. Domestic violence specialists are also responsible for training other hospital personnel on how to identify and sensitively respond to domestic violence cases.

The wide range of domestic violence related injuries that victims experience mean that they come in contact with a wide range of medical specialists. These include surgeons, anesthesiologists, radiologists, ER doctors, gynecologists, pediatricians, pain specialists, ophthalmologists, chiropractors, psychiatrists, and dentists. Therefore, domestic violence training in health care settings, once limited to ER staff, has increasingly been extended to specialists as well as to all direct care providers. Almost half of the victims we interviewed said that they had sustained eye injuries due to being punched or hit with an object and therefore seen an ophthalmologist. One woman said that, on two different occasions, her abuser had fractured bones in the orbits around one of her eyes. Five women had required dental care due to damage to their teeth from being punched, knocked into something, or hit with an object. Several women talked about damage to their genitals. Two women had miscarried babies due to injuries sustained while they were pregnant.

Battered Women's Programs

More than three-quarters (80%) of the victims of attempted homicide had sought the services of a battered women's program. Half of these women, however, had only contacted such a program following the attempts on their lives. Eight victims said they had previously called a battered women's program. Only one woman had sought emergency shelter at the program. Despite this, six of the women who had sought help from a battered women's program credited the program with providing her with useful information and support. For three women, this primarily consisted of having an advocate who went to court with her to obtain a protective order or to file criminal charges. Two additional women said they had been referred to a lawyer who specialized in domestic violence cases. Both of these women had filed for divorce after the homicide attempts. Six of the eight women who had contacted a battered women's program said that someone at the program had talked with them about their safety. The other two women said that they had only spoken with the program once or twice over the phone and had declined to see a victim advocate in person. One of these women said this was because she had reconciled with her husband. The other said she did not feel that she needed their help after she had left her husband. We asked women who had not previously called a battered women's program why they had not done so. Their responses are summarized in Table 8.8.

Five of the women said that they had mistakenly assumed that battered women's programs are primarily for women who require emergency shelter. For the most part, these women said that they wanted to remain in their own homes. All five had obtained at least one protective order prior to the attempted homicide that had required their abusive partner to vacate the home. For three of the women, these orders were still in effect when the homicide attempts occurred. Three women said that they had not believed that an emergency shelter would have made them any safer.

Children were prominent factors in women's decisions about seeking or not seeking emergency shelter. The most commonly cited reason for not seeking shelter was that women did not want to uproot their children from their communities and their schools. Some women said they sought a more permanent solution than what an emergency shelter could pro-

Table 8.8: Reasons why victims had not sought services from a battered women's program

Reasons given	Percent who cited this as a reason*
Did not want children to live in shelter	66
Did not wish to quit her job	66
Felt that she did not need it (because she was taking other steps)	55
Did not know that nonemergency services were available	55
Felt too embarrassed or ashamed	44
Felt that she was not in danger	33
Did not wish to leave her abuser	33
Feared that she might lose custody of her children	33
Did not want children to not see their father	33
N=9	

* Six of the women gave more than one reason.

vide. Typically, battered women's programs provide emergency shelter for periods ranging from thirty days to six months. Though some programs provide assistance in finding longer-term housing, some women said they were unaware of this or skeptical that affordable housing was available. One woman had been on a waiting list for subsidized housing for one year when the homicide attempt occurred. Other women said they were making their own efforts to find long-term housing, and several had already done so. Two women had relocated and were living with their children and their new partners. In both cases, their ex-partners continued to have legal contact with the children.

Some women said that depriving their children of contact with their fathers was also a factor in their not seeking emergency shelter. Over half of the mothers said that they wanted their children to continue to have contact with their fathers, if it could be done in a way that did not put them or their children at risk. Some said that, although they had reservations about their abusers having continued contact with the children, they believed the men's violence would become worse if they were denied such contact outright.

Besides not wanting to disrupt their children's lives, another common reason victims gave for not seeking emergency shelter was that it would have disrupted their own lives in major ways. A number of the women said that they did not wish to leave their jobs, for instance. Other women said that they did not want to relocate and felt safer and more secure in their own communities.

Virginia said, "It was where my family and my friends was and they was always looking out for me. If I had to pick up and leave, me and the kids would have just been in a strange place with no one. . . . And I knew I would always be looking over my shoulder expecting him to show up, so no, that wouldn't have been good for me or them."

Counselors

Just under half of the victims had spoken with a therapist at least once prior to the homicide attempt. The number of counseling sessions attended by these nine women ranged from once or twice to weekly counseling that had extended over several years. Five of the women were still seeing a counselor at the time that the homicide attempt occurred. For the most part, these women were not seeking therapy because of domestic violence but for other problems such as depression or anxiety. Three women sought therapy after making suicide attempts. In retrospect, most of the women acknowledged that the problems for which they were seeking therapy were caused or greatly exacerbated by domestic violence. Despite this, not all of the women revealed to their therapists that they were victims of abuse. Six of the nine women said that they revealed domestic violence to their therapists. However, two of these women said that they minimized the extent of the abuse. In both of these cases, the women attended couples counseling with their abusers while alternately attending individual sessions with the same therapist. Each woman said that she only disclosed to the therapist her husband's verbal or emotional abuse, such as yelling or criticism or infidelity. She did not disclose his physical abuse for fear that this would provoke retribution.

Carol said, "I guess I was half hoping he [the couples counselor] would read between the lines and talk to him [her abusive husband]—you know, man to man—but I didn't have to guts to say what was really happening. I think he was pretty shocked by what happened [the homicide attempt]."

Therapists who see battered women face two major challenges. The first is to identify the domestic violence while the second is to provide useful interventions for it. Some researchers who have investigated mental health responses to domestic violence have noted that many therapists fail to assess adequately for abuse among their clients, particularly those who do not self-identify as victims or perpetrators.[6] This often reflects a lack of specific training in domestic violence. Only in recent years have graduate programs for social workers, psychologists, and counselors included coursework on domestic violence. This coursework has emphasized the importance of proactive screening for domestic violence for all clients. Effective screening protocols include looking for common effects of abuse such as depression, suicidality, anxiety, substance abuse, and post-traumatic stress disorder.[7]

Three of the victims of attempted homicide said that they had been psychiatrically hospitalized at least once during their relationship with their abusive partner. In all three cases, the women admitted themselves or were admitted to the hospital following a suicide attempt. While two of the women revealed that they were victims of abuse, neither received any referrals to battered women's programs during or following their release. Instead, both women were advised to leave their abusive partners and to call the police if new acts of violence should occur. One woman who told her psychiatrist that her husband was beating her was referred to an Alcohol Anonymous group as well as a community mental health center for outpatient therapy.

All told, only three of the six women who disclosed abuse to their therapists said that they were given referrals to programs for battered women. All three of these women followed through with these referrals and credited both their therapists and the battered women's programs with helping to make them safer. Each of these women felt that her therapist cared about her safety and well-being. Of her therapist, April said, "She said she was worried about me and that made me worry about myself more. 'Cause at that point, I guess I had given up a little bit and Esther [her therapist] motivated me and gave me hope to keep trying."

Interestingly, few of the victims of attempted homicide said that they had blamed themselves for their abusive partner's violence. This may be because the violence they experienced was so frequent and severe. I've found that victims of less severe violence sometimes mistakenly blame themselves to some degree or feel that they bear some responsibility for problems in the relationship. This reflects the manipulation skills of many abusers who are able to successfully assign blame or responsibility to their partners. When the abuse is more severe, however, the victims seem less ambivalent about who is responsible. Severe abusers appear to provoke more of a "he's just crazy" or "he's just bad" response from their victims.

Clergy

Half of the victims said that they regularly or occasionally attended religious services at a church, synagogue, or temple. Table 8.9 summarizes the religious affiliation and participation of these women. Even though half of the women were still regular or occasional members of their houses of worship, only three of the women (15%) said that they had ever sought clerical help because of domestic violence, and one did so following the attempted homicide.[8]

Mindy approached her priest following her divorce to ask for his blessing and was told, "You did the right thing," in ending the relationship.

Patricia did not tell her priest about the domestic violence that she was experiencing but talked generally of "problems in the family," and asked him if he would talk to her husband and her. Though the priest was agreeable, her husband, Winston, refused to see the priest.

Monica told her priest about her husband's violence. His only response that she could recall was to ask if she had sought help.

We did not ask the remaining seventeen women their reasons for not seeking clerical help. Two women, however, volunteered that they did not think that their priest or pastor would have been responsive or helpful. One said that her pastor was "very traditional about men and women . . . and he probably would have told me to just pray more."

Carolina said that her priest was "dead set against divorce." Asked if it would matter to her priest that she was being battered, she said, "Oh no, that wouldn't have mattered." She added that her husband was well-regarded within their church and that they "were shocked at what he did" (referring to her husband's attempt to kill her). Carolina went on to say that she had left her church after finding that no one had reached out to her following this. Carolina had remained loyal to her faith, however, and subsequently joined another church that she found to be more understanding about domestic violence.

Table 8.9: Religious affiliations of the victims of attempted homicide

Religious denomination	Percent who were raised in this denomination	Percent who still participated*
Catholic	55	30
Protestant	30	15
Jewish	5	5
Buddhist	5	0
None	5	5
Total	100	50
N=20		

* This is the percent of victims who were still regularly or occasionally attending religious services of this denomination while still involved with their abusive partner.

Family

Not surprisingly, victims were more likely to have sought help from their own relatives than from any other source. Eighty-three percent of the victims said that one or more of their relatives knew about the domestic violence. Half of these women said that a relative had witnessed their partners being violent toward them. Three-quarters of the women said they had asked for assistance from a relative at least once during their relationships with their abusive partners. Victims typically asked their siblings and/or parents for help. Overwhelmingly, victims reported that relatives had responded positively to their pleas and had provided at least one type of help. The most common form of assistance cited by the victims was that a relative let them stay at their house for a period of time. One-third of the victims said they had received this kind of help prior to the homicide attempt and one-half afterwards. One woman said that she had been staying with her sister for four months when her estranged partner tried to kill her. Another said she had stayed with her parents off and on for two years leading up to the near-fatal assault. All told, five women had been staying with relatives when the homicide attempts occurred.

By providing temporary housing, some relatives had put themselves at risk. By the victims' accounts, the majority of the relatives who had provided such refuge (83%) were threatened by the abusers. This compares to 22% of the relatives who had not provided refuge.

Lynette said that her abuser, William, would call and threaten to kill her parents every day when she was staying with them. William would also threaten to Lynette that he would burn her parents' house down. Fearful that he would make good on this, Lynette returned to William shortly before his final assault on her when he held her and the children hostage and tried to kill her. Besides her parents, William also held a vendetta against Lynette's brother, Vincent, for assisting Lynette and for threatening him. Just prior to the homicide attempt, William had demanded that Lynette call Vincent over to their house so he could ambush him. When Lynette refused, William began bludgeoning her with the bat.

Lynette's brother was one of five relatives of the victims who had threatened the abuser or physically intervened in some manner, usually in response to witnessing an act of abuse. In three of these cases, the abuser subsequently threatened to kill the relative. Several victims said that they had pleaded with family members not to intervene for fear that their abusers would retaliate against them and/or the intervening relatives. Most of the victims said that their fear of retribution had led them to curtail contact with relatives. Reinforcing this fear, half said that their abusers had forbidden contact with particular relatives. Three victims said that such injunctions and threats had been stated on a daily basis, while six additional women said their abusers had stated them every week or every month.

Some victims said that they had avoided contact with certain relatives because of their abusive partners' threats. Others said that they had maintained contact with relatives but did not disclose the violence they were experiencing. All but two of the victims said that they had not reported some acts of violence to their relatives. Some victims said this was for fear that relatives might respond in a manner that would further antagonize their abusers. Victims also said that they had downplayed the violence to avoid worrying their relatives. Some also said that they had denied or minimized the violence out of embarrassment or shame. Three victims said that they never told a relative that they were in an abusive relationship. Two of these women said that they were estranged from their parents and therefore would not have turned to them for help in any event. The third woman said that she believed her parents "would have just blamed me for everything." She went on to say that even after her abuser's arrest for attempted homicide, her parents "didn't believe me" and continued to defend her husband.

Five women who had told relatives about the violence complained that the relatives' only response was to tell them to "leave him" or to "call the police." Most of these women said that they felt that their relatives were "blaming" or "judgmental" towards them, either for choosing an abusive partner or remaining with him. One woman, Kay, complained that her mother had threatened to go to court to seek custody of her two children "if I didn't leave him [her abuser]." Kay went on to say that she felt more support from her abuser's family than from her own. A few women said that their relatives had sided with their abusive partners.

Two days before Wilberto tried to kill her, Annabel had fled him to stay with her mother, Maria. Even knowing about Wilberto's prior acts of severe violence toward Annabel, however, Maria had told Annabel, "Your place is with your husband" and refused to take her in. She had reminded Annabel that no one in their family had ever gotten a divorce and that "divorce is a sin in the eyes of God." Maria had called Wilberto on the phone and insisted that Annabel talk with him. At Maria's invitation, Wilberto had then come over and convinced Annabel to give him another chance.

In contrast, many of the victims said that the emotional support that they had received from parents or siblings had helped to comfort and sustain them during their abusive relationships. One woman, April, said that even though her mother could do little to keep her safe, "she helped to keep me sane." April also said that her mother had taken her children for extended periods and that this had helped to keep them out of the line of fire from their father. Altogether, five mothers said that they had left their children with relatives for periods of time that ranged from one overnight to several months. One woman said it had been particularly helpful to have this kind of refuge for her children when she was in the hospital for several days after her husband had broken her jaw. Another woman said that she could often count on her mother or sister to take the children during the many times that she went to court to obtain a protective order or to file charges against her estranged partner. Twelve women said that they had received money from relatives. One woman said that this money had enabled her to pay for her lawyer during her divorce proceedings. Two said that they had received money from relatives to put deposits on a new apartment. Over half of women said that they had relied upon relatives for transportation.

Abuser's Relatives

A surprising source of help for some of the victims was relatives of their abusive partners. Seven women (35%) said they had received some form of assistance from one of the men's relatives. Compared to that provided by their own relatives, this help tended to be more short-lived, and was more often counteracted by hostile and otherwise hurtful responses. Two-fifths of the victims said that they had appealed for help from their abusers' relatives, usually one or more of their partners' parents. Two women had stayed with the abusers' parents while separated from their abusers. One of these women said that she felt it was safer to stay with his parents than with her own since her abuser was on good terms with his parents and was more likely to heed their advice to stay away. The other said that his parents were more supportive than her own parents who had not offered such assistance. Four women had let their children stay with their abusers' parents during periods of estrangement from the abusers.

Two women reported that their abusive partners' parents had warned them about his violence toward previous partners. One of these women said that this warning had come before she was married to her husband and that she had not believed them. The other woman, Amy, said that Carmen's parents had told her that "Carmen has always been violent." Amy credited Carmen's parents with being very supportive, even after she left Carmen for another man. She said that his parents had often offered to let her stay at their house after Carmen had been violent toward her. She added that Carmen's father and brother had "pulled him off of me a couple of times" when Carmen was beating her and had often urged Carmen to get help for his violence.

Five victims said that one or more of their abusers' relatives had intervened to protect them while they were being attacked. In four cases, victims said that the relatives had physically intervened by separating the victim from the abuser. The most dramatic intervention took place when Sylvie's brother came to blows with Edgar when he was hitting Sylvie. This fight resulted in injuries to both men, including a broken leg for Sylvie's brother.

Rather than intervening, however, abusers' relatives were more likely to do nothing or to blame them, according to the women. In half these cases when violence was witnessed, victims said that his relatives ignored it. Annabel reported that Wilberto's parents first witnessed his violence toward her at a bar when the couple was still dating. Enraged after finding out that Annabel had spoken with another man, Wilberto slapped her several times in the face. Annabel said that "I kept expecting his folks to say something or do something but they didn't. They just went into another room and never did anything."

Lydia said that Albert's "whole family" once observed him slapping her at a family gathering. Though one guest pulled Albert off her and told him to "calm down," Albert's father and brother later blamed Lydia for embarrassing him in front of his family.

After witnessing her son, Roger, assault Mindy at a family party, Roger's mother approached Mindy in private to advise her, "Never complain about Roger, that just makes him madder." She went on to advise Mindy to "take better care of him sexually."

Some victims said there was a price to be paid for any assistance provided by their abusers' parents. While sometimes chastising their sons for violence, for instance, some parents also sought to discourage the victims from ending the relationships. Some victims also complained that even while acknowledging their sons' violence, the parents had conspired with them to seek custody or guardianship of the grandchildren.

Dolores said that she was initially relieved that Elston's mother would offer to take care of their two-year old son when the couple was separated. Following the couple's final separation, however, Elston's mother sought legal custody of her grandson, claiming that Dolores was an unfit mother. According to Dolores, she also claimed never to have seen Elston be violent to Dolores, even though she had witnessed it on numerous occasions.

Neighbors

While victims were not inclined to ask their neighbors for help, neighbors were a resource nonetheless. Three victims credited neighbors with saving their lives.

Conrad attacked Lucy in her kitchen while she was cooking with a crock-pot. He forced her head into the crock-pot, badly burning her face and neck. Conrad then began grinding Lucy's head into the shards of crock-pot on the floor and banging her head into the floor. Overhearing the racket, Lucy's next-door neighbor, Jim, burst in and pulled Conrad off Lucy. Conrad then attacked Jim, but this diversion gave Lucy time to call the police. Conrad was subsequently convicted of assault with intent to murder.

Annabel is the woman whose mother, Maria, had convinced her to go back to her husband, Wilberto. On the day of her return home, Wilberto was furious that Annabel had left him. He demanded to know why she had not come when he had summoned her two days earlier. When she did not answer, he told her, "Now I must kill you." He knocked Annabel down with several punches and then began kicking her in the head and hitting her head with a metal fan. Annabel said that at this point she "heard a voice that told me to play dead." As she lay still, trying not to breathe, Annabel felt Wilberto feeling for her breath. Finding one, he continued kicking and hitting her head with the fan, stopping only when he apparently thought he had finished her off. Annabel waited until she could not hear anything and then began to get up, thinking that Wilberto had left. Still watching her, however, Wilberto resumed his assault, even continuing when their three-year-old daughter, Michelle, begged him to stop. Michelle ran out of the house calling for help. A female neighbor came in and yelled at Wilberto, "Stop! Stop! Don't you think she has had enough?" Wilberto stopped and left the house. He was arrested one hour later.

In both of these cases, the victim had had little prior contact with the intervening neighbor and had not previously sought help from this person. These particular neighbors just happened to be in the right place at the right time to help the victim. To their credit, these neighbors were willing to become involved, and to put themselves at risk in doing so. Judging from all the victims' accounts, neighbors were evenly split in their willingness to become involved. Six victims reported that one or more of their neighbors had "ignored" a prior act of violence by their abusers that the neighbors had witnessed or overheard. In contrast, seven other victims said that neighbors had called the police to report prior acts of violence. In half of these cases, the victim had previously asked for help from the neighbor. In these cases, neighbors were acting at the behest of the victim in calling the police. In other cases, however, neighbors called police without knowing the victims' wishes. Two victims said that they believed that their neighbors had called the police not out of any concern for the victim's well-being but rather because they were bothered by the noise. These kinds of calls to police are sometimes referred to as "disturbing the peace" calls. Prior to domestic violence pro-arrest policies in the early- to mid-1980s, police used to make arrests primarily only when neighbors made such complaints.[9] Alleged abusers in these cases, especially those judged to be intoxicated, were often not formally charged with a crime but simply held for the night in protective custody so that they could "sleep it off."

Most victims did not ask for help from neighbors. Their reasons included not knowing or trusting their neighbors enough to ask for help, not wanting neighbors to know about their problems, and believing that the neighbors would take their abusers' side. Three victims who said that their abusive partners were well-liked by the neighbors cited this last factor. One woman said, "They thought he was a darling. He was always plowing their driveways and helping to move things and whatnot."

Table 8.10: Kinds of help provided by neighbors to victims

Type of help provided	Percent of victims who received this
Called the police	35
Let her use phone to call police or other services	30
Provided transportation	30
Gave support or advice	30
Watched the children	25
Testified in court	20
Let her stay overnight	10
Loaned or gave money	10
Accompanied her to court	10
N=20	

For the most part, victims who had asked neighbors for help were satisfied with the response. This may be because victims were discerning about whom to ask, only asking those who they already knew or strongly believed would be helpful or sensitive to their situation. For instance, some victims asked for help only from neighbors who had reached out to them with offers of help. One victim said that she sought help from a particular neighbor who had a reputation for helping other women in the neighborhood. Table 8.10 summarizes the kinds of help provided by neighbors.

Friends

Next to their relatives, victims were most likely to have sought help from friends.[10] Three-quarters of the women said they had asked for help from at least one friend. The kind of help given was similar to that provided by relatives. Victims had turned to their friends for support and advice but also for more concrete things like transportation, money, and childcare. About one-quarter of the women had also stayed at a friend's house prior to their final breaks from their abusers. The duration of these separations ranged from one night to several weeks. Victims reported that these times not only provided a refuge from their abusers but also a time to consider their options in a more calm atmosphere—"without him hovering all over me" as one woman put it. By providing this refuge, however, some friends of the victims put themselves in the line of fire from the abusers. Several victims reported that their abusers had physically assaulted friends with whom they were staying.

Dolores was previously cited as the woman whose husband, Ellston, broke into the apartment of her friend, Brenda, to abduct Dolores and rape her in his car. While he was dragging Dolores down the stairs to his car, Ellston punched Brenda in the jaw when she attempted to intervene. Ellston also told Brenda, "It's not your business, bitch. I'll kill you if you come between us again."

Cheryl was still living with Rodney when he attacked her with a hot iron, severely burning her in the face. Five months previously, Cheryl had left Rodney and was staying at her friend Janina's house. On her first night there, Rodney broke down Janina's door and then slapped Janina several times in the face when she tried to prevent him from abducting Cheryl. While hitting Janina, Rodney kept yelling at her, "You're going to get yourself killed, bitch." Rodney then pushed Cheryl down the stairs and forced her into his car. Cheryl reported that she avoided any contact with Janina following this incident for fear that Rodney would make good on his threat to kill her.

Cheryl and Dolores were two of the five victims who reported that their abusive partners had physically assaulted a friend in response to the friend coming to their assistance. All five women said that they had subsequently curtailed or avoided contact with these friends out of concern for the friends' safety. Three additional women said that they had never sought help from a friend for the same reason. In all cases, these women were not only protecting their friends but also themselves. Nearly all of the victims said that they had become more socially isolated during their relationships with their abusive partners.

Nearly all the victims said that they had been advised by at least one friend to leave their abusive partners. In about half the cases, victims said that this advice had not been accompanied by any offers of help. For the most part, these victims felt that these friends were critical of them for remaining with their abusive partner. Discussing one such friend, Virginia said, "She said I was crazy [to stay with him] and I must have a 'death wish' or something." A smaller number of victims said they had friends who were critical of them for leaving their abusive partner. Carolina, for instance, appreciated that her friend, Roxie, would often come over to cook for her. One time, Roxie let Carolina and her children stay with her while she was separated from Angel. It was during this time, however, that Roxie told Carolina that she was "lucky to have such a good man who loves you and provides for you."

In contrast, most of the victims said that they were satisfied with the help they had received from friends. About one-third of the women credited friends for giving them the strength or the support to leave their abusers. Wanda talked of a friend, Trina, who would "tell me I'm a good person, regardless," adding that Trina "kind of helped me to go on when I was feeling real low. She would come over and cook for me, whatever I needed." Wanda said that Trina also gave her contact information for a battered women's program and a legal advocacy program for low-income women. Summing up her feelings about Trina, Wanda said, "I know she was worried for me and kind of frustrated that she couldn't do more but she was helping me a lot. She kind of kept me feeling sane for awhile when I was so low. And I wouldn't have never called [the emergency shelter program] if it wasn't for her. She understood on account of what she went through with her ex, and that gave me courage." Though Trina's help didn't prevent Wanda's partner, George, from trying to kill her, Wanda did credit Trina with keeping her from killing herself. "I was ready to give up and Trina would just keep telling me that my children love me and God loves me. God didn't want me to go and she was God's angel."

9 | **Conclusions and Recommendations**

No previous study has so painstakingly examined the lives of men who kill their partners. Moving backwards from the murders they committed through their relationship histories and their childhoods, I sought to understand what motivates them to kill. Embedded in their histories, I found strong patterns in how these men sought to establish and maintain relationships. These patterns reveal that, for the most part, the murders they committed were neither random nor spontaneous. These killings were triggered as much by long-term factors in the men's histories as they were by the immediate situation. The history of these crimes is one in which these men become increasingly predisposed to kill.

I saw no strong predictors in the men's upbringings that they would grow up to murder their partners. There were, however, strong omens of their future violence. In most cases, their upbringings seemed indistinguishable from those of other abusive men I've counseled. As with most abusive men, the seeds for their abusive behavior had been planted by abusive fathers, and in some cases, abusive mothers. The intergenerational roots to domestic violence have been well established by prior research. It appears that early exposure to domestic violence by one's father provides a powerful role modeling for boys, though clearly many men do not follow this example as adults. The men's behavior in intimate relationships is mediated by a variety of other influences in their lives, and is further influenced by their own personalities. Depending on these other factors, early exposure to domestic violence can become a negative or a positive example over time. I have known of many men who grew up with abusive fathers who ultimately recognized the negative example and followed a different path. In contrast, some of the killers I interviewed talked of coming to admire or love the fathers that they once feared. These men said that they had conquered their fear by developing an aggressive and tough exterior.

Other researchers have suggested that boys exposed to domestic violence are more likely to be attracted to and influenced by violent social peers.[1] Many of the killers in this study, particularly the substance abusers and career criminals, said that most of their peers were also violent toward their partners. Some of the killers admitted sharing a contempt of women with their male friends. Disdain for women was strongly evident among many of the killers, particularly the materially motivated men and the career criminals. Even more prevalent among the killers, especially the jealous ones, was a strong distrust of women. For the most part, this distrust seemed only to increase over time and to inspire increasing levels of surveillance and violence. This distrust could well have its origin in family upbringings. Experts on children who are exposed to family violence say that one common effect of such exposure is the development of insecurity and anxiety about intimacy.[2] This in turn can lead to difficulty establishing relationships that rely upon intimacy and trust. Most of the jealous killers appeared to have been perpetually vigilant toward their intimate partners, and this only seemed to escalate over the course of their relationships.

It appears that intimate partner femicides are the end result of an interaction between the perpetrator and the victim. From the victim's perspective, there were fairly clear turning points in the relationship. These began with the first appearance of violence and the abuser's initial apologies and promises that it would not happen again. This was followed by the reappearance of violence. By this stage, many perpetrators had stopped apologizing for their violence and instead began blaming their victims. In response, many victims expressed dissatisfaction and talked of ending the relationships. This seemed to trigger increased monitoring, and particularly for the jealous types of perpetrators, stalking of the victim. And while most victims had already been subjected to rape and sexual humiliation prior to separation, some said that this became more severe afterwards. Some women recounted incidents during which they had been sexually or physically assaulted in public. For the perpetrator, committing violence in public not only served to reassert ownership claims on his partner, but also to scare off her potential helpers. Besides escalating their violence, most perpetrators began to make more frequent and explicit threats to kill their partners, and often her children, relatives, and friends as well. The threats appeared to serve two functions for the perpetrator. One was to deter his partner from taking actions such as ending the relationship or seeking custody of the children. The second function of making threats was to embolden himself, or as one killer put it, "to psych myself up." Disclosing one's wishes or fantasies to others is often a key step toward committing oneself to action. Career counselors, for instance, often recommend this as a first step toward changing jobs or careers. Many people say that once they communicate their nascent plans to others, they are more likely to carry them out since to not do so would potentially disappoint others. Other people say that announcing their own dreams or plans, even if just to themselves, helps to make them "more real." Experts say that both thinking and stating one's plans are ways of rehearsing future actions. Thoughts and words pave the way for preliminary actions, which further cement one's resolve. Criminologists who study serial killers say that many rehearse their actions by first killing animals and practicing how they will approach their human targets. Each action along this road is not only a way of emboldening themselves but also of ensuring success.

Judging from the explicit death threats made by the perpetrators in this study, murder was already on their minds long before they committed or tried to commit it. Having made death threats, these men had already distinguished themselves from the majority of batterers. Though many batterers make threats to harm their partners, the explicitness and frequency of threats made by the more severe batterers further separates them from the pack of other abusers. In the minds of many of the perpetrators I interviewed, killing their partner had always been an option, even if only one of last resort. Recall John, who said, "The idea that I could always kill her was just a comforting thing for me to say to myself." Many of the other killers and would-be killers similarly did not keep these kinds of thoughts to themselves. In all but a few cases, the perpetrator had already threatened to kill his partner or committed violence that could have easily resulted in her serious injury or death. In their words and actions, these men had already advertised their willingness to kill. These threats appeared to be an integral part of the perpetrators' repertoire of control. However, I found that rarely did their death threats appear until well after the onset of their physical violence. This makes sense since threats are usually viewed as empty or even "harmless" unless they have been preceded or are accompanied by physical assaults. Once violence has been established in a relationship, verbal and nonverbal threats serve to remind the victim of the perpetrator's potential for violence.

Though threats of violence would logically seem to lessen the need for physical assaults, this did not appear to be the case for the perpetrators interviewed. Not only did their threats become more frequent and serious over time but so too did their physical violence. This was because their usual threats and level of violence had failed to prevent their partners from seeking to end the relationship or from otherwise defying them. Over time, even their increasingly brutal levels of physical violence were no longer working for these men. Already having failed in their primary goal of maintaining the relationship, many concluded "the next best thing" was to kill their estranged partner. As several killers stated, killing at least ensured that "no one else would have her."

Killing one's partner communicates not only the ultimate act of control but also of ownership since one prerogative of ownership is to destroy that which is no longer of use to us. I am reminded of John's chilling words about the importance of having had sex with his wife, Debra, shortly before killing her: "It was a way of preserving us as a couple forever." Further, by letting the man whom he assumed to be Debra's new partner know that "I was the last to have her," John was attempting to communicate his eternal ownership of her.

For most of the killers, proprietary ownership was intertwined with jealous anger toward their partners, and appeared to have been the emotional trigger for murder as well as for many of their previous assaults of their partners. This was most evident among the jealous, suicidal, and substance-abusing types of killers. For other types of killers, attitudes of ownership were also evident but did not always arise out of jealousy. The financially possessive killers, for example, appeared more interested in retaining ownership or exclusive access to material assets rather than to their estranged partners. For the financially exploitative men, proprietary ownership did not arise out of jealousy so much as their wish to retain the goods and services that their partners provided. These men seemed to view women as disposable objects of sex and money. Despite the considerable differences between the five types of killers, all appeared to have had a history of possessively controlling their intimate partners.

Recommendations

I began this study hoping to better identify how women's murders might be prevented. I found that in some of the murder and attempted murder cases, it was easy to spot potential deterrents. In others, it was much harder. Some men proclaimed that nothing would have deterred them from killing their partners or ex-partners. Not able to ask the deceased, we did the next best thing by asking the survivors of near-fatal assaults. These women had sought help from a wide variety of sources and as a result provided valuable perspective about what might have made a difference. The killers also offered useful information about their own help-seeking, as well as their responses to the help sought by, or offered to, their partners. From these accounts, a picture emerges about potential deterrents. Many deterrents have already been identified in the sections about each type of killer and in the chapter about victim help-seeking. Beyond these, I'd like to conclude with the following broad recommendations aimed at reducing the incidence of intimate partner homicides. These recommendations span six major realms of institutional practice and public policy.

Removing the Guns

Forty-five percent of the men I interviewed used guns to kill their partners. The highest rates of gun use were among the materially motivated (80%), suicidal (67%) and substance-abusing (42%). By comparison, the rates among the career criminal and jealous types were 33% and 32% respectively. The high rate of gun use among the substance abusers makes sense given the more impulsive nature of the murders they committed. Most of these killers said that they would not have killed their partner had it not been for the easy availability of a gun. Recall Kevin, who shot first his male roommate and then his girlfriend with his assault rifle following a night of heavy drinking. Another example is Edward, who shot his wife, Sylvia, in the head while she slept after injecting heroin. When asked if he would have still killed Sylvia were it not for his easy access to a gun, Edward is the man who said, "A gun depersonalizes, doesn't it?"

The use of guns clearly did not always indicate lack of premeditation, however, even among the substance abusers. Some men (like Michael, who had driven to Maine to obtain a Civil War vintage sidearm three weeks prior to killing his wife) were very calculating. Three of the materially motivated killers used guns to kill in a manner that could only be seen as premeditated. It appears that gun use by killers represents two ends of the continuum of premeditation. This ranges from killers who appear to have no forethought to kill to those who plan their partners' murders for weeks and even months. Even in these cases, however, their ability to kill is greatly enhanced by the availability of a gun, and that is why some of these men took considerable pains to obtain one.

Evidence is mounting that many battered women's lives would be saved if stronger and more consistent efforts were made to remove the guns of abusive men and to make it far more difficult for them to obtain new ones. As mentioned earlier, guns are used in nearly two-thirds of all intimate partner homicides of American women. This nation's high rate of gun use in femicides is unique among industrialized nations. One large research study of femicides in England, for instance, found that only 5% of the women had been killed with a gun. By comparison, 35% had been strangled and 31% had been stabbed.[3] In Canada, the rate of gun use in intimate partner homicides is less than half than the rate in the United States (30% versus 63%), while in Australia the rate is nearly three times lower (22%).[4] The other notable difference between women's homicides in the United States and these three countries is that the overall rate of femicides in the United States is three to eight times higher.[5] Canada, Great Britain, and Australia each have more restrictive laws about gun ownership than this country. It has also been found that within the United States, those states with the fewest restrictions on gun ownership tend to have the highest intimate partner homicide rates. For instance, the intimate partner homicide rates in Arkansas, Nevada, and South Carolina, where gun ownership laws are permissive, are two to eight times higher than in the six New England states, where gun laws are considerably more strict.[6] Over the past five years, a number of states have enacted more restrictive gun laws pertaining to recipients of court protective orders, and there is strong evidence that this new legislation has saved lives. One team of researchers that tracked intimate partner homicide rates in states that have enacted such legislation found an ensuing 8% reduction in intimate partner homicides per ensuing year.[7]

One intended remedy to the inadequacies of state laws has been the enactment of federal legislation. By a federal statute enacted in 1994 as part of the Violent Crime Control Act, recipients of domestic violence protective orders are prohibited from owning or possessing firearms.[8] An amendment to this law in 1996 extended this prohibition to anyone convicted of certain misdemeanor crimes concerning domestic violence, including the use of physical force and the threatened use of a deadly weapon.[9] Not all domestic violence crimes are covered and therefore some states have enacted legislation to include all domestic violence crimes. The federal law also does not require police to confiscate firearms at the scene of domestic violence crimes and is otherwise vague about enforcement of the gun prohibition. At this writing, less than half of the states require police to seize guns at the scene of domestic violence crimes, and in some of these states, the guns must be "visible" to the police.[10] Less than half of the states require courts that issue restraining orders against abusers to specify on such orders that firearms are hereby prohibited and must be surrendered to police. Victim advocates have complained that these legal loopholes have enabled many batterers to retain their weapons and even to purchase new ones. But even in states that require gun seizures and court orders to surrender firearms, there are problems with enforcement. One study of restraining orders issued in California conducted by the Attorney General's Task Force on Domestic Violence found substantial rates of court noncompliance with this law. Overall, just over 5% of the restraining orders did not include firearms prohibitions, but it fluctuated from 0% to 43% from county to county.[11] The rate of noncompliance was highest in small, more rural counties. The researchers also found that some judges, "contrary to the law, had crossed the firearms prohibition language off the mandatory Judicial Council form order."[12]

Even though a small proportion of gun-owning batterers use them to kill their intimate partners, a much greater proportion use them to terrorize their partners. An interesting study of over 8,500 men who attended batterer intervention programs in Massachusetts provided more specific information about gun use by abusive men. This study found that batterers who owned firearms were eight times more likely than non-gun owners to have made "gun-related threats" against their partners.[13] These threats included not only explicit death threats but also nonverbal threats such as displaying a weapon; cleaning, loading or holding a gun during an argument; firing a weapon during an argument; and threatening to shoot a pet or object that the victim cared about.[14] A survey of women staying in seventy-two battered women's shelters found that gun threats against them were startlingly common. Two-thirds of the women whose partners kept a firearm in the house said that their abusers had used the weapon to threaten, terrorize, or harm them.[15] In our study, 45% of the victims of attempted homicide said that they had been explicitly threatened with a gun. Two additional women disclosed graphic and terroristic nonverbal threats that had been made by their abusers. These were Lynette, whose partner had forced her to play Russian roulette with him, and Sylvie, whose partner had once held a gun to the head of her young daughter. Independently of whether they are physically harmed or killed by guns, battered women and their children who are exposed to gun threats are emotionally traumatized. A number of the women in our study said that they felt suicidally depressed. Almost all said that they felt extremely anxious and fearful. Most said that they and their children had difficulty sleeping.

Conducting More Comprehensive Threat Assessment and Risk Management

As already noted, very few of the victims were passive, and most engaged in a wide variety of coping strategies and forms of resistance. This included pleas for help from others. Judging from the reports of homicide victims, the assistance provided varied from helpful to harmful in its impact. Reassuringly, victims were most likely to rate positively the criminal justice responses to domestic violence that occurred prior to 1995, when domestic violence statutes in Massachusetts were enhanced. Despite this, most victims felt that the criminal justice system could have done more to protect them. If nothing else, homicides and attempted homicides are evidence of the need to better detect and reduce the danger posed to victims of abuse. Only recently has the criminal justice system considered ways to do this in a more systematic and coordinated manner. In its response to domestic violence, the criminal justice system has often been characterized by progressive criminologists as a "blunt instrument." Even proponents of "get tough" or "zero tolerance" policies admit that making arrests and winning convictions is not always the same thing as protecting victims of abuse. For this reason, criminal justice systems in some jurisdictions have moved to incorporate threat assessment and risk management into their overall responses to domestic violence crimes. While also investigating whether there is sufficient evidence to make an arrest, for instance, police officers are also taught to assess the danger posed to the victim. In doing this, some police use laminated palm-sized cards that include critical threat assessment questions, such as whether the suspect has made past threats, used a weapon, or recently escalated his violence. Some courts have also developed dangerousness assessment protocols. For instance, courts in Connecticut and Colorado now routinely assess for dangerousness for all arraignments of domestic violence offenders. Usually such assessments are conducted by probation officers or prosecutors. The results of these assessments inform the sentencing of perpetrators. Perpetrators who are judged to be of high risk can be held pending their trials. If not sentenced to jail, a high-risk perpetrator can be mandated to a batterer intervention program, and if appropriate, to a substance abuse program. They can additionally be assigned to strict monitoring by their probation officers. This monitoring can include unscheduled home visits by the probation officer, random drug screenings, frequent communication between the probation officer and the mandated treatment programs, and regular court hearings to review program compliance. Some jurisdictions also hold regular meetings of criminal justice personnel and victim advocates to pool information about particularly dangerous offenders and to strategize ways to better protect their victims. The rationale for this information pooling and coordination of effort is that each member of the team—whether the victim advocate, the batterer intervention counselor, the police officer, the probation officer, or the prosecutor—tends to have unique information about the cases that contributes to a better picture of the situation. These high-risk response teams recognize that the dangerousness assessment should never be a one-time process since the level of danger posed to the victim may rise and fall over time. For some victims, the danger clearly increases when they are taking steps to end the relationships, file for child custody, or file criminal complaints against their abusers. The perpetrator may be increasing his use of drugs or alcohol, making more frequent or more graphic threats to kill the victim or himself, surveilling or stalking the victim, or escalating his violence. With this new intelligence about the situation, team members can collectively strategize what additional safety and monitoring measures are needed.

Dangerousness assessments are only as effective as the people conducting them. As a coordinator of national trainings on domestic violence threat assessment, I've found there to be a wide range of practices. Ironically, in some cases, the technology of threat assessment is offered in place of true victim advocacy. The same can be said about aggressive investigation and prosecution of domestic violence crimes. The quality of information that victims will provide about the danger they face depends a great deal upon how much they trust the law enforcement professionals who are asking the questions.[16] Many of the victims of attempted homicide said that they feared that the police officer, prosecutor, or judge with whom they interacted did not have their best interests in mind. Some said that they felt police and prosecutors were more interested in "building a case" than in protecting them, or in considering how prosecution of the case might further endanger them. This was one strong factor cited among the 30% of victims who said that the prosecutors' actions in prior domestic violence cases had "made the situation worse." In appraising the effects of judges' actions, an even higher proportion of victims (47%) said that their situations had gotten worse as a result. Some victims said the same thing about the victim advocates with whom they had interacted, although to a much lower extent. It bears noting that many of these were police- and prosecutor-based advocates who cannot grant confidentiality to the victims they help. This means that the information they reveal can be presented as evidence in the court hearing or trial and therefore becomes known to their batterer as the defendant. In the best case practices, police- and prosecutor-based advocates proactively inform victims of the limits to their confidentiality so that victims can make informed choices about what to disclose. Because they are not employed by the criminal justice system, community-based victim advocates can grant confidentiality to victims. Community-based advocates also do not have the dual role of advocating for victims while at the same time assisting their employer in a crime investigation or a criminal prosecution. Theoretically, this enables them to better weigh the pros and cons of criminal prosecution with victims without being seen as having a strong bias.

A substantial number of the victims of attempted homicide said that they were put off by criminal justice professionals whom they felt had been judgmental toward them for not wishing to proceed with criminal prosecution of previous domestic violence incidents. Other victims said that they felt that police, prosecutors, or judges had been judgmental toward them for remaining with their abusers. More troubling, some of these victims said that because of these experiences, they did not turn to the criminal justice system for help following subsequent incidents.

One larger study also found evidence of this. The researchers in this study examined over 350 court cases of domestic violence in Quincy, Massachusetts, and subsequently conducted one-year follow-up interviews with the victims to see if they were satisfied with how the criminal justice system had handled their cases, whether any new assaults had occurred, and if so, whether they had continued to use the legal system.[17] They found that the majority of victims were satisfied with the police, prosecutor, and court actions, and most reported that they had not experienced any new acts of domestic violence during the follow-up period. About one-quarter of the women reported that new acts of abuse had occurred, and whether or not they reported this to the police depended a great deal on their degree of satisfaction or dissatisfaction with how the system had handled the initial case. The researchers found that those victims who were dissatisfied with the initial police or court response were six times less likely to call the police in response to subsequent domestic violence incidents.[18] Most troubling, the dissatisfied victims were those who had experienced the most severe abuse. The researchers found that victim dissatisfaction was not related to actions that the court had taken in the initial case. Rather, victims' dissatisfaction was strongly correlated with whether they believed that their concerns were respected by police, prosecutors, and judges. Paramount among these concerns was the victim's safety and fears of offender retribution in response to court actions. Another strong concern was disruptions in the victim's economic stability as the result of the offender's arrest or incarceration. The researchers conclude that aggressive or mandatory prosecution policies are not always in the best interests of victims, particularly those in the most dangerous situations, since they sometimes severely curtail some victims' sense of control.[19] Tracking trends in federal intimate partner homicide rates from 1976–1996, one other set of researchers found that the death rate among unmarried women has actually increased.[20] They attribute this increase to more aggressive prosecution policies that have sometimes created abuser retaliation. These researchers attribute the overall reduction in intimate partner homicide rates to other legal reforms, particularly laws that enable police to apprehend offenders who violate protective orders without first having to obtain a warrant. The Quincy study found that, overall, victims were satisfied with strong and consistent court actions, since these appear to deter ongoing violence by their partners and ex-partners, particularly for victims of low to moderate levels of abuse.[21] Clearly, these have resulted in enhanced safety for most battered women. What is needed, I believe, are swift and consistent criminal justice responses that are accompanied by the availability of strong victim advocacy at the police, court, and community levels. The victims of attempted homicide in our study who had not been directed to a victim advocate were the most dissatisfied with the legal system's response. Specifically, those without advocates were most likely to complain that no one had asked them about dangerousness or assisted them in devising a safety plan. They were most likely to say that the legal process had not been sufficiently explained to them, and that they were not fully appraised about the status of pending cases.

Victim advocates play a crucial role in the criminal justice system for victims who often experience it as bewildering and hostile. Victim advocates often have the time to explain the legal process more fully to victims. Victim advocates tend also be more attuned to signs of victim trauma and how this affects their ability to give and to process information. Victim advocates often play a key role in training other first responders on how to better recognize and sensitively respond to victims of serious trauma. For instance, police officers are advised to introduce themselves when interviewing the victim, make eye contact, explain their role, and to repeat information. Many of the victims we interviewed confirmed that they felt more trusting of police, prosecutors, and judges who exhibited this kind of demeanor.

Improving Community Responses

Clearly, not all solutions to dangerous domestic violence cases can be provided by the criminal justice system. More than half of the victims of homicide never used the criminal justice system. Instead, many turned to other systems or individuals for help. The other institutional helpers included health care workers, therapists, clergy, child welfare providers, and battered women's programs. As with the criminal justice system, workers in these institutions have only recently received training and guidance on how to identify and protect victims of abuse. This training often includes how to recognize and to respond sensitively to victims. In their ratings of past helpers, the victims of attempted homicide said that they responded most positively to helpers whom they perceived to be caring as well as competent. Being asked the right questions by a doctor or nurse, for instance, is of limited benefit unless these questions are asked in a sensitive and nonjudgmental manner. Victims consistently said that they were more likely to disclose abuse to those whom they felt to be nonjudgmental. Conversely, it also appeared that bad experiences with particular institutional helpers often discouraged victims from turning to these systems for help in the future.

The victims of attempted homicide were most likely to have sought informal help from friends, relatives and neighbors. Victims credited these individuals as important sources of support and validation. Friends and relatives also provided concrete assistance such as money, transportation, and a refuge for the victims and their children. Besides this, friends and relatives were often vital links between victims and more professional sources of help. Over time, however, most victims of attempted homicide said that they had become more and more socially isolated, due in large part, to the abusers' apparent efforts to prevent their contact with others. Very often, supportive friends and relatives of the victim came within the abuser's line of fire.

I found that neighbors were often the "wild cards" as potential sources of help or harm for victims. Due to their proximity, they are potentially the most well positioned to help the victim of abuse. Several victims credited neighbors with saving their lives. Recognizing this largely untapped resource, victim advocates in some communities have attempted to foster more community awareness about domestic violence, and beyond this, more information about how to help victims of abuse. The Family Violence Prevention Fund has developed a resource kit called Neighbor To Neighbor, which shows individuals and community groups how to organize such a program.[22] The stated goal of these programs are to mobilize neighborhood blocks to become "Domestic Violence-Free Zones."[23] For instance, store and house signs are posted that proclaim, "There's NO ROOM for domestic violence in this neighborhood." The kit also includes handouts, flyers, bumper stickers, and posters as well as suggested activities to bring neighbors together to address domestic violence.[24] Initiatives in other communities have included education and outreach to men in order to mobilize the silent majority of men who do not condone domestic violence to add their voices to efforts to end it.[25] Such campaigns have included annual men's marches in support of battered women, men's educational forums, male participation in preventive education programs aimed at children, and fundraising events for battered women's programs.[26] In some cases, these men have also become "big brothers" to boys who grew up with abusive fathers. Serving as coaches, teachers, and community volunteers, others have served as positive role models to larger numbers of boys.

Educating Young People about Abusive Behavior

Children exposed to domestic violence are not doomed to become victims or perpetrators in their adult relationships. Much depends upon the information and guidance they receive from others. Schools can play a critical role in teaching young people the differences between healthy and harmful relationships. In my own experience as a member of an early intervention program, I found that much confusion exists among teens about what constitutes abusive behavior. For example, teenage girls sometimes interpret possessive jealousy as a positive sign of their dating partner's strong affection for them rather than as an early warning sign of abuse. For boys and girls, confusion often exists about what constitutes sexual coercion. Rather than from informed adults, we found that teens often get their information about relationships from the popular media, such as movies, fashion magazines, and music videos. The messages conveyed in these media often glamorize violence, alcohol, drugs and sex. They also frequently present exaggerated notions of masculinity and femininity, along with an inflated emphasis on physical appearance and sex appeal. Teen dating violence prevention programs often help young people to develop a more critical consciousness such messages and to recognize more important values. Schools and other youth programs, such as those for teen parents, can also help young people to identify the early warning signs of abusive relationship.

Rates of intimate partner violence among teens are alarmingly high. One survey of high school students found that one-fifth reported having been physically or sexually abused by a dating partner.[27] A survey of male high school students found that one-fifth had witnessed a fellow student physically assault a dating partner.[28] A third survey, this one of fourteen- to seventeen-year-olds, found that one-third had witnessed such an event.[29] Unfortunately, funding for preventive education curricula in schools has been reduced over the past ten years due in part to the emphasis on improving standardized test scores.

Teen dating violence prevention programs not only raise awareness about dating violence but of domestic violence as well. One common result is that children who are exposed to such violence in their homes will disclose this to a teacher or a counselor who is able to refer these students for appropriate services. Children exposed to domestic violence are known to be at higher risk to drop out of school and to otherwise underachieve.[30] Often, the preventive education programs have been accompanied by counseling and advocacy services for such children as well as those who have already become victims or perpetrators in their dating relationships. In evaluating the impact of one such program, one school counselor noted that the participating girls and boys whom she thought were at high risk to drop out of school had remained in school and become better students.[31] More formal evaluations of these programs have shown them to be effective in helping teens to become more aware of how to recognize and avoid dating and domestic violence.[32]

Some people have argued that education and interventions for teens exposed to domestic violence is already too late, and that earlier interventions are needed. Child trauma experts have pushed for better training of pre-school and elementary school teachers to recognize signs of trauma. Recognizing this potential, there is a growing push in some states to expand capacity of schools to provide early intervention to traumatized children based on a model of trauma-informed care.[33] Often, children who are exhibiting behavior or academic problems in school are victims of trauma at home. According to one expert, trauma-informed training for teachers should include:

information about child development and the effects of exposure to violence on children of different ages. It should include an overview of the dynamics of domestic violence and. . . . . media violence. It should emphasize practical problem-solving strategies. [34]

Creating More Options for Battered Women

Though the victims of attempted homicide had sought help from a variety of places, most said that they came to feel more isolated over time. Social isolation is a primary control tactic used by many abusers. Most of the victims we interviewed said that their abusers had verbally or physically assaulted one or more of their friends and relatives. Only a small proportion of the victims had sought help from a battered women's shelter program. Though they clearly serve a critical role, emergency shelters can contribute to some victims' social isolation since they require women to uproot their own and their children's lives and to disconnect from their regular communities. Clearly, they are an option of last resort for many victims, and considering that most limit stays to one month, not even that for victims of the most pernicious batterers. Despite these limitations, many battered women's shelters are continuously full, and due to underfunding, cannot provide emergency housing to many women and their children who seek it. There is an urgent need for affordable medium-term housing for battered women (sometimes referred to as "transitional housing") as well as long-term housing. Currently, waiting periods for federally subsidized public housing exceed two years in many cities and states. Many more services are now available for battered women, but the options for the most severely abused are still limited, and this may be one reason why the intimate partner death rates for American women have only marginally decreased over the past twenty years. One research team that has tracked this trend has suggested that improvements in the criminal justice response to domestic violence may have been counteracted by the loss of economic benefits for poor women and children. In particular, they attribute the increase in homicide rates among unmarried poor women to reductions in Aide for Dependent Children (AFDC) benefits.[35] They also speculate that reduced welfare benefits have led to more poor unmarried women killing their abusive boyfriends since their opportunity to live independently of their abusers is severely limited.[36] Increased protections for battered women have come during a time of eroding social and economic supports for women in general, and for poor and immigrant women in particular. Increased public attention to domestic violence may have only increased the social stigma felt by women still entrapped in these relationships. At the same time, there appears to be a disproportionate public policy focus on those victimized rather than those who perpetrate these crimes. Consistent identification, monitoring and rehabilitation of the most dangerous abusers continue to lag far behind, meaning that many battered women and their children remain in the line of fire. Domestic violence has emerged from behind closed doors but women continue to be killed in broad daylight. With better intelligence about the chronic abusers, we will be better able to identify and stop those most likely to kill.

Notes

Chapter 1

1. "The plague strikes home," *People*, August 29, 1994: 34–40.
2. "Witnesses, on the stand, detail how woman was slain in Quincy," *Boston Globe*, April 8, 1997.
3. "Amherst man is held without bail in ex-girlfriend's slaying," *Boston Globe*, March 23, 1993.
4. One study in Britain also conducted interviews with killers, including men who had killed their intimate partners. Relying primarily on case file reviews, this study compared 106 intimate partner killers with 424 killers of others. In-depth interviews of 200 male and female inmates serving time for homicide were conducted, though the authors do not specify how many of these were men who had killed their intimate partners. The study did not include those who had committed manslaughter. See Dobash et al. 2004, 577–605.
5. Roehl et al. 2005, 12.
6. Rennison 2003, 1.
7. Browne 1987, 65–70.
8. Websdale 2000, 2; Roehl et al. 2005, 9–13.
9. Rennison 2003, 1.
10. Websdale et al. 1999, 61–74.
11. Campbell et al. 2003, 1089–97.
12. These other tools included the Psychological Maltreatment of Women Inventory, developed by Richard Tolman; the Beliefs about Wife Beating Scale, developed by Daniel Saunders et al.; and the Addiction Severity Index (ASI) and the Jealousy Scales, developed by Gregory White. We also used two tools that we developed to measure acts of physical abuse toward partners and children, as well as one to measure jealous beliefs. All but the ASI were administered to both the killers and the victims of attempted homicide.
13. Bureau of Justice Statistics 2004, 6.
14. Violence Policy Center 2002, 1.
15. Campbell et al. 2003, 1092. To gain more detailed information about the killer's

behavior toward the victim, as well as other situational factors, the researchers conducted telephone interviews with "proxy informants" who were primarily relatives and friends of the deceased.

Chapter 2

1. Coleman and Straus 1983, 104–124; Leonard et al. 1985, 279–82; Kaufman-Kantor and Jasinski 1998, 1–43.
2. Batterer Intervention Programs 2006.
3. Gondolf 2002, 97.
4. Gondolf 2002, 96–97.
5. Gondolf 2002, 187.
6. Gondolf 2002, 171–72.
7. Holtzworth-Munroe et al. 1997, 286–87.
8. Gondolf 2002, 95.
9. Rothman and Perry 2004, 238–46.
10. D. Adams 1996, 123–26.
11. Emerge, personal communication, 2004.
12. D. Adams 1991, 76–82.
13. Emerge, personal communication, 2003.
14. Emerge, personal communication, 1999.
15. Batterer Intervention Programs, 2006.
16. Emerge, personal communication, 1988.
17. Emerge, personal communication, 1984.
18. Emerge 2000, 26.
19. D. Adams 1989, 25.
20. Emerge, personal communication, 2004.
21. Davis and Steiner 1999, 69–93.
22. Babcock and Steiner 1999, 52.
23. Aldarondo 2002, 3–1 to 3–20.
24. Aldarondo 2002, 3–11 to 3–12; Moyer 2004, 17; Bennett et al. 2005, 21–22.
25. Gondolf 2002, 152–54.
26. Gondolf 2000, 433.
27. Hamberger and Hastings 1993, 193.
28. Babcock and Steiner 1999, 56.

Chapter 3

1. Hare 1993, 32–34.
2. Hare et al. 1993.
3. Emerge, personal communication, 2001.
4. Aldarondo 2002, 3–15 to 3–17.
5. Addiction Severity Index, Treatment Research Institute. www.tresearch.org/asi.htm.

6. Sharps et al. 2003, 3.
7. Ibid.
8. Gondolf 2002, 183–92; Sharps et al. 2003, 3.
9. Pernanen 1991, 192; Bushman 1997, 227–43.
10. MacAndrew and Edgerton 1969, 88; Collins and Messerschmidt 1993, 93–100.
11. Taylor et al. 1979, 73–81.
12. Kantor and Straus 1987, 213–30.
13. D. Adams 1991, 43–51.
14. Campbell 2003, 1093; Dobash et al. 2004, 594–96.
15. Block 2002, 7.
16. "Domestic abuse comes into focus in Stuart death," *Boston Sunday Globe*, January 14, 1990.
17. "Risk Factors for Femicide in Violent Intimate Relationships: Preliminary Findings" (PowerPoint presentation, 2003). www.son.jhmi.edu/research/homicide/prelim/index.htm
18. See *Domestic violence homicides in Massachusetts* (Peace At Home annual reports, 1995–2005). www.peaceathome.org.
19. Arizona Coalition Against Domestic Violence 2002, 5.
20. Florida Domestic Violence Fatality Review Team 2004, 9.
21. Esteal 1994, 140; Violence Policy Center 2002, 4–5.Centers for Disease Control 1991, 652–59.
22. Violence Policy Center 2002, 6.
23. Koziol-McLain et al. 2006, 7.
24. Koziol-McLain et al. 2006, 8.
25. Koziol-McLain et al. 2006, 14.
26. Arizona Coalition Against Domestic Violence 2002, 6.
27. Koziol-McLain et al. 2006, 8.
28. Koziol-McLain et al. 2006, 11.
29. West 1967, 64.
30. Rosenbaum 1990, 1036–39.
31. Koziol-McLain et al. 2006, 10.
32. Polk 1993, 35–53.
33. Jacobson and Gottman 1998.
34. Wilson and Daly 1995, 197.
35. Emerge, personal communication, 2002.
36. Hare 1993, 34.
37. Babcock and Steiner 1999, 46; Gondolf 2002, 139–46.
38. Bocko et al. 2004, 5–7.
39. Gregory and Erez 2002, 206–32.
40. Pence and Shepard 1999, 24–50; Gondolf 2000, 428–37; Babcock and Steiner 1999, 46–59.
41. Gondolf 2000, 428–30.
42. Langford et al. 1999.

43. Campbell et al. 2003, 1091.
44. Campbell et al. 2003, 1094; Wilson and Daly 1992, 189–215; Websdale 1999, 594.
45. Southern Hilltown Domestic Violence Task Force 2004.
46. Farley and Barkan 1998, 37–48; Farley, et al. 1998, 405–26.

Chapter 4

1. Straus et al. 1980; Dobash and Dobash 1979.
2. Kalmuss 1984, 11–19.
3. Straus et al. 1980, 114–22.
4. Whitney and Davis 1999, 158–66.
5. Dutton and Hart 1992, 101–12.
6. Robinson and Taylor 1994.
7. Straus et al. 1980, 205–18.
8. Dube et al. 2002, 3–17.

Chapter 6

1. Wilson et al. 1995, 275–91.
2. Campbell et al. 2003, 17.
3. Saltzman et al. 2003, 31–43.
4. Block 2000, 140–49.
5. Campbell et al. 2003, 1094.
6. Block 2000, 149.
7. Hollander 2004, 44–45.

Chapter 7

1. S. Adams 1999.
2. Wilson and Daly 1995, 286–90.
3. Hart 1999.
4. Polk 1994, 28.
5. Hochschild 1989, 19.
6. Dobash and Dobash 1979, 122.
7. Emerge, personal communication, 1981.
8. Campbell et al. 2003, 1094.
9. Block 2000, 151–53.
10. Emerge, personal communication, 1999.
11. Meloy 1996, 147–62.
12. Tjaden and Thoennes 1998.
13. Miller 2001, 8.
14. Campbell 2003, 1094.
15. Personal communication, 2000.

16. Websdale 1999, 89–90.
17. Wilson and Daly 1993, 3–16.
18. Campbell 2003, 1093.

Chapter 8

1. See Bowker 1986 and McFarlane et al. 2001.
2. Massachusetts General Laws, Chapter 209A, Section 6. www.mass.gov/laws.
3. See Klein 2004, 89–130; Police Executive Research Forum 1998; and Shepard and Pence 1999.
4. See Klein 2004. For a specific examination of judicial practices and demeanor, including recommendations, see Ptacek 1999. For national guidelines for family and juvenile court judges, see National Council of Juvenile and Family Court Judges 1995.
5. An excellent set of recommended guidelines for medical responses to domestic violence is Family Violence Prevention Fund 2002.
6. See, for instance, Harway et al. 1997.
7. See Warshaw and Moroney 2002 and New York State Office for the Prevention of Domestic Violence 2001. For guidelines on child protection and child custody evaluations concerning allegations of domestic violence, see American Psychological Association Committee on Professional Practice and Standards 1998.
8. See Volcano Press staff 1995. See also the training initiatives and written resources provided by Safe Havens: Interfaith Partnership Against Domestic Violence, available at www.interfaithpartners.org.
9. Buzawa and Buzawa 1996.
10. Additional findings about support networks of battered women are available in Block 2000.

Chapter 9

1. Dutton 1995, 138.
2. Dutton 1995, 114–16.
3. Dobash et al. 2004, 599.
4. Shackelford and Mouzos 2005, 1309–24; Mouzos and Rushforth 2003, 3–4; Sev'er, et al. 2004, 1–14; Hemenway et al. 2002, 100–104.
5. Hemenway et al. 2002, 101.
6. Premack 2005.
7. Vigdor and Mercy 2006, 337.
8. 18 U.S.C. 922 [g] [8].
9. 18 U.S.C. 922 [g] [9].
10. Frattaroli and Vernick 2006, 296–312.
11. Seave 2006, 245–65.
12. Seave 2006, 256.

13. Rothman et al. 2006, 62–68.
14. Rothman et al. 2006, 64.
15. Sorenson and Wiebe 2004, 1412–17.
16. See, for example, an interactive training guide on danger assessments, *Domestic violence dangerousness assessment and safety planning*, produced by Emerge in 2006; www.emergedv.com. Another training resource is Jacquelyn Campbell's website, www.dangerassessment.org.
17. Hotaling and Buzawa 2003a.
18. Hotaling and Buzawa 2003b.
19. Hotaling and Buzawa 2003a, 33.
20. Dugan et al. 2003, 20–25.
21. Hotaling and Buzawa 2003a, 4.
22. Available at www.endabuse.org, the website for the Family Violence Prevention Fund.
23. See, for instance, Domestic Violence Free Zone Initiative at www.cambridgema. gov/WOMEN/womensafety.cfm.
24. Family Violence Prevention Fund 2002.
25. A national Harris Poll of American adults conducted in 2006 found that 54% of men, compared to 72% of women, considered domestic violence to be a "very serious" or "extremely serious" problem. The overall rate was 63%. Results accessed at the National Domestic Violence Hotline, www.ndvh.org.
26. See, for instance, the activities listed for the Men's Initiative at Jane Doe, Inc. at www.mijd.org and the Men's Resource Center at www.mensresourcecenter.org. See also Newton-Poling and Cozad-Neuger 2002.
27. Silverman et al. 2001, 572
28. Zwicker 2002, 131.
29. The poll was conducted by Knowledge Networks in 2000 for the Empower Program, and sponsored by Liz Claiborne and the Empower Program.
30. Advocates of Children Domestic Violence Project 2004, 22; see literature review provided by Edleson 1999, 839–70.
31. Carole Sousa, personal communication, 1998.
32. See overview of prevention programs and their outcomes by O'Keefe 2005, 7–8.
33. See Hodes 2006 for a comprehensive overview of the trauma-informed care model for children. A good source of information about resources for traumatized children is the website of the Child Witness to Violence Project at www. childwitnesstoviolence.org.
34. McAlister Groves 2002, 95.
35. Dugan et al. 2003, 22.
36. Dugan et al. 2003, 24.

References

Adams, D. 1989. Identifying the assaultive husband in court: you be the judge. *Boston Bar Journal* 33, no. 4: 23–25.

———. 1991. Empathy and entitlement: a comparison of battering and nonbattering husbands. Doctoral dissertation, Northeastern University.

———. 1996. Guidelines for doctors on identifying and helping their patients who batter. *Journal of American Medical Women's Association* 51:123–26.

———. 2004. Excuse-making strategies of abusive men. Presentation at *Why Doesn't She Just Leave?* Conference in Belfast, N. Ireland, November 24.

Adams, S. 1999. Serial batterers. *Probation Research Bulletin*, December 13. Boston: Massachusetts Trial Court, Office of the Commissioner of Probation.

Advocates for Children Domestic Violence Project. 2004. Children in crisis. Education Advocacy Project, 1–34. www.advocatesforchildren.org.

Aldarondo, E. 2002. Evaluating the efficacy of interventions with men who batter. In *Programs for men who batter: Intervention and prevention strategies in a diverse society*, ed. E. Aldarondo and F. Medoros, 3–1 to 3–20. Kingston, NJ: Civic Research Institute.

American Psychological Association Committee on Professional Practice and Standards. 1998. Guidelines for psychological evaluations in child protection matters. www.apa.org/practice/childprotection.html

Arizona Coalition Against Domestic Violence. 2002. Arizona domestic violence fatality review: a review of 2000 and 2001 murder suicides. www.azcadv.org.

Babcock, J., and R. Steiner. 1999. The relationship between treatment, incarceration and recidivism of battering: A program evaluation of Seattle's coordinated community response to domestic violence. *Journal of Family Psychology* 13, no. 1: 46–59.

Batterer Intervention Programs. 2006. Preliminary FY05 report on intake data. Boston: Massachusetts Department of Public Health.

Bennett, L., C. Call, H. Flett, and C. Stoops. 2005. Program completion, behavioral change, and re-arrest for the batterer intervention system of Cook County,

Illinois. Final Report to the Illinois Criminal Justice Information Authority, February, 1–67.

Block, C. 2000. The Chicago women's health risk study: risk of serious injury in intimate violence. Illinois Criminal Justice Information Authority. www.icjia. state.il.us.

———. 2002. The Chicago women's health risk survey at a glance. Illinois Criminal Justice Information Authority. www.icjia.state.il.us.

Bocko, S., C. Cicchetti, L. Lempicki, and A. Powell. 2004. Restraining order violators, corrective programming, and recidivism. Boston: Massachusetts Trial Court, Office of the Commissioner of Probation.

Bowker, L. 1986. *Ending the violence: A guidebook on the experiences of 1,000 battered wives.* Holmes Beach, FL: Learning Publications.

Browne, A. 1987. *When battered women kill.* New York: The Free Press.

Bureau of Justice Statistics. 2004. *Intimate partner homicide: 1976–2002.* U.S. Department of Justice. www.ojp.usdoj.gov/bjs.

Bushman, G. 1997. Effects of alcohol on human aggression: Validity of proposed explanations. In *Recent developments in alcoholism*, Vol. 13: *Alcoholism and violence*, ed. M. Galander, 227–43. New York: Plenum Press.

Buzawa, E., and C. Buzawa. 1996. *Domestic violence: the criminal justice response.* Thousand Oaks, CA: Sage.

Campbell, J., D. Webster, J. Koziol-McLain, and J. McFarlane. 2003. Risk factors for intimate partner femicide. *American Journal of Public Health* 93:1089–97.

Campbell, J., D. Webster, J. Koziol-McLain, C. Block, D. Campbell, M. Curry, F. Gary, J. McFarlane, C. Sachs, P. Sharps, Y. Ulrich, and S. Wilt. 2003. Assessing risk factors for intimate partner homicide. *NIJ Journal* no. 250. www.ojp.usdoj. gov/nij/journals.

Centers for Disease Control. 1991. Current trends: homicide followed by suicide-Kentucky, 1985–1990. *Morbidity and Mortality Report* 40, no. 38: 652–59.

Coleman, D., and M. Straus. 1983. Alcohol use and family violence. In *Alcohol, drug abuse and aggression*, ed. E. Gottheil et al., 104–124. Springfield, IL: Thomas.

Collins, J., and P. Messerschmidt. 1993. Epidemiology of alcohol-related violence. *Alcohol Health and Research World* 17, no. 2: 93–100.

Davis, R., and B. Taylor. 1999. Does batterer treatment reduce violence? A synthesis of the literature. *Women and Criminal Violence* 10:69–93.

Dobash, R. E., and R. P. Dobash. 1979. *Violence against wives: a case against the patriarchy.* New York: Free Press.

Dobash, R. E., R. Dobash, K. Cavanagh, and R. Lewis. 2004. Not an ordinary killer—just an ordinary guy. *Violence Against Women* 10, no. 6: 594–96.

Dube, S., R. Anda, V. Felitti, V. Edwards, and D. Williamson. 2002. Exposure to abuse, neglect, and household dysfunction among adults who witnessed intimate partner violence as children: implications for health and social services. *Violence and Victims* 17, no. 1: 3–17.

Dugan, L., D. Nagin, and R. Rosenfeld. 2003. Do domestic violence services save lives? *NIJ Journal* no. 250: 20–25. www.ojp.usdoj.gov/nij/journals.

Dutton, D. 1995. *The batterer: a psychological profile.* New York: Basic Books.

Dutton, D., and S. Hart. 1992. Risk markers for family violence in a federally incarcerated population. *International Journal of Law and Psychiatry* 15:101–112.

Edleson, J. 1999. Children's witnessing of adult domestic violence. *Journal of Interpersonal Violence* 14, no. 8: 839–70.

Emerge. 2000. Emerge batterers intervention group program manual. www.emergedv. com.

Empower Program. 2000. Social control, verbal abuse, and violence among teenagers. www.empowered.org.

Esteal, P. 1994. Homicide-suicides between adult sexual intimates: an Australian study. *Suicide and Life-Threatening Behavior* 24:140.

Family Violence Prevention Fund. 2002. National consensus guidelines on identifying and responding to domestic violence victimization in health care settings. www.endabuse.org.

Farley, M., and H. Barkan. 1998. Prostitution, violence and post-traumatic stress disorder. *Women and Health* 27, no. 3: 37–48.

Farley, M., I. Baral, M. Kiremire, and U. Sezgin. 1998. Prostitution in five countries: violence and post traumatic stress disorder. *Feminism and Psychology* 8, no. 4: 405–26.

Florida Domestic Violence Fatality Review Team. 2004. Annual Report 2004, 1–60. www.fdle.state.fl.us/CitResCtr/Domestic_Violence/index.html.

Frattaroli, S., and Vernick, J. 2006. Separating batterers and guns: a review and analysis of gun removal laws in 50 states. *Evaluation Review* 30, no. 3: 296–312.

Gondolf, E. 2000. Mandatory court review and batterer program compliance. *Journal of Interpersonal Violence* 15, no. 4: 428–37.

———. 2002. *Batterer intervention systems: issues, outcomes and recommendations.* Thousand Oaks, CA: Sage.

Gregory, C., and E. Erez. 2002. The effects of batterer intervention programs: the battered women's perspectives. *Violence Against Women* 8, no. 2: 206–32.

Hamberger, K., and J. Hastings. 1993. Court-mandated treatment of men who assault their partners: Issues, controversies and outcomes. In *Legal responses to domestic violence,* ed. N. Hilton. Thousand Oaks, CA: Sage.

Hare, R. 1993. *Without a conscience.* New York: Pocket Books.

Hare, R., Strachan, K, and Forth, A. 1993. Psychopathy and crime: A review. In *Clinical approaches to mentally disordered offenders,* ed. K. Howells and C. Hollin, 165–78. New York: Wiley.

Hart, B. 1996. Rule Making and Enforcement/Rule Compliance and Resistance. In *I Am Not Your Victim: Anatomy of Domestic Violence,* ed. B. Sipes and E. J. Hall, 258–63. Thousand Oaks: Sage Publications.

————. 1999. Rule-making and enforcement, the violent and controlling tactics of men who batter, and rule-compliance and resistance, the response of battered women.

Harway, M., M. Hansen, and N. Cervantes. 1997. Therapist awareness of appropriate awareness in treatment of domestic violence: a review. *Journal of Aggression, Maltreatment and Trauma* 1, no. 1: 27–40.

Hemenway, D., T. Shinoda-Tagawa, and M. Miller. 2002. *Journal of American Medical Women's Association* 57, no. 2: 100–104.

Hochschild, A. 1989. *The second shift: working parents and the revolution of the home.* New York: Viking.

Hodes, G. 2006. Responding to trauma: the promise and practice of trauma-informed care. www.nasmhpd.org.

Hollander, D. 2004. Reports to police of abuse during pregnancy signal risk of adverse outcomes. *Perspectives on Sexual and Reproductive Health* 36, no. 1: 38–39.

Holtzworth-Munroe, A., N. Smutzle, and L. Bates. 1997. A brief review of the research on husband violence, part III: sociological factors, relationship factors, and differing consequences of husband and wife violence. *Aggression and Violent Behavior* 2:285–307.

Hotaling, G., and Buzawa, E. 2003a. Victim satisfaction with criminal justice case processing in a model court setting. Report prepared for Grant # 2000-WT-VX-0019, National Institute of Justice, Violence Against Women Programs. Accessed via Victim satisfaction with the criminal justice system (summary article) in *NIJ Journal* no. 253 (2006). www.ojp.usdoj.gov/nij/journals.

————. 2003b. Forgoing criminal justice assistance: the non-reporting of new incidents of abuse in a court sample of domestic violence victims. Report prepared for Grant # 2000-WT-VX-0019, National Institute of Justice, Violence Against Women Programs. Accessed via Victim satisfaction with the criminal justice system (summary article) in *NIJ Journal* no. 253 (2006). www.ojp.usdoj. gov/nij/journals.

Jacobson, N., and J. Gottman. 1998. *When men batter women: new insights into ending abusive relationships.* New York: Simon and Schuster.

Kalmuss, D. 1984. The intergenerational transmission of marital aggression. *Journal of Marriage and the Family* 46:11–19.

Kantor, G., and M. Straus. 1987. The "drunken bum" theory of wife beating. *Social Problems* 34:213–30.

Kaufman-Kantor, G., and J. Jasinski. 1998. Dynamics and risk factors in partner violence. In *Partner violence: a comprehensive review of 20 years of research*, ed. J. Jasinski and M. Williams, 1–43. Thousand Oaks CA: Sage.

Klein, A. 2004. *The criminal justice response to domestic violence.* Belmont, CA: Wadsworth.

Koziol-McLain, J., D. Webster, J. McFarlane, Y. Ulrich, N. Glass, and J. Campbell.

2006. Risk factors for femicide-suicide in abusive relationships: results from a multisite case control study. *Violence and Victims* 21, no. 1: 3–21.

Langford, L., N. Isaac, and S. Kabat. 1999. Homicides related to intimate partner violence in Massachusetts, 1991–1995. www.peaceathome.org.

Leonard, K., E. Bromet, D. Parkinson, N. Day, and C. Ryan. 1985. Pattern of alcohol use and physically aggressive behavior in men. *Journal of Studies in Alcohol* 46:279–82.

MacAndrew, C., and R. Edgerton. 1969. *Drunken comportment: A social explanation.* Chicago: Aldine.

McAlister Groves, B. 2002. *Children who see too much.* Boston: Beacon Press.

McFarlane, J., J. Campbell, and K. Watson. 2001. The use of the criminal justice system prior to intimate partner femicide. *Criminal Justice Review* 26, no. 2: 193–208.

Meloy, R.1996. Stalking (obsessional following): A review of some preliminary studies. *Aggression and Violent Behavior* 1:147–62.

Miller, N. 2001. Stalking laws and implementation practices: a national review for policymakers and practitioners. Institute for Law and Justice. www.ilj.org

Mouzos, J., and Rushforth, C. 2003. Family violence in Australia. *Trends and issues in crime and criminal violence*, no. 255:3–4. www.aic.gov.au/publications

Moyer, R. 2004. To BIP or not to BIP? Paper presented to York/Springvale (ME) Domestic Violence Coordination Project, June 8.

National Council of Juvenile and Family Court Judges. 1995. Improving court practice in child abuse and neglect cases. www.ncjfcj.org.

Newton-Poling, J., and C. Cozad-Neuger. 2002. *Men's work in preventing violence against women.* New York: Haworth Press.

New York State Office for the Prevention of Domestic Violence 2001. Mental health and human services. www.opdv.state.ny.us.

O'Keefe, M. 2005. Teen dating violence: a review of risk factors and prevention efforts. www.vawnet.org/DomesticViolence/Research.

Pence, E., and M. Shepard 1999. Developing a coordinated community response. Shepard and Pence, 24–50.

Pernanen, K. 1991. *Alcohol in human violence*, 192–224. New York: Gilford Press.

Police Executive Research Forum 1998. *Community policing to reduce and prevent violence against women: training curriculum and resource guide.* www. mincava.umn.edu.

Polk, K. 1993. A scenario of masculine violence: confrontational homicide. In *Homicide: patterns, prevention and control*, ed. H. Strang and S. Gerull, 35–53. Canberra: Australian Institute of Criminology.

Premack, E. 2005. New England intimate partner violence murder rate 2 to 8 times lower than south or west, federal crime data show. www.umass.edu/journal/car/studentwork/premack.

Ptacek, J. 1999. *Battered women in the courtroom: the power of judicial responses.* Boston: Northeastern University Press.

Rennison, C. 2003. Intimate partner violence, 1993–2001. Crime data brief, Bureau of Justice Statistics, U.S. Department of Justice.

Robinson, D., and J. Taylor. 1994. The incidence of family violence perpetrated by federal offenders: a file review study. Correctional Service of Canada.

Roehl, J., C. O'Sullivan, and D. Webster. 2005. Intimate partner violence risk assessment validation study, final report. Document # 209732, U.S. Department of Justice.

Rosenbaum, M. 1990. The role of depression in couples involved in murder-suicide and homicide. *American Journal of Psychiatry* 147:1036–39.

Rothman, E., and M. Perry. 2004. Intimate partner abuse perpetrated by employees. *Journal of Occupational Health Psychology* 9:238–46.

Rothman, E., D. Hemenway, M. Miller, and D. Azrael. 2006. Batterers' use of guns to threaten intimate partners. *Journal of the American Medical Women's Association* 60, no. 1: 62–68.

Saltzman, L., C. Johnson, B. Gilbert, and M. Goodwin. 2003. Physical abuse around the time of pregnancy: a examination of prevalence and risk factors in 16 states. *Maternal and Child Health* 7:31–43.

Saunders, D., A. Lynch, M. Grayson, and D. Linz. 1987. The inventory of beliefs about wife beating: the construction and initial validation of a measure of beliefs and attitudes. *Violence and Victims* 2, no. 1: 39–57.

Seave, P. 2006. Disarming batterers through restraining orders: the promise and reality in California. *Evaluation Review* 30, no. 3: 245–65.

Sev'er, A., M. Dawson, and H. Johnson. 2004. Lethal and nonlethal violence against women by intimate partners: trends and prospects in the United States, United Kingdom and Canada. *Violence Against Women* 9, no. 10: 1–14.

Shackelford, T., and J. Mouzos. 2005. Partner killing by men in cohabitating and marital relationships: a comparative, cross national analysis of data from Australia and the United States. *Journal of Interpersonal Violence* 20, no.10 (October): 1309–24.

Sharps, P., J. Campbell, D. Campbell, F. Gary, and D. Webster. 2003. Risky mix: Drinking, drug use and homicide. *NIJ Journal* no. 249: 2. www.ccjrs.gov

Shepard, M., and E. Pence. 1999. *Coordinating community responses to domestic violence: lessons from Duluth and beyond.* Thousand Oaks, CA: Sage.

Silverman, J., A. Raj, L. Mucci, and J. Hathaway. 2001. Dating violence against adolescent girls and associated substance use, unhealthy weight control, sexual risk behavior, pregnancy and suicidality. *Journal of the American Medical Association* 286:572–79.

Sorenson, S., and D. Wiebe. 2004. Weapons in the lives of battered women. *American Journal of Public Health* 94:1412–17.

Southern Hilltown Domestic Violence Task Force. 2004. The domestic violence murder of Karen Trudeau: a review of the judicial system response. Internal report.

Straus, M., and R. Gelles. 1980. *Behind closed doors: violence in the American family.* Garden City, NJ: Anchor/Doubleday.

Taylor, S., G. Schmutte, K. Leonard, and J. Cranston. 1979. The effects of alcohol and extreme provocation on the noxious electric shock. *Motivation and Emotion* 3:73–81.

Tjaden, P., and N. Thoennes. 1998. Stalking in America: findings from the national violence against women survey. National Criminal Justice Resource Source. www.ncjrs.org.

Tolman, R. 1989. The development of a measure of psychological maltreatment of women by their male partners. *Violence and Victims* 4, no. 3: 159–77.

Vigdor, E., and J. Mercy. 2006. Do laws restricting access to firearms by domestic violence offenders prevent intimate partner homicide? *Evaluation Review* 30, no. 3: 313–46, 337.

Violence Policy Center. 2002. American roulette: the untold story of murder-suicide in the United States. www.vpc.org/studies/amertrend.htm.

Volcano Press staff. 1995. *Family violence and religion: an interfaith resource guide.* Volcano, CA: Volcano Press.

Warshaw, C., and G. Moroney. 2002. Mental health and domestic violence: collaborative service models and curricula. Domestic Violence and Mental Health Policy Initiative. www.dvmhpi.org.

Websdale, N. 1999. *Understanding domestic homicide.* Boston: Northeastern University Press.

———. 2000. Lethality assessment tools: a critical analysis. National Online Resource Center on Violence Against Women Online Resources. www.vawnet. org.

Websdale, N., M. Town, and B. Johnson. 1999. Domestic violence fatality reviews: From a culture of blame to a culture of safety. *Juvenile and Family Court Journal* 50 (Spring): 61–74.

West, D. 1967. *Murder followed by suicide.* Cambridge: Harvard University Press

White, G. 1981. Some correlates of romantic jealousy. *Journal of Personality,* 49: 129–47.

Whitney, P., and L. Davis. 1999. Child abuse and domestic violence in Massachusetts: can practice be integrated in a public child welfare setting? *Child Maltreatment* 4:158–66.

Wilson, M., and M. Daly. 1992. Who kills whom in spouse killings? On the exceptional sex ratio on spousal homicides in the United States. *Criminology* 30, no. 2: 189–215.

———. 1993. Spousal homicide risk and estrangement. *Violence and Victims,* 8, no. 1: 3–16.

———. 1995. An evolutionary perspective on male sexual proprietariness and violence against wives. In *Interpersonal violent behaviors: social and cultural aspects,* ed. R. Ruback and N. Weiner, 109–133. New York: Springer.

Wilson, M., Daly, M. and Daniele, A. 1995. Familicide: the killing of spouse and children. *Aggressive Behavior* 21: 275–91.

Zwicker, T. 2002. Education policy brief: The imperative of developing teen dating violence and intervention programs in secondary schools. *Southern California Review of Law and Women's Studies* 12, no. 1: 131.

Index

Canada, 123, 159, 256, 273 n. 4, 274 n. 1
child abuse.
   as linked to domestic violence, 121,
      272 n. 4
   by perpetrators, 12, 121, 124, 148–
      61, 162, 193, 210, 211, 272 n. 2
   by victims, 121
   definition of, 123, 124
   in general public, 123, 124, 133
   of perpetrators (as children), 121–26,
      131, 132, 133, 149, 272 n. 5,
      272 n. 7
   of victims as children, 42, 144–45.
   See also children, child sexual abuse
children
   abduction of, 158, 159
   custody of, 118, 152, 158, 159, 160,
      166, 190, 198, 201, 237, 243,
      246, 253, 259, 273 n. 7
   impact of abuse on, 127, 136,
      150, 155, 156, 215, 265, 266,
      274 n. 33–34
   killing of, 13, 91, 159, 197, 269 n. 14,
      271 n. 34, 272 n. 1
   sexual abuse of, 42, 121, 122, 124,
      125, 132, 145, 150, 157–58, 162
   witnessing of abuse, 121, 122, 123,
      127, 128, 131, 133, 154, 155–56,
      159, 272 n. 2–3, 272 n. 6.
   See also child abuse
choking. *See* strangulation
clergy, 52, 67, 220, 221, 240–41, 263,
   273 n. 8
Colorado, 24, 259
Connecticut, 259
court
   as deterrents, 89, 102, 104, 103, 259,
      270 n. 21–28, 272 n. 1, 273 n. 4,
      274 n. 16–21
   sentences of perpetrators, 3, 14, 20,
      33, 34, 41, 46, 58, 61, 68, 89,
      93, 96, 97, 102, 103, 104, 114,
      115–16, 125, 146, 157, 167, 188,
      191, 206, 226, 228, 229, 230,
      259, 270 n. 28
criminal records of perpetrators, 7, 17,
   24, 37, 80, 96, 98, 101, 103, 144,
   163, 164, 272 n. 1

Daly, Martin, and Margo Wilson, 91,
   165, 271 n. 34, 272 n. 2, 272 n. 44,
   273 n. 17
Danger Assessment (Jacquelyn
   Campbell), 8
dangerousness assessment, 5–9, 184,
   229, 258–59, 260, 274 n. 16
depression
   of children, 154–55
   of perpetrators, 1, 24, 42, 43, 57, 65,
      66, 81, 91, 92, 94, 116–17, 118,
      217, 218, 269 n. 6, 271 n. 29–32
   of victims, 26, 155, 210, 219, 239,
      273 n. 7
Diaz, John, 1, 269 n. 2
divorce. *See* estrangement
Dobash, Russell and Rebecca, 171,
   269 n. 4, 271 n. 14, 272 n. 1, 6,
   273 n. 3
domestic homicides
   media accounts of, 1, 39
   methods of, 12, 13, 256, 269 n. 13
   rates of, 4–6, 83–84, 108, 111, 261,
      269 n. 6, 271 n. 17, 271 n. 18,
      272 n. 43, 274 n. 20
   risk factors to, 6–8, 56, 110, 194,
      253, 269 n. 11, 271 n. 6, 272 n. 44,
      273 n. 16, 273 n. 17
drugs. *See* substance abuse

economic
   abuse 38, 64, 164, 185, 211
   benefits, 70, 72, 79, 216, 217, 266,
      267
   dependency, 62, 158, 182, 210
   exploitation, 62, 64, 72–74, 79, 100,
      198, 216, 217, 254
   grievances, 32, 68, 69, 70, 73, 74,
      75, 78, 79, 100, 216, 217
   level, 25, 64, 104, 130
   loss, 59, 70, 188, 193, 217
   motive to kill, 68, -72, 80, 207
   possession, 72, 74–77, 79, 166, 216,
      217, 254
   support, 174, 244, 248, 263
   theft, 18, 65, 72, 101, 112, 143, 165,
      217